Land of Volcanic Ash

Land of Volcanic Ash
火山灰地
A Play in Two Parts

Kubo Sakae
久保栄

REVISED EDITION
Translated and with an Introduction by
David G. Goodman

East Asia Program
Cornell University
Ithaca, New York 14853

The *Cornell East Asia Series* publishes manuscripts on a wide variety of scholarly topics pertaining to East Asia. Manuscripts are published on the basis of camera-ready copy provided by the volume author or editor.

Inquiries should be addressed to Editorial Board, Cornell East Asia Series, East Asia Program, Cornell University, 140 Uris Hall, Ithaca, New York 14853.

CAUTION: Inquiries regarding the use of this play in any manner whatsoever should be addressed to David G. Goodman in care of the Cornell East Asia Series, East Asia Program, 140 Uris Hall, Cornell University, Ithaca, New York 14853.

For My Mother

Contents

Land of Volcanic Ash

Part One

Part Two

Photographs appear as a group following page 124.

Acknowledgments

I am indebted to many people and institutions for the help they gave me in preparing this translation. I began work in 1983 with the support of an Undergraduate Instructional Award from the University of Illinois at Urbana-Champaign (UIUC). In 1984, the Research Board of UIUC made it possible for me to visit Hokkaido, the site of the play. The translation was completed in December 1985, while I was studying in Japan under the auspices of a grant from the National Endowment for the Humanities; and I was assisted in the preparation of this revised edition by Laurie Wesselhoff, a research assistant provided by the Program in Arms Control, Disarmament, and International Security (ACDIS) at UIUC.

Special thanks must go to Professor Ted Hymowitz at the University of Illinois for his technical advice. I consulted Maurice Friedberg, head of the Slavic Department at UIUC, about some of the Russian references in the play; and Eric J. Gangloff read Part I and made helpful criticisms of the translation. In Tokyo, Okamura Haruhiko and Kubo Masa, the playwright's student and his daughter, provided unstinting support. Nakayama Toshihiko and Horiguchi Hayao, both former directors of the Tokachi Agricultural Station, helped me understand agricultural conditions in Hokkaido during my visit to Sapporo. And Kondō Yūko, professor of soil science at Obihiro University, and Kubo Yoshiharu (no relation to the playwright) made my stay in Obihiro and Otofuke as enjoyable as it was enlightening. Professor Kondō's detailed technical knowledge and Mr. Kubo's profound understanding of the culture of "the land of volcanic ash" were particularly helpful in preparing this translation.

This translation is one in a series I have prepared as part of an introduction to modern Japanese drama. Readers interested in other modern Japanese plays may wish to refer to the works I have translated in *After Apocalypse: Four Japanese Plays of Hiroshima and Nagasaki* (Columbia University Press, 1986); *Japanese Drama and Culture in the 1960s: The Return of the Gods* (M. E. Sharpe, 1988); and *Five Plays by Kishida Kunio*, Cornell East Asia Papers, #51 (Cornell East Asia Program, 1989).

Introduction

David G. Goodman

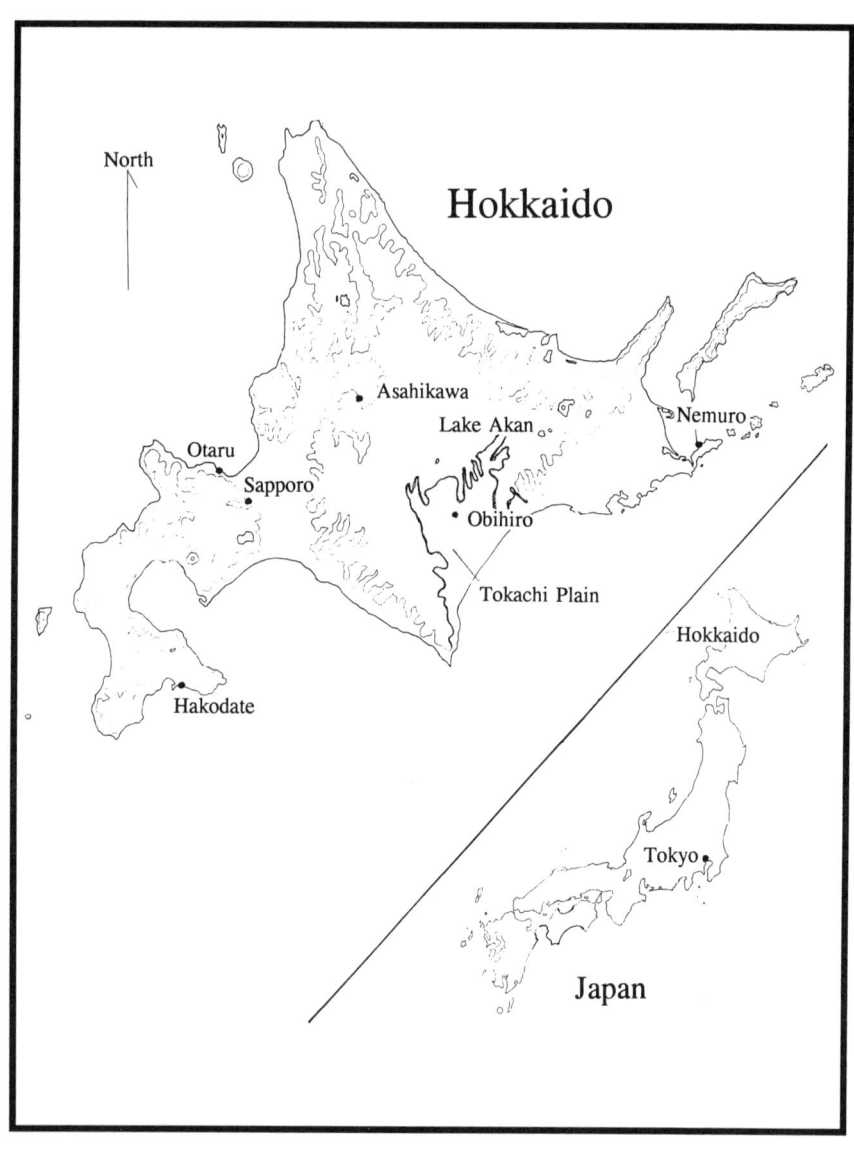

A Modern Classic

No work of modern Japanese drama has had greater impact than Kubo Sakae's *Land of Volcanic Ash (Kazanbaichi)*. More has been written about the play than any other modern Japanese dramatic work.[1] Abe Itaru, an unsympathetic critic, relates that for better or worse, "its reputation as the finest realistic drama of the prewar period in both its staged and printed versions is firmly established";[2] and its influence has extended beyond the theatre to all of Japanese intellectual life. The list of contributors to *Kubo Sakae   kenkyū* (Kubo Sakae Studies), a journal dedicated to Kubo's life and work, reads like a *Who's Who* of the postwar intellectual community.[3] Indeed, no work of modern Japanese drama recommends itself to our attention more than *Land of Volcanic Ash*.

First published in the magazine *Shinchō* in 1937-38 and first staged by the Shinkyō (New Cooperative) Troupe the year it was completed,[4] *Land of Volcanic Ash* became an immediate classic. It has been included in numerous anthologies of modern Japanese literature,[5] and despite its forbidding scale, it has been restaged twice in the postwar period.[6]

---

[1] Two book-length compilations of criticism about the play have been published: Kazanbaichi *hihyō sukurappu*, 1937-1960, ed. Kubo Sakae kenkyū (Gekidan Mingei, 1961); and Kazanbaichi *hyōron, shiryō*, ed. Gekidan Mingei (Gekidan Mingei, 1963). The latter volume covers the period November 1959 to March 1962.

[2] Abe Itaru, *Kindai gekibungaku no kenkyū* (Ōfusha, 1980), p. 195.

[3] Ten issues published between November 1959 and January 1969.

[4] Part I appeared in the December 1937 issue; Part II was published the following July. The original production of the play was directed by the author and was performed at the Tsukiji Little Theatre in Tokyo. Part I ran from June 8 to June 26, and Part II was performed from June 27 through July 8, 1938.

[5] These anthologies include *Shōwa bungaku zenshū* (Complete Works of Shōwa Literature; Kadokawa shoten, 1953); *Gendai nihon gikyoku senshu* (Collection of Modern Japanese Plays; Hakusuisha, 1955); *Gendai nihon bungaku zenshū* (Complete Works of Modern Japanese Literature; Chikuma shobo, 1956); and two editions of Kubo's own collected works, one published by Chūō kōron beginning in 1949 and the other, a posthumous compendium edited by Hani Gorō, Kuno Osamu, Taketani Mitsuo, Noma Hiroshi, and Uno Jūkichi, which was published by San'ichi shobo beginning in 1961.

[6] Haiyūza (The Actors' Theatre) performed Part I in 1948. The entire play was restaged by Gekidan Mingei (The People's Theatre Company) between August 1961 and January 1962.

Land of Volcanic Ash is a major landmark in the history of *shingeki*, the modern Japanese theatre movement. From its inception in the first decade of the twentieth century, *shingeki* struggled to establish a realistic theatre in Japan modeled after the the theatres of Ibsen, Chekhov, and Stanislavsky. With *Land of Volcanic Ash*, that goal was achieved, and the subsequent history of modern theatre in Japan may be explained in terms of the reaction to the dramaturgy of historical realism *Land of Volcanic Ash* epitomized.[7] Heroes like Kubo's Amamiya, who wage a tragic struggle to preserve their intellectual integrity against all the forces of society, became the mainstay of orthodox *shingeki* drama after the war. So prevalent did these plays become, one critic has suggested, that in effect postwar playwrights systematically rewrote the entire history of modern Japan as an omnibus drama centering on a single Amamiya-like, tragic figure who is reincarnated in each work and historical period.[8] Kinoshita Junji's first play, *Furō* (Turbulent Times, 1939-1947), for example, concerns a young ex-samurai who tests and is eventually destroyed by the new ideologies that proliferated in Japan in the 1870s. Miyamoto Ken's *Meiji no hitsugi* (A Coffin for Meiji, 1963), dramatizes the struggle of politician and early environmental activist Tanaka Shōzō (1841-1913) in the next historical period; and Fukuda Yoshiyuki, a disciple of Kinoshita, wrote *Nagai bohyō no retsu* (A Long Row of Tombstones, 1957) about the experience of economist Kawai Eijirō, who was forced out of his post at Tokyo Imperial University in the 1930s because of his liberal views.

Playwrights have not been uncritical of *Land of Volcanic Ash*. As early as the late 1940s, when Kinoshita began writing "folktale dramas" like his famous *Yūzuru* (Twilight Crane, 1949; tr. 1956), there was an incipient recognition that Kubo's uncompromisingly realistic approach to Japanese life and history excluded important aspects of Japanese tradition and belief. After 1960, when a full-scale revolt against *shingeki* orthodoxy developed, playwrights like Kara Jūrō, Betsuyaku Minoru, and Satoh Makoto rejected, not only Kubo's realism, but the entire tragic interpretation of Japan's modern history that had been crystallized in his work.

---

[7]For a fuller explication of this view, see my article on modern Japanese theatre in *The Cambridge Guide to World Theatre* (New York: Cambridge University Press, 1988), pp. 515-521. Kubo's work did not appear *ex nihilo* by any means. See Eric J. Gangloff, "Kinoshita Junji: A Modern Japanese Dramatist" (Ph.D. diss., University of Chicago, 1973), pp. 1-116, for a discussion of Kubo's antecedents.

[8]Saeki Ryūkō, *Ika suru jikan* (Shōbunsha, 1973), pp. 79-87.

The influence of *Land of Volcanic Ash* has been been felt outside the theatre as well. The play electrified the generation of Japanese intellectuals who came of age in the 1930s, and it is not hard to find a Japanese even today who can recite from memory the play's opening lines. "If my thought today is left-wing," says critic Uryū Tadao, "that is clearly due to the influence of *Land of Volcanic Ash*";[9] and the renowned political scientist Maruyama Masao recalls,

> The play appeared at a time when people like me were very pessimistic about the future of the social sciences, and so Amamiya's struggle to maintain his integrity as a scientist really moved me. Any impulse I may have had to criticize the organization of the play or the acting became secondary, and I remember inexplicably breaking into tears as I watched.[10]

In short, *Land of Volcanic Ash* is a highly influential *tour de force* that represents the culmination of the *shingeki* movement in the prewar period and the starting point for modern Japanese drama after the war.

The Playwright and His Times

Kubo Sakae was born in Sapporo on December 28, 1900, the second son in a family of seven children born to Kubo Hyōtarō, who had migrated to Hokkaido in 1898 to assist his father with the brick foundry he had established there.

With the exception of the first three grades of elementary school, Kubo was educated in Tokyo. He was adopted by his father's youngest brother and taken to Tokyo in April 1903. Even after his adoptive family was ruined in the stock market in 1915 and he was officially readopted into his family of birth, he did not return to Sapporo but took up lodgings near Tokyo Imperial University. Kubo nevertheless remained attached to Hokkaido, and it exerted an important influence over him throughout his life. Indeed, it would be hard to imagine Kubo conceiving

---

[9]*Gendai nihon gikyoku senshū*, v. 9 (Hakusuisha, 1955), p. 410.

[10]*Gendai nihon gikyoku senshū*, v. 9, pp. 409-410.

a drama on the momentous scale of *Land of Volcanic Ash* in any Japanese environment but Hokkaido.[11]

Kubo's father wanted him to become a doctor, but Kubo refused and dropped out of Tokyo's prestigious First High School in 1919 rather than continue his study of the physical sciences. He had begun publishing poetry in *Hototogisu* and *Mizugame*, leading poetry magazines of the day, and in 1918 he won the Kitamura Tōkoku Prize awarded by *Chūō bungaku* (Central Literature) magazine for a story entitled *Sannin no yamago no hanashi* (The Tale of Three Woodcutters). Kubo was intent on pursuing a literary career, but his rebellion against his father had a high psychological cost. Shortly after dropping out of the First High School, he began experiencing the spells of nervous prostration that were to plague him to the end of his life. He was forced to withdraw to Sapporo and Kamakura, where he studied oil painting and classical Japanese literature, prefiguring the character Amamiya Tōru in the play. Kubo's "scientific" approach to playwriting, his almost obsessive concern with empirical data, may have been his way of fulfilling the conflicting psychological demands he felt to pursue a literary career and fulfill his father's wish that he become a scientist. The tensions this solution set up in his mind may have contributed to Kubo's tendency to depression.

Kubo entered the German department of Tokyo Imperial University in April 1923. While at the university, he began translating works of German drama and wrote a senior thesis on "The Historical Plays of Georg Kaiser." Over the course of his career, Kubo translated some thirty German naturalist and expressionist plays, including works by Kaiser, Wedekind, and Hauptmann. His crowning achievement was a translation of Goethe's *Faust*, which strongly influenced his conception of *Land of Volcanic Ash*.[12]

While in college, Kubo came under the influence of Osanai Kaoru, and he entered the literary department of the Tsukiji Little Theatre in March 1926. Osanai had founded the Tsukiji two years earlier as Japan's first theatre devoted exclusively to the production of modern drama.[13]

---

[11]Paul Anderer describes the special place Hokkaido occupies in modern Japanese literature in *Other Worlds: Arishima Takeo and the Bounds of Modern Japanese Fiction* (New York: Columbia University Press, 1984), pp. 19-40. See also, Ogasawara Masaru, *Kindai Hokkaidō no bungaku* (Nihon hōsō kyōkai, 1973), esp. pp. 8-17.

[12]Kubo Sakae, Shingeki no sho (Shinchōsha, 1955), p. 12.

[13]For details concerning the Tsukiji, see Brian Powell, "Japan's First Modern Theater: The Tsukiji Shōgekijō and Its Company, 1924-1926," *Monumenta Nipponica* (1975), 30(I):69-85

Kubo was deeply influenced by Osanai, to whom *Land of Volcanic Ash* is dedicated, and he spent the enforced leisure of the war years writing a biography of his mentor. The nature of Osanai's influence on Kubo is complex, but certainly he was the source of Kubo's conception of *shingeki* as a movement with a historical mission.

Osanai died on December 25, 1928 at the age of 47, and the Tsukiji company split immediately into political and literary camps. Kubo, who had been converted to Marxism, became a leader of the politically engaged group, editing, translating, and directing for a variety of left-wing troupes.

In 1934, Kubo was instrumental in founding the Shinkyō Troupe, and he formulated the new company's philosophy in the journal *Teatro* the following year:

> Our realism captures the innermost truths of man and society and, cutting through all facades, shows how—while antagonistic, contradictory, and interacting in complex ways—they develop toward a higher stage of unity. Without reducing them to stereotypes and without vulgarization, we clarify them in terms of the typical form of [class] conflict and formulate them with artistry and style.[14]

The Marxist character of this statement is unmistakable. The Shinkyō manifesto was clearly influenced by the notion of "socialist realism" introduced at Stalin's behest by the Union of Soviet Writers in 1932. It is important to emphasize, however, that Kubo's approach to socialist realism was critical and independent and that he was not merely a Soviet dupe. In his famous article "Mayoeru rearizumu" (Misguided Realism), serialized in the *Miyako shimbun* between January 20 and 23, 1935, Kubo argued strenuously against writers, including the Marxist poet Nakano Shigeharu, who, he charged, had "plotted the mechanical transplantation of socialist realism because they have failed to see it in its relationship to Soviet society." Kubo understood the word "socialist" in the term socialist realism to refer specifically to postrevolutionary Soviet society, not as a concept relevant to *pre*revolutionary Japan. Japanese realism, Kubo insisted, had to be strictly faithful to conditions prevailing in Japan and thus could not be "socialist" but had to be "anticapitalist" and "revolutionary."[15] Because

---

[14]Quoted in Sugai Yukio, *Kindai nihon engeki ronsōshi* (Miraisha, 1979), pp. 210-211.

[15]Sugai, pp. 206-207.

of the   author's independent approach, the well-known critic Yoshimoto Takaaki cites Kubo's work as   the   only socialist realism in Japan worthy of serious consideration.[16]

Land of Volcanic Ash conforms to the   guidelines set forth in the Shinkyō manifesto. As Kubo explained them in a letter to members of the Shinkyō Troupe, his aims in writing the play were twofold. First, he sought "to evoke the unique conditions of Japanese agriculture"; and second, he wanted to achieve "a unification of scientific theory and poetic form."[17] Kubo hoped to describe the complex interaction of all the forces active in Japanese society and show how they moved ineluctably toward a higher stage of unity and truth in consonance with the Marxist law of dialectical materialism.   He sought to sought to evoke the general reality of Japanese agriculture through a scientifically accurate portrayal of the particular conditions prevailing in a certain rural locale; and he sought to do this in a way that would be artistically compelling.

Kubo's precise description of agricultural conditions in eastern Hokkaido   in   the   mid-1930s   is impressive. Moreover, he succeeds admirably in describing members of all classes "without reducing them to stereotypes and without vulgarization." The conditions motivating exploitative Komai Tsuta are therefore described as fully those that shape the behavior of the hotheaded but sympathetic Izumi Jirō. Indeed, as Eric J. Gangloff has noted, "In [Land of Volcanic Ash] we find the first real struggle of a socialist dramatist to master the art of charac-terization."[18]

Nevertheless,   Land   of   Volcanic   Ash   is   a   difficult, often elliptical   work.   This   quality resulted in part from the playwright's uncompromising desire to be absolutely faithful to the data at hand, but it was also the result of the need to satisfy government censors in a period of increasingly intense repression. Kubo began writing Land of Volcanic Ash in mid-1937, just as the Incident at Marco Polo Bridge plunged Japan into full-scale war with China. Hundreds of newspapers were being drummed out of existence at this time, and the number of periodicals fell from   11,400 in 1936   to 7,700 in   1939.[19] Liberal

[16]Yoshimoto Takaaki, "Shakaishugi rearizumu hihan," *Itan to seikei* (Gendai   shichōsha, 1960), p. 83.

[17]*Shingeki no sho*, p. 43.

[18]"Kinoshita Junji: A Modern Japanese Dramatist," p. 100.

[19]Thomas R. H. Havens, *Valley of Darkness: The Japanese People and World War Two* (New York: Norton, 1978), pp. 22-23.

professors like Yanaibara Tadao and Kawai Eijirō were hounded out of
their positions during this period; and on August 19, 1940, the Shinkyō
troupe was ordered to disband, and Kubo was arrested along with more
than one hundred other theatre people and imprisoned for "thought
crimes."

Kubo wrote after the war that the threat of censorship had forced
him "to write as a secondary theme what by rights should have been
primary" and to indicate by indirection what he would otherwise have
stated outright. Kubo had set out to write a play that would make a
scientific case for the necessity of revolution in Japan, but circumstances
forced him to conceal this message. What emerged instead as the play's
principal theme was Amamiya's struggle to maintain his integrity and his
gradual acceptance on purely empirical grounds of the validity of socialist
ideas.

The threat of censorship had a significant impact on the style of
the play. There is only one reference to Communists or Communism in
the work, although Ichihashi Tatsuji, Adachi Kimi, and Teramachi
Tamaki are clearly of that ilk. "Going to Kamikawa" becomes a trope for
joining the army; and army units leaving for Manchuria are referred to
euphemistically as "immigrants." More to the point, Kubo intentionally
buried significant lines in masses of less important verbiage; and his
insistence on constantly interrupting conversations, picking up the train of
thought later in an unrelated context, was also intended to distract the
censors.[20]

Various opinions of Kubo's style in *Land of Volcanic Ash* have been
forwarded. Murayama Tomoyoshi, who directed the 1961-62
production, wrote that Kubo was in any case a didactic individual given to
obscurantism and that censorship simply exacerbated this tendency,
making *Land of Volcanic Ash* "almost impossible to understand."[21]
Maruyama Masao's view, quoted above, is by far the more prevalent,
however. Whatever the play's technical flaws (and they are not incon-
siderable), the audience seems to have been inspired by the intellectual
rigor of the work.

Kubo's struggle to write an intellectually rigorous, scientifically
accurate play was mirrored in the struggle of Amamiya Akira, the
embattled scientist in *Land of Volcanic Ash*, who tries to maintain his

---

[20]*Gendai nihon gikyoku senshū*, v. 9, p. 409.

[21]"Kubo Sakae to rearizumu no gikyoku," quoted in Abe, p. 200. "*Nankai o kiwameta
gikyoku*" is the way Murayama put it.

integrity in the face of overwhelming social pressure. At the time the play was written, this was a timely theme, to say the least. The 1930s were the period of tenkō, "intellectual apostasy," when Japanese intellectualsrecanted their former left-wing convictions in droves and proclaimed their allegiance to the mystical *Kokutai*, Japan's inimitable "National Polity." Amamiya's struggle to stand by his convictions, with its echoes in the drama of his son Tōru and Tōru's friend Sugai, took on added significance in this climate.[22]

Kubo's struggle to maintain his integrity did not go unnoticed, by the authorities as by his peers. Arrested in 1940, he refused to cooperate in the war effort and was consigned to a life of imprisonment and house arrest for the duration of the struggle. When the conflict finally ended, Kubo emerged a hero. *Shingeki* had resisted the rush to war more successfully than any other cultural movement, and Kubo's role in this had been large. For a time it seemed that *shingeki* would become the center, not only of Japanese theatre, but of all Japanese culture in the postwar world and that Kubo's position of leadership was secure.[23]

These halcyon days did not last, however. Kubo became embroiled in internecine struggles within the shingeki and Communist movements, and although he published two plays after the war, *Ringoen nikki* (Apple Orchard Diary, 1947) and *Nihon no kishō* (Weather Conditions in Japan, 1953), it was hard to avoid feeling that he was living in the past. In 1949, he began editing his own collected works for Chūo Kōron; in 1952, he published *Noborigama*, a novelistic treatment of the themes in *Land of Volcanic Ash*; and in the same year he directed a production of *Goryōkaku kessho* (Blood Petition from Goryōkaku Castle), a play he had written in 1933.

Kubo was hospitalized repeatedly for nervous exhaustion after 1953. On the morning of March 15, 1958 he took his own life.

Thirty years to the day earlier, the mass arrest of Japanese Communists had begun what was to be the most difficult and the most rewarding period of his life. Kubo's suicide seems to have been timed as a calculated protest against a growing sense of obsolescence and stasis

---

[22]For analyses of the phenomenon of tenkō, see Kazuko Tsurumi, *Social Change and the Individual* (Princeton: Princeton University Press, 1970), pp. 29-79; and Patricia Golden Steinhoff, "*Tenkō*: Ideology and Societal Integration in Prewar Japan" (Ph.D. diss., Harvard University, 1969).

[23]Okuno Takeo, "Kaisetsu," *Gendai nihon gikyoku taikei*, v. 1 (San'ichi shobō, 1971), pp. 453-454.

and a reaffirmation of the movement in which he had been a prime mover.

Agricultural Background

The events described in *Land of Volcanic Ash* take place in Hokkaido from late 1935 through the autumn of 1936 in the area between the city of Obihiro and the village of Otofuke on the Tokachi plain. Kubo was of course familiar with Hokkaido, and he had made several visits to Tokachi, where his sister Shige lived with her husband Tamayama Yutaka, director of the local agricultural station. Kubo's last visit before writing *Land of Volcanic Ash* was from mid-August to late September 1936.

Kubo's purpose in writing the play was to present a picture of the situation in Tokachi that would be both scientifically accurate and artistically compelling. It would not be a pretty one. There had been a series of disastrous crop failures in 1931, 1934, and 1935 that, combined with the overall depression in the Japanese economy, had caused great hardship among Japanese farmers, especially in the northern provinces. In 1934, the rice crop was 61 percent of the average yield for the previous five years. There were more tenant-landlord disputes after 1934 than at any previous time, and in Iwate prefecture in northeastern Japan, about half of the 900,000 residents were on the verge of starvation. In 1934 alone, 4,521 girls were sent to work in brothels from the six northern provinces of the country, the basis for Teruko's comments on the subject of prostitution in Act One.[24]

Land of Volcanic Ash describes the life of an agricultural community in one of the most inhospitable climates in Japan. Hokkaido is Japan's northernmost and second largest island. It has an area of 83,514 square kilometers and comprises 22 percent of Japan's land area. Located in the eastern part of the island, the Tokachi plain has an area of 9,025 square kilometers; it is bounded by mountains on three sides and the Pacific Ocean to the south. The average temperature in Obihiro is 5.7 degrees centigrade, 14.6 degrees between May and October. The climate thus resembles southern Canada or northern Europe more than the rest of Japan. Temperatures in the spring and fall are low; and long,

---

[24]Mikiso Hane, *Peasants, Rebels, and Outcasts: The Underside of Modern Japan* (New York: Pantheon, 1982), pp. 110-115.

cold springs cause crop damage on the average every four years. There are only 124 frost-free days in Obihiro during the course of a year, which contrasts with about 180 days in northeastern Honshu and 220 days in the Kanto area around Tokyo. Amamiya's desire to find some means to predict a cool growing season derives from these conditions.[25]

Nevertheless, certain crops thrive in this environment. There are 2,149 hours of accumulated sunshine in Obihiro during the year; about 830 hours during the growing season. Annual precipitation is 940 millimeters; 550 millimeters during the growing season. Ample sunshine and relatively little rain provide good growing conditions for legumes, but rice cultivation is difficult. Thus, from the end of World War One, when prices were high, there was intensive cultivation of various bean varieties, but attempts such as those of the elder Igarashi in the play to grow rice were frequently unsuccessful. Amamiya's attempts to help Seki Tamekichi grow rice on the "bucket land," so named because its paddies lost water like a leaky bucket, were also unsuccessful.

Tōru's sense of affinity for Brueghel's snowscapes is natural considering that in Tokachi there are an average of 115 days of continuous snow cover and 97 days when the accumulation exceeds ten centimeters. Accumulations of 40 to 50 centimeters are common. Temperatures frequently dip below minus 20 degrees centigrade, and in January 1902 the temperature dropped to minus 38.2 degrees, the lowest in recorded history.

The development of Hokkaido is both recent and unique. While indisputably part of Japan, Hokkaido was all but ignored by the Japanese before modern times and was treated like a foreign colony after the Meiji Restoration of 1868. In 1869, the new Imperial government established a Colonial Office (*Kaitakushi*) to oversee the development of Ezo, which was renamed Hokkaido (Northern Sea Circuit). In 1882, a scandal involving the disposition of government-owned land closed the Colonial Office; and in 1886, a new local administration was set up with a governor appointed by Tokyo. The central government continued to treat the island as a colony, however, and in 1895 it was even placed under the jurisdiction of the Ministry of the Colonies before being transferred eventually to the Ministry of Home Affairs. Hokkaido competed for government resources and public attention with other

---

[25]Unless otherwise noted, the statistics presented in this section are taken from Kondō Yūko, "*Kazanbaichi no nōgyō ritchiteki haikei*," Kubo Yoshiharu, ed., *Kazanbaichi* (Otofuke-chō, Hokkaido, Japan: Kazanbaichi kenshōkai, 1974), pp. 328-343; and figures prepared by the Tokachi Agricultural Experiment Station, Memuro, Hokkaido, Japan.

Japanese colonies like Taiwan, acquired in 1895, and Korea, annexed in 1910; and its situation became especially precarious in the period treated by the play, because the colonization of Manchuria, acquired by Japan in 1931, drained the island of human and financial resources. Conditions were so bad, in fact, that one scholar reports, "Some foreign observers were already saying in the nineteen-thirties that, owing to climatic and topographical limitations, the limits of settlement in Hokkaido had nearly been reached."[26]

Japanese farmers had never been enthusiastic about migrating to Hokkaido, and beginning in 1872 a variety of laws were promulgated, first by the Colonial Office and then by the central government, to encourage immigration and development. These laws provided for the lease of tax-exempt government lands to developers who would receive title after a period of years provided that the land had been successfully developed. In 1908, the "Law Concerning the Disposal of Undeveloped Government Lands in Hokkaido" (*Hokkaidō kokuyu mikonchi shobun hō*, 1897) was amended to make land available to independent farmers as well, and plots of ten hectares were offered to squatters willing to cultivate them.[27] Before becoming a charcoal burner, Ichihashi Tatsuji had worked land in northern Hokkaido on this basis.

In *Land of Volcanic Ash*, three other kinds of farms appear. The Igarashi and Hayakawa farms are large parcels of land originally acquired from the government and worked by tenant farmers. Igarashi is a local developer; Hayakawa an absentee landlord represented on the scene by his mistress, Komai Tsuta. Komai's father was killed by his fellow farmers because he was suspected of having "sold out" to the landlord; and Tsuta, having lost any sense of loyalty to her class as a result, is determined to lift herself out of poverty at any cost, even if it means collaborating with her oppressors.

In addition to these large agglomerations of tenant farms, there are some small, independent farms like that of Seki Tamekichi. These were established in the 1920s when economic conditions forced large developers to divest themselves of some of their holdings and long-term government loans made it possible for farmers to purchase the

---

[26]F. C. Jones, *Hokkaido: Its Present State of Development and Future Prospects* (London: Oxford University Press, 1958), p. 22. Jones's brief introduction to the history of Hokkaido is valuable, particularly pp. 10-23.

[27]*Shingeki no sho*, pp. 36-38; Jones, pp. 14, 20.

land.[28] By the time the action of the play takes place, however, most of these farms have been reabsorbed into the Hayakawa and Igarashi holdings, and the former owners have reverted to being sharecroppers.

The tractor farm set up by the sugar company represents a third type, an attempt to establish large-scale, mechanized agriculture along capitalist lines. This experiment has already failed as the play begins.

Land of Volcanic Ash painstakingly describes how both small, independent farming and large-scale capitalist agriculture inevitably fail in Hokkaido and why land necessarily comes to be concentrated in the hands of a small number of rich landlords. Kubo's hero Amamiya reluctantly arrives at the conclusion that, given the failure of small-scale independent farming and large-scale agricultural development on the capitalist model, the only practical way to improve conditions in Hokkaido is through collectivization. That this conclusion is consistent with socialist theory and Soviet practice (the 1930s were, after all, the heyday of the *kolkhoz*, the collective farms) horrifies Amamiya and leads him to question the validity of his findings.

One of the primary factors affecting the situation Kubo describes in *Land of Volcanic Ash* is the colonial status of the island. With governors appointed by the central government to implement decisions made in Tokyo, development policy for Hokkaido inevitably reflected national priorities rather than local needs. The cultivation of certain crops was encouraged, for example, because of central government policies, regardless of deleterious local effects. Thus, as the play's opening narration suggests, flax cultivation was encouraged because of the need to produce canvas for military applications; and sugar beets were originally grown in Hokkaido to provide avenues of investment for the sugar industry, which had already saturated colonial Taiwan.

Land of Volcanic Ash details the consequences of this situation. In Tokachi during the 1930s, there was a heavy concentration on a few crops, particularly legumes, which rapidly depleted the soil. In 1936, the Tokachi region produced 47.5 percent of the soybeans grown in Hokkaido; 30.4 percent of the adzuki beans; 67.1 percent of the kidney beans; and 44.7 percent of the peas. It also produced 24.9 percent of the sugar beets and 38 percent of the flax. This dependence on relatively few crops not only depleted the soil but made the farmers of the region highly vulnerable to fluctuations in climatic and market conditions.

---

[28]Takakura Shinichirō, "Jisakunō sōtei," *Sono go no kazanbaichi* (Obihiro, Japan: NHK, 1965), pp. 15-16.

Amamiya's efforts to encourage diversification are based on an appreciation of the consequences of this kind of depletion farming.

As the chart below indicates, agriculture is much more diversified in Tokachi today. Dependency on legumes has been drastically reduced, and no flax is grown at all. There has been a significant increase in dairy farming, and the amount of land devoted to sugar beet cultivation has also increased.

Land Use in the Tokachi Region

	1936	1968	1982
Total land area (ha.)	1,083,000	1,083,000	1,083,000
Arable land (")	209,231	217,800	
Paddy fields (")	7,659	5,200	
Dry fields (")	201,57	212,600	
Cultivated land (%)	19.3	20.1	
Households (#)	18,101	16,830	

Crops Grown in the Tokachi Region

	1936	1968	1982
Wet rice (ha.)	6.207	4,810	
Oats (")	25,695		
Potatoes (")	5,515	23,500	25,10
Soybeans (")	38,347	11,800	5,600
Adzuki (")	11,612	23,200	13,200
Kidney beans (")	54,283	38,400	19,300
Peas (")	17,517	827	0
Sugar beets (")	4,839	25,000	28,700
Flax (")	6,085	0	0
Grasses (")	2,602	75,000	96,300
Dairy cattle (head)	9,294	73,250	
Dairy farmers (households)	3,325	8,676	

The quality of the soil in the Tokachi region made the problem of depletion farming, the "rape of the land," as Amamiya puts it, all the more urgent. About 53 percent of the land area of Hokkaido is covered with ash and pumice deposits from volcanic eruptions, and the concentration of these andosols is particularly high in the Tokachi plain, where 80 percent of the topsoil is relatively infertile volcanic ash soil.[29]

The inspection of the flax harvest in Act Five illustrates the consequences of the government's colonialist agricultural policy and exploitative industry practice for the farmers of Tokachi. Flax was first introduced to Hokkaido in 1886, when the Hokkaido Flax Company was founded and Constant Huybrecht, a Belgian expert, was invited to instruct the Japanese in its cultivation. Flax, however, makes many demands on the soil and requires heavy fertilization, especially in the relatively poor volcanic ash soil of Tokachi. Annual replanting rapidly depletes the soil, resulting in inferior crops in each succeeding season. The poor quality of the flax being inspected in Act Five is the result of improper fertilization and the failure to rotate crops. The point is, however, that the farmers cannot rotate crops because of government policy; and and they cannot fertilize properly because of the social and economic pressures to use the improperly formulated company brand of fertilizer. Thus, when Izumi Jirō uses Amamiya's alternative fertilizer, he is denied access to the co-op's shared transport, which makes it difficult for him to move his crop and leads to the run-away horse incident in Act Five.

The controversy over the lack of potassium in the flax company's fertilizer that is central in *Land of Volcanic Ash* actually took place. The fertilizer distributed by the Imperial Flax Company in Tokachi did not, in fact, contain potassium, and test results published by the Hokkaido Agricultural Station in 1933 showed that the company's fertilizer did not yield results significantly different from generic chemical fertilizers formulated from ammonium sulfate and superphosphate. As in the play, Tamayama Yutaka, the model for Amamiya Akira, argued the need to supplement the company fertilizer with potassium. He was opposed by Miyake Kōji, professor at Hokkaido University, the model for Professor Takimoto in the play, and his student, Ōnuki Yoshinosuke, the model for Karasawa Katsumi.[30]

Kubo uses the controversy over potassium to illustrate that agricultural policies and people's lives were being governed, not by

---

[29]Quarternary pyroclastic deposits account for at least 20 centimeters of the topsoil over almost the entire area of the plain. By contrast, alluvial soils with their high native fertility account for only about 13 percent of the topsoil and are found along the Tokachi River and its tributaries. Kondō, p. 330; and Lokugamage Gnanapala Yapa and Yūko Kondō, "Comparative Studies on Some Chemical Properties and Water Relations of Volcanic Ash Soils in the Tokachi District, Hokkaido, Japan," *Research Bulletin of Obihiro University*, 12 (1980), p. 42.

[30]Kondō, pp. 340-342.

objective science or a sincere interest in their welfare, but by the capitalist system and its preparations for war. The importance of the Neubauer seedling method that occupies such a prominent place in the play is that it provides Amamiya with a means to demonstrate definitively the relationship between potassium absorption and flax quality. His findings do not impress his opponents, however, since their reasons for perpetuating the status quo have little to do with the quality of the flax crop, as becomes clear in the following exchange from Act Four:

AMAMIYA: Potassium fertilizer is one of the most expensive fertilizers people can buy. That's why, sir, that's why, you see, we should encourage people to grow red clover, which is the most effective green manure crop, so that they can save as much money as possible on nitrogen fertilizer and use the money instead to buy a mixture with a higher proportion of potassium. Do you see what I mean? In other words, all I'm saying is that for the same amount of money we could set up a system where the proportions in fertilizer of, say, ammonium sulfate, superphosphate, rice bran, and potassium sulfate would be scientifically appropriate. Karasawa, that's the point!

KARASAWA: In other words you're suggesting a boycott, a boycott of ammonium sulfate, is that it?

AMAMIYA: Boycott? Well, I suppose you could look at it that way.

KARASAWA: You can't do that. Fertilizer isn't the only thing ammonium sulfate is used for. The farmers already have a system, and it's allowed them to buy ammonium sulfate up to now. You can't just go out and upset that system.

Ammonium sulfate supplies nitrogen in chemical fertilizers, but it is also an important ingredient in explosives. Amamiya's scheme for making it economically feasible for farmers to purchase expensive potassium fertilizer impinges on the economy of an important war industry and is therefore unacceptable regardless of its agricultural merits.

Kubo goes on to show how Amamiya's well intentioned efforts to aid the farmers alienate them from their fellows, put them at a disadvantage in their social milieu, and ultimately hurt rather than help them. Without revolutionary change in the economic system, Kubo implies, the farmers will remain at the mercy of the capitalist state and bourgeois entrepreneurs, who will do anything, including wage war, to maximize their profits. Despite their "correctness," the efforts of people like Amamiya Akira only exacerbate the situation. Kubo's conclusion is, however, that, faced with a choice, it is better to serve the truth than concede, and thus in the final moments of the play, Amamiya courageously sets off for Sapporo to argue his case at a conference of agricultural station directors despite the assurance of certain defeat.

Conclusion

History has vitiated whatever claim to predictive scientific value Kubo may have wanted to make for his play. Despite his faith in dialectical materialism and his belief that the contradictions in Hokkaido agriculture in the 1930s could only be resolved through the advent of socialism, events developed otherwise. Unlike his fictional alter ego, Tamayama Yutaka eventually won the argument over potassium. He was promoted to the directorship of the main agricultural station when his principal opponent, Amano Fumisuke, the model for Saegusa in the play, left Hokkaido for Manchuria. Ironically, although potassium fertilizer came to be used in the late 1930s as a result of Tamayama's efforts, imports of potassic salt from Germany, France, and the Soviet Union ended with the outbreak of the Second World War, and the controversy quickly receded into oblivion.[31]

Today it is conventional wisdom that the soil of Hokkaido is low in potassium. When I visited Sapporo in 1984, a former director of the Tokachi Agricultural Station even went so far as to suggest that Kubo had invented the whole controversy and no such argument had ever taken place. Moreover, far from being the desolate, ashen expanse suggested by the title of Kubo's play, the Tokachi region is today a rich agricultural area that produces delicious wines and which in 1983 surpassed northern Europe in overall productivity.[32]

Nevertheless, *Land of Volcanic Ash* continues to hold our interest today. The playwright's methodological rigor is impressive still, and his meticulous description of the structure of rural life in the 1930s remains an important sociological document and a valuable corrective to the tendency to view modern Japanese economic development as painless and preordained for success. Moreover, the image of Amamiya Akira, the embattled intellectual hero, continues to fascinate and disturb. Ironically, it is not the inevitability of revolution but these

---

[31]Kondō, pp. 341-342.

[32]Conversation with Hanabusa Masao, deputy mayor of Obihiro, May 22, 1984.

supposedly ancillary themes that give *Land of Volcanic Ash* its lasting value.

Land of Volcanic Ash

Cast of Characters

Act I: A New Year's Market (Late December)

Kawabe	Photographer for *The Northern Japan Daily News*
Miyake Tetsuya	Reporter for *The Northern Japan Daily News*, former speed champion from Meiji University
Funatsu Hidematsu	Farmer who operates a stall selling new years ornaments
Funatsu Ishi	Hidematsu's wife
Funatsu Matsue	Hidematsu's daughter
Seki Tamekichi	Independent farmer. Hold-out on bucket land and member of the east-two coop
Henmi Shōsaku	Farmer who works during the off-season as a laborer
Henmi Shino	Shōsaku's pregnant sister, maid for Amamiya family
Jimpo Yasohachi	Farmer working in dredging project; heavy smoker who plays the "demon" in the annual festival
Ichihashi Tatsuzō	Charcoal burner from the marshes, head of the charcoal burners' guild
Nose Kiyoji	Charcoal burner also working on the dredging project
Izumi Jirō	Rebellious charcoal burner from the marshes
Izumi Hidema	Jirō's younger brother
Izumi Kametarō	Jirō's father
Izumi Toku	Jirō's mother

Amamiya Akira	Head of the experimental station
Amamiya Teruko	Amamiya's wife, daughter of Professor Takimoto
Amamiya Tōru	Their son
Amamiya Reiko	Their daughter
Komai Tsuta	"The Lady Landlord," mistress of absentee landlord Hayakawa Sentarō
Komai Ayako	Tsuta's daughter
Komai Nenokichi	Tsuta's brother
Teramachi Tamaki	School teacher
Sagara Tomoyoshi	Foreman of the Igarashi Lumber Mill
Morita Otozō	Elderly lumber mill worker
Fyodor Kovankov	White Russian expatriate, operates a hard cider bar
Yoshimitsu Yosaburō	Charcoal burner

Act II: A New Year's Party (Early January)

Tsuji Shōhei	Senior worker at the experimental station
Aoki Yoshie	Young technician at the experimental station; wife's name is Michiko
Karasawa Katsumi	Manager of the flax mill; like Amamiya a student of Professor Takimoto

Act III: Inspection at the Kilns (ca. February/March)

| Adachi Kimi | Daughter of grocer in town, formerly a member of the Hokkaido Council, a left-wing organization |
| Tashirogi Ryōkichi | Tsuta's enforcer |

Act IV: The Experimental Fields (May)

Workers 1-5	Female laborers
Maintenance Man	
Dr. Nakaide	Amamiya family physician
Watari Junzō	Farmer, member of the east-two coop who tries to use Amamiya's method
Takimoto Toshiaki	Professor of agriculture, mentor of Amamiya and Karasawa, father of Teruko

Act V: The Flax Mill (Early September)

Daymen	Female laborers at the flax mill
Laborers	Male workers at the flax mill (Laborer 1 is named Akutsu)
Tora	Tenant farmer, friend of Seki Tamekichi
Tadokoro	Agricultural inspector
Hatano	Clerk who assists Tadokoro
Sue	Friend of Matsue
Igarashi Shigeo	Young owner of the Igarashi Lumber Mill

Act VI: The Festival (Mid-September)

Vendors	Ice cream, fruit, and balloon vendors; baker and haberdasher
Children	
Village Notables	
Priest	Shinto priest
Kaneyo	Friend of Matsue and Sue
Youths 1-3	Members of the Young Men's Association
Shinji	Tenant farmer on Hayakawa farm
Saichi	Tenant farmer on Hayakawa farm
Takashi	Tenant from the Igarashi farm
Sango	Tenant from the Igarashi farm
Mother and Child	
Man with Bicycle	

To the memory of Osanai Kaoru.

This play is by one of your less able students, who has tried to accept your legacy and articulate it, not in its contemporary form, but in the form of the future.

—Kubo Sakae

Part One

Time: The 1930s. (From the end of one year until the harvest season of the next.)

Place: Northern Japan. (A town and a farming village in a certain rural district.)

Act One: A New Year's Market

It is still dark as the overture begins. Slides are projected on a screen: the title of the play, then the insignia of the troupe.

The voice of the Narrator overlaps with the play's musical theme:

NARRATOR: The original inhabitants[1] called this town/ "The place where the rivers part."/ It lies nestled in the acute angle/ At the confluence of Japan's sixth largest river and its tributary,/ Which flow together at the tip of the town/ Like a swallow's severed tail.

An agricultural town in the northernmost part of Japan,/ It lies in a plain/ Where the snow thaws later/ And the frost falls earlier than anywhere else;/ A town small as a kernel of grain/ In a peasant's wrinkled palm.

But the soybeans that are transported to market here by rail and wagon/ From the twenty thousand hectares[2] that surround the town/ Are nonetheless shipped across the sea/ To vie with the produce of Holland and the vicissitudes of the world market./ Each day thousands of sugar beets,/ The soil still clinging to their skins,/ Are flushed with iron rakes/ Onto the trade route of a company that makes sugar/ With distant Taiwan./ And the fibers that pass through the rollers of the flax company's mill/ Are shipped to the industrial areas of the south/ To be woven into the wings of airplanes/ And to canvas the decks of ships.

Pause. Music.

NARRATOR: The main street of the town/ Extends from the train depot to the river,/ Where a single bridge links it with the surrounding villages.

---

[1] The Ainu, a group racially distinct from the rest of the Japanese, were the original inhabitants of northern Japan.

[2] Measurements are given in their approximate metric equivalents.

Across the river/ Lies the village with the largest tillable area on the plain./ The original inhabitants called it "Tresses,"/ After the river that flows like black hair streaming in the wind.

But even as they are ravaged by cold, famine, crop failures, and floods,/ All the menaces contrived by nature and man to dissuade them,/ The people who live on this land persevere like the nameless grass/ That springs from rocks in desolate terrain.

Our drama centers on this town,/ This village./ It moves from the time/ When the stall selling new year's ornaments/ Appears at the foot of the bridge/ To the harvest season of the next year.

The final portion of the Narrator's introduction assumes the rhythm of a speeding train; and as the sound of real train wheels drowns it out, a slide appears: ACT ONE: A NEW YEAR'S MARKET.

The deafening screech of approaching wheels. A long, high-pitched steam whistle. The title fades, and the stage lights come up.

The train passes, shaking the new year's stall to its foundations. It is a makeshift affair built of logs and covered on three sides with straw matting. Its roof is cantilevered and opens toward the audience.

Kawabe, a photographer for The Northern Japan Daily News, *has been standing on the snow-covered, concrete embankment at the edge of the stage, taking pictures of the people in the stall.*

KAWABE *(choking on the trail of smoke from the passing train)*: Pyuuu! Damn!

He has been photographing Funatsu Matsue, who is tending the stall.

MATSUE *(watching the train pass)*: Hey! Who was that?

As the crossing barrier rolls away, the pool of people, horses, and sleighs dammed up behind it begins to flow. There are the sounds of sleigh bells, hoofs, whips, and the hubbub of the crowd.

VOICE: Giddyap there! Giddyap! Giddyap!

The harsh voice of someone scolding his horse; laughter; conversation.

The stall is ostensibly selling ornaments to decorate homes for the impending new year, but there are few pines in this snow-covered region, and the fir branches used in the traditional ornaments make them look more like Christmas trees. The wreaths are also made of sedge dyed an unnatural green and lack the soft fullness of the usual straw. Clumsily fired clay prawns and masks of the plump, happy Okame are displayed on the stall's roughly hewn counter along with the half-frozen mandarin oranges that substitute for the traditional citrons. Forlorn branches of poplars decked with dumplings and candies have been inserted in the drifts at the edge of the road, their vulgar pastels strangely lovely in the arsenic-white light of the snow. Octopuses and whole salted salmons hang from the eaves, frozen stiff like so much lumber. In short, everything about the stall testifies that its customers are impoverished farmers and poor people from the outskirts of town.

A family of three operates the stall: Funatsu Hidematsu, a farmer of moderate means from the village, his wife Ishi, and their daughter Matsue. Usually they are busy filling customers' orders, lowering goods from the eaves with a long pole, untying bunches of ornaments, and retreating to the stove in the recesses of the stall when their hands grow stiff with the cold, but just now they are being dragged out into the blinding light of this snowy morning by the photographer for The Northern Japan Daily News.

MATSUE (*looking over her shoulder*): Papa!

KAWABE (*from atop the embankment*): Face a little more this way, would you, miss?

MATSUE (*doing as she's told*): Like this? (*Without moving her face*): Didn't you see him? There was someone in the train just now, looking this way and shouting out the window.

HIDEMATSU: Probably some drunk. They're giving the new immigrants to Manchuria[3] a big send-off today. The depot's filled with people laughing and crying and carrying on.

KAWABE (*changing the position of his camera*): Damn! Reflection's too strong. Everything's going to be too dark.

Laughing voices. As only a small portion of the road before the stall is shown in the proscenium, the remainder should be understood to extend to the audience's left and right. These voices of excited young men come from across this road.

VOICE: Looking good! Looking good!

ANOTHER VOICE: You're a regular Queen of Sheba!

MATSUE (*looking in the direction of the voices*): It's the boys from the lumber mill. (*Shouting*): Mind your own business! Push that wagon to the warehouse like you're supposed to!

There is more excited shouting, and snowballs come flying toward the stall.

---

[3] Soldiers on their way to the front. See introduction.

MATSUE: Jerks! (*In a loud voice*): If you've got so much energy, come over here and put your arms around me! We'll get our picture taken together!

ISHI: Matsue!

Miyake Tetsuya, a reporter for the same newspaper as Kawabe, is interviewing people for a story on preparations for the new year. He approaches Seki Tamekichi, a customer who is wrapping his purchases in a large cloth.

MIYAKE: How about getting in the picture, too?

SEKI: Lay off me!

MIYAKE: The smiling face of a satisfied customer. . . . (*Turning toward the embankment*): That's what you want, isn't it?

SEKI: Just let my smiling face show up in the paper: there'll be hell to pay!

ISHI (*handing him his change from a basket suspended from the roof*): Here you go. Can't afford to be too careful when you're loaded with cash, right?

MIYAKE: Come on, how about it?

SEKI (*looking down the road*): Where's that damn bus!

MATSUE: What bus? You know perfectly well the one that just passed has to make a stop at the station first.

MIYAKE (*toward the embankment*): What do you want to do?

KAWABE: Never mind. We'll have to forget about the picture.

ISHI: Poor Seki, never did make it home. The weight of the snow twisted Suzuran bridge, and the bus slipped right off! Wrapped chains around the tires and everything, but it didn't help!

SEKI (*taking her seriously*): Hey!

ISHI (*trying to keep a straight face*): I can hear people talking now: What a shame! they'll say. And he just deposited all that money in the bank, too! If he'd only stopped to have his picture taken, he'd have lived!

SEKI: Trying to make a fool out of me, eh! (*To Hidematsu*): Funatsu, let me stay here until the bus comes, all right?

HIDEMATSU: Be my guest.

Seki goes to the stove.

MATSUE (*spying someone coming down the road, she signals for the photographer to hide his camera*): Shōsaku! (*There is a distant response.*) Come here a minute. (*She beckons to him.*)

Henmi Shōsaku approaches the stall. It is obvious from his clothing that he is a farmer working as a laborer in the off-season.

MATSUE: What are you doing wandering around here?

SHŌSAKU: You want something?

MATSUE: I thought you were washing down the beets.

SHŌSAKU: We finished yesterday, but what with this snow. . .

MATSUE: Come here and give me your hand.

SHŌSAKU: What for?

MATSUE: I've got something for you. Come on!

SHŌSAKU: What is it? (*He begins to put out his hand.*)

KAWABE (*releasing the shutter*): Got it!

Everyone around Shōsaku bursts out laughing. The young men across the street also clap their hands and shout.

VOICE: You really got him that time!

ANOTHER VOICE: Gal's a regular con artist!

Shōsaku looks around in confusion.

MATSUE (*holding her sides with laughter*): Look at this! He still doesn't know what happened! Hah-hah-hah!

KAWABE: Hold this for me, will you? (*He hands the camera to Miyake and jumps to the ground.*)

ISHI: Get tomorrow's newspaper from somebody and you'll see. You'll be in there big as life. Hah-hah-hah!

HIDEMATSU: A real big-spender, getting your picture taken out shopping and all!

MIYAKE (talking to Kawabe at the foot of the embankment): There isn't enough time to go back to the office and still make it to the station. . .

KAWABE: You have to. The chief said. . . . (He continues talking.)

HIDEMATSU (to the disgruntled Shōsaku, who has begun to walk away): How about buying something while you're here? You just got paid by the sugar company. You must be loaded.

ISHI: Come on, we'll give you a discount.

MATSUE: You better buy something. You're gonna make a liar out of the newspaper!

Shōsaku starts to walk away without responding.

SEKI (from beside the stove): Hey, Henmi!

Shōsaku looks back.

SEKI: You said you were going to get in touch with me. What happened?

SHŌSAKU: About what?

SEKI: The allocation of your fields for flax.

SHŌSAKU: I haven't decided yet.

SEKI: I see. I guess you've just got so much land you don't know what to do with it, huh? Maybe you're thinking of planting five hectares in flax next year!

Everyone bursts out laughing.

SEKI: You know the incentive policy's changed. If we don't let them know early in the spring, our co-op won't be able to borrow fertilizer from the company. You got that?

SHŌSAKU: All right. (*He goes over the railroad crossing toward the bridge and exits.*)

KAWABE (to Miyake): Then you wait here. I'll go discuss it with the chief, and if he wants you to go too, I'll pick you up in the car.

MIYAKE: Damned waste of time, if you ask me.

KAWABE (*to the people in the stall*): Thanks. (*He runs off.*)

MIYAKE (*obviously annoyed, he enters the stall*): All right, let's get this over with.

SEKI (*looking after Shōsaku*): That man's more damned trouble! Phew, it's cold! Spent every last cent I made last year, and now there's a damned draft through my pockets!

HIDEMATSU: Look who's complaining. You're the only independent farmer left up there. All the others lost their land three years ago.

SEKI: Yeah, well, I'm different from the rest. I slept over there last night because of the snow. . . (*he indicates the lumber mill across the road*): and old man Igarashi said the same thing: so long as Seki survives, nobody'll be able to say the landlord made a killing when he sold us the land.

MATSUE (*reacting to one of Miyake's questions*): Look, if I say I'm not going to tell you, I'm not going to tell you. Now, if you were a policeman or something. . . (*she pretends to twirl a mustache*): it'd be a different story! Hah-hah-hah!

MIYAKE: Come on, don't give me a hard time.

MATSUE: Listen, when you ask a young girl's age, you don't just say, "Age?" You've got to be tactful and polite.

There is the sound of a bus filled with passengers pulling up to the stop.

SEKI: Finally! Hey, wait for me!

CONDUCTOR (*a female voice*): If you've got a lot of luggage, wait for the next bus.

SEKI (*raising his bundle with one hand*): This is it. (*He bows to the people in the stall and exits at a run.*)

ISHI: Come again!

The bus revs its engine and struggles through the snow. The sound fades into the distance.

ISHI: Sleighs used to stop here for passengers too. Wasn't but two or three years ago. Now everything's buses!

MATSUE (*to Miyake*): Now that you mention it, I used work out at the sugar company's tractor farm. You're from the newspaper, so you ought to know—about that incident with Adachi Kimi, I mean.

MIYAKE: That must have been back when they divided the farm into tenant plots.

MATSUE: That's right. Anyway, you look just like the man who questioned me then.

MIYAKE: Don't be silly!

HIDEMATSU (*as he works*): I never saw anybody as restless as that Seki. First he's out to the exchange to see them select the beans for export, then he's off to the beet farm, and after that. . . .

MATSUE: You better watch what you say: you're going to get written up in the newspaper.

ISHI: Let him write us up. They come around here asking all these questions and never write anything anyway.

MATSUE: Whatever happened to those tractors, I wonder?

MIYAKE: I heard they were sold to the town and the agricultural school. Some wheeler-dealer from the company named Shimura made the arrangements. They're probably using the one at the school in their experimental fields, but what use the town has for a tractor, I don't know.

Carrying a shovel in one hand, Jimpo Yasohachi appears over the embankment. One of the poorest peasants from the village, he has been dredging gravel in the riverbed as part of a public works project. He is dressed lightly, with boots up to his thighs.

YASOHACHI: Damned snow's everywhere. (*He leaps down from the embankment and comes to the stall.*) Sorry, but let me warm myself by the stove again, will you?

HIDEMATSU (*looking displeased*): Again? You're going to get caught if you're not careful.

YASOHACHI: Damn, it's cold! (*He goes to the stove.*)

MATSUE: How's it going?

YASOHACHI: Today? Look at these legs. I wrapped a red woolen blanket around them under my boots. But when you're standing in the water. . . . Hey, what's this? (*He removes the cover from the pot on the stove.*)

MATSUE: Don't be getting any ideas in your head now, Mr. Demon.

YASOHACHI: Cod fish stew, eh? (*He starts to take off his cotton gloves.*) Oops, I'll rip them like that. Damn, that hurts!

ISHI: Those gloves have seen better days. Why don't you get a used pair from the bunk house?

MATSUE: Your hands are red as a lobster! (*She feels them.*) They're freezing!

YASOHACHI: Listen, I dig in the snow, right? So today I dig down, and I'll be damned if it's not frozen solid. So I use a pick and chop away at it until, whadya know, there's the gravel looking up at me. So first I use a shovel to dig a hole in the gravel, and then I go down in the hole and dig around inside. And how do you like that? Before I know it, I'm frozen in all around my ass and can't budge. So I get up a head of steam and . . . (*he demonstrates as he speaks*): Give my ass a good shake, and I'll be damned if the ice doesn't break right away.

ISHI: Like hell!

YASOHACHI (*obscenely*): My little helper here caught a cold, too. He'll die for sure if we don't warm him up. Matsue, you wouldn't be able to nurse him back to health, would you?

MATSUE: The cold's gone to his head! Ah-hah-hah! (*To Miyake*): Now here's something for the papers!

YASOHACHI: Hey, quit it! Say, Funatsu, sorry to trouble you, but you wouldn't have a . . . a cigarette, would you?

HIDEMATSU: Sorry.

MIYAKE (*taking out a pack*): I have some, if you don't mind "Bats."[4]

YASOHACHI: Say, thanks! (*He lights up.*) Oh, that's good. You know what they say, the finest things in life are a borrowed smoke and a stranger's . . . I forget what. Anyway. . . . (*He drops the cigarette.*)

MATSUE: See, your hands are so stiff, you can't even hold it. Your mouth works well enough, but. . . .

YASOHACHI (*picking up the cigarette*): Thanks to these weeds, everything takes me a day longer than anybody else. If you work six days on the dredging project, you usually get a bushel of rice. But I get cigarettes from the bunk house, so I have to work a day extra. I can't ask for gloves, either.

Hidematsu has finished his work for the moment and sits down behind the counter at the front of the stall where he makes entries in his ledger while he warms himself with a brazier made from an oil can set between his legs.

From the other side of the road, Ichihashi Tatsuzō, a charcoal burner from the marshes, bounds over the snow carrying a gunny sack.

ICHIHASHI: Howdy!

HIDEMATSU: What can we do for you?

---

[4]"Golden Bats," a cheap brand of cigarettes.

ICHIHASHI: Sorry, I didn't come to buy. Listen, how'd you like to sell charcoal in your stall here? (*Looking around*): You've got a good location. You'd do a good business.

HIDEMATSU: Charcoal?

ICHIHASHI: I just got an order for twenty bags from the Igarashi Lumber Mill across the way. Of course, you don't need any charcoal for indoor use, but. . . . How about it? I can let you have a forty-kilo bag of first-class oak charcoal wholesale for forty sen.

ISHI (*extricating herself from near the stove*): How come it's so cheap?

ICHIHASHI: Hah-hah-hah! We're having a year-end sale. The only thing is, all sales are cash in advance.

HIDEMATSU: Cash? Where's this charcoal from?

ICHIHASHI (*taking a piece of charcoal from his sack*): Here, just take a look at this sample. I live over in the marshes, and I'll bring your order by about noon. It doesn't cost anything to look.

ISHI: Let me see that. (*She takes the charcoal and examines it.*)

MATSUE (*to Miyake*): Why? They call him "Mr. Demon" because at the carnival he always wears a demon mask.

ICHIHASHI: You're a regular expert, aren't you?

ISHI: Why do you say that?

ICHIHASHI: I can tell by the way you handle it.

ISHI: I'm no match for you. You'd say anything to make a sale. Doesn't this spark and crackle when you burn it?

ICHIHASHI: It'll spark and crackle a little bit. It's oak after all.

ISHI: You mean to tell me first-class oak's going to spark and crackle?
Everyone bursts out laughing.

ICHIHASHI: Whoops! Well, you'll have to give me credit for honesty anyway! Hah-hah-hah! This stuff's going for one yen twenty or thirty sen on the open market.

ISHI: What do you think? (*She looks back at Hidematsu.*)

HIDEMATSU (*without responding*): You said you were from the marshes? You a burner?

ICHIHASHI: That's me!

HIDEMATSU: I thought Hayakawa had a concession on all the charcoal from the marshes?

ICHIHASHI: Oh, if that's what's bothering you, don't worry. We've got permission.

HIDEMATSU: Hmmmm.

ICHIHASHI: We've got permission to sell a limited number of bags. There's nothing to worry about. (*To Ishi*): See?

HIDEMATSU: We'll pass this time.

ICHIHASHI: You're missing a good opportunity.

HIDEMATSU: I said we don't need any.

Ishi returns the sample.

ICHIHASHI: Hah-hah-hah! Listen, you don't think we're selling this without permission, do you?

HIDEMATSU: I said we don't want it!

ICHIHASHI: All right, I'll tell you what: I'll drop by again when I make my deliveries, so think it over. (*Exits.*)

ISHI: We'd make a nice profit, you know.

HIDEMATSU: Don't be a fool. In the first place, I don't like his looks.

YASOHACHI (*to Miyake*): At the moment I'm working construction, but I go way back to the pioneer days. Why, I'm a regular institution around here. They can't hold the festival without me.

ISHI (*going to the stove*): Yeah, and he'll drive you crazy, too! Every time the procession stops, he's got his mask up and a fag in his mouth!

YASOHACHI: You must know something about haiku, being from the newspaper and all. Mr. Hayakawa wrote one about me once. You think it's any good? Let me see, it went, "Pushing up his mask . . . " And then how did it go? Oh yeah: "He smokes a cigarette/ Face of a demon."

MIYAKE: Face of a demon?

YASOHACHI: No, that can't be right, can it?

Nose Kiyoji, a charcoal burner from the marshes who is also working on the dredging project, descends from the embankment.

KIYOJI (*at the entrance to the stall*): You bastard, I thought it was taking you a hell of a long time to piss!

YASOHACHI (*spinning around*): Hey, don't sneak up on me like that!

KIYOJI: Every time I turn around you're running off somewhere, and now I see you found yourself a nice cozy little hole to curl up in.

YASOHACHI: The sleigh isn't back for another load yet, is it?

KIYOJI: Just never mind about the sleigh. They want you over at the bunk house.

YASOHACHI: Yeah?

KIYOJI: Well, since I'm here, I might as well warm myself, too. Let me through there. (*He approaches the stove.*)

YASOHACHI: You son-of-a-bitch!

KIYOJI: Go ahead. I'm numb from the waist down. I could care less. (*He leans on Yasohachi, rocking him as he sings*):

It's new year's eve

And cold in the water.

But the boss's pockets,

Lined with green,
Seem more like May.
Oh, give some back to me!
Yes, give some back to me!

MATSUE: Ah-hah-hah!

HIDEMATSU: That's about enough. This isn't a saloon. Now out with the both of you!

YASOHACHI (*to Kiyoji*): Now see what you've done! In the first place, Funatsu here doesn't know you. You've got a lot of nerve barging in.

HIDEMATSU: Before you know it, someone from the bunk house is going show up to chew me out.

KIYOJI (*to Hidematsu*): Sorry. Look, I'm Nose from the marshes.

YASOHACHI: Come on, let's go. (*They start to leave.*)

HIDEMATSU: You say you're from the marshes?

KIYOJI: That's right.

HIDEMATSU: Okay, then you can stay—if you don't make a ruckus. I've got something I want to ask you. (*He takes a pack of cigarettes from inside his coat.*)

YASOHACHI (*spying the cigarettes*): Why, you! . . . Okay, this is for holding out on me. (*He takes one from the pack.*)

HIDEMATSU: I understand they've arranged for the burners to sell charcoal on their own?

KIYOJI: Is that so? I don't know anything about it. Of course, I've been staying in the bunk house for ten days, so I wouldn't know if the roof on one of the kilns had caved in, but it sounds strange to me.

HIDEMATSU: Hmmm. You know a burner with a scar on his forehead that splits his right eyebrow in two?

KIYOJI: That'd be Ichihashi. Him and Izumi Jirō are the biggest troublemakers in the marshes. Bastard, when I get home, I'll give him a licking he won't forget!

HIDEMATSU: Jirō? Kametarō's son?

KIYOJI: You know his old man? I heard he ran off to Otaru and is sponging off some dame. She runs a little restaurant, they say.

Amamiya Teruko appears at the front of the stall. Her attire—an elegant coat, a silver fox muffler, and a velvet scarf across her face—contrasts sharply with her surroundings. She is accompanied by her maid, Henmi Shino, who wears the modest cotton shawl she saves for special occasions.

TERUKO: Pardon me.

HIDEMATSU: Yes ma'am! What can I do for you?

TERUKO (*looking around at the stall's wares*): My word! . . . (*Turning around*): Shino, is this the place?

SHINO: Yes, ma'am.

TERUKO: This won't do at all. We'll have to go into town after all.

MIYAKE (*rising*): Mrs. Amamiya?

TERUKO: Why, Mr. Miyake, what are you doing in a place like this?

MIYAKE: I was just about to ask you the same thing. When did you get back from Tokyo?

TERUKO (*uncovering her face*): I returned some time ago, but I've been staying at my father's house in Sapporo. I got back here just this morning.

MIYAKE: You were lucky to get through Karikachi Pass[5] with all this snow.

TERUKO: Yes, indeed. And what about you?

MIYAKE: The paper's doing a special on these new year's stalls. Year-end local color, that sort of thing.

TERUKO: I'll be most cross with you if you write about me in your article.

MIYAKE: Hah-hah-hah, now you've given me an idea! The wife of the head of the local agricultural station rushes back at the last minute from the home of her father, Professor Takimoto, and, totally unprepared to greet the new year, shows up in a place like this!

TERUKO: You're awful! We were on our way to the Kikumaru Department Store, weren't we, Shino?

ISHI: Excuse me, ma'am, but isn't there something here that would interest you?

TERUKO (*looking around*): Well. . . . My land, look at this prawn! Why it's made out of clay, isn't it? With wire for whiskers! And what about this mask? Shino, do you display this sort of thing in your home?

SHINO: Yes, ma'am. Please, ma'am, watch your head.

TERUKO: Heavens! (*Ducking, she looks up at the objects hanging from the eaves.*) Why, the legs of this octopus are frozen stiff as a board! Hah-hah-hah. (*Sensing the eyes of those around her*): I'm sorry. I shouldn't laugh. I suppose in peasant households people eat this sort of thing as a special new year's delicacy. (*Her grimace has a double meaning.*)

---

[5] The mountain pass between the Tokachi Plain and the Ishikari Plain, where Sapporo is located.

HIDEMATSU: Ma'am, how about one of these decorated branches? These here are too small, of course, but we could make up a big one for you by tomorrow and deliver it if you like.

TERUKO: No, we really couldn't do with anything less than willow branches from the mainland. Let me see now. . . . Mr. Miyake! Stop laughing!

Miyake is enjoying her predicament.

TERUKO: Shino, shall I buy you one of these paddles with the portrait of a geisha on the back?[6]

SHINO: No, thank you, ma'am. Miss Reiko gave me her's from last year.

TERUKO: Well . . . I wonder if they've already done their new year's shopping at your brother's place?

SHINO: I don't know, but. . . .

TERUKO: Let me see . . . (*To the stallkeepers*): You people return to the village at night, don't you?

ISHI: Yes, ma'am. You didn't think we slept. . . .

TERUKO: Is the Henmi house far from yours? Henmi . . . (*She looks at Shino*): Shōsaku, wasn't it?

SHINO: Yes, ma'am.

ISHI (*signaling to Hidematsu with her eyes*): Psst!

HIDEMATSU: Oh, no, ma'am. It's not far, but. . . .

TERUKO: In that case . . . (*Pointing at nothing in particular*): Please deliver this branch to their home. If it's not too much trouble.

HIDEMATSU (*vaguely*): I see.

SHINO: You really don't have to bother, ma'am.

TERUKO: That's perfectly all right. How much will it be?

ISHI: Thirty sen, please.

TERUKO: Here you are. (*She pays.*) Please keep the change for your trouble. Mr. Miyake, please drop by the house, won't you? I have some delightful stories to tell you about the national convention.

MIYAKE: Oh, yes, "Supporters of Women in Society." Of course, I'll drop by as soon as I get the chance.

MATSUE (*who's been staring at her for some time*): Shino!

SHINO (*their eyes meet*): Matsue!

MATSUE: You look so different! I hardly recognized you!

---

[6]*Hagoita,* a traditional implement used in a badmintonlike game but now primarily for decoration.

SHINO: I'm sorry. I was thinking about something else. Have you seen Sue and Kaneyo lately?

There is the sound of a bus crossing the railroad tracks from the other side of the bridge.

TERUKO: Here's the bus, Shino. Let's take it and save some money.

HIDEMATSU AND ISHI: Thank you. Come again.

Teruko and Shino exit. The sound of the bus driving off.

MATSUE (*watching the bus pull away*): Who does she think she is? These paddles are too good for her!

YASOHACHI (*rising*): Well, I guess we'd better get going. (Going to the entrance of the stall and imitating Teruko): "My heavens, look at this mask!" Where does she get off talking like that? She's the spitting image!

Everyone laughs.

YASOHACHI: Or even . . . (*He was thinking of some other insult, but*): Monkey! Mr. Newspaperman, that was it!

MIYAKE: What?

YASOHACHI: "He smokes a cigarette/ Face of the monkey god!"[7] That's how it went. I was thinking of "monkey" and it came back to me. Ah-hah-hah!

KIYOJI: Oh, I'm cold again already! And for what? We pay out the rice we receive the minute we get it. I'm about at the end of my rope.

The two men climb over the embankment.

MATSUE: Mother, who was that lady?

ISHI: Don't be silly. Don't you know where Shino's working? That was Mrs. Amamiya from the agricultural station.

MATSUE: The agricultural station? Rats! Why didn't you ask her about me?

ISHI: Why me? Talk to that newspaper fellow.

MATSUE: Good idea! (*To Miyake*): Say, mister? I've been wanting to work as a field hand over at the agricultural station. I sent in my application and everything. Put in the good word for me, will you?

MIYAKE: All right. (*Looking across the way*): I wonder if the coffee's any good over there? Listen, when they come from the paper, tell them I'm over next to the bicycle shop, all right? (*Making scribbling motions with his hand*): I'll be working on my article.

---

[7]Sarutahiko, a traditional demon character. Saru means monkey. Here, Sarutahiko is identical with the demon (*tengu*) mentioned earlier. Both are known for their long nose. Cf. Act Six.

MATSUE: All right. But in exchange, remember what I asked you.

MIYAKE (*to the others in the shop*): Thanks very much. (*Exits.*)

Led by two teachers, a group of children from the village school enters over the railroad crossing. One of the teachers is comforting a crying girl. The teacher, the girl, and one of the boys separate from the group and come to the stall. They are Teramachi Tamaki, Komai Ayako, and Izumi Hidema.

TERAMACHI (*to the other teacher*): Mr. Yamamura, I'll leave the rest of them to you.

The group of children exits toward the depot.

TERAMACHI: Do you mind if we rest here a minute? One of the children is sick.

HIDEMATSU: Mr. Teramachi?

TERAMACHI: Oh, Funatsu! Perfect!

ISHI: That's Ayako, Komai's little girl.

TERAMACHI: Half-way here she had to get this tummy ache, and. . .

Ayako is whimpering.

HIDEMA: I'll take her to the stove.

TERAMACHI: I'll see to it. Izumi, you go ahead with the others.

HIDEMA: All right. See you later, Aya. Hope you feel better. (*He runs off.*)

TERAMACHI (*with a sardonic smile*): This is what I get for opening my big mouth. I told the principal it would destroy the whole point of the exercise to let Komai here go by car when the other children had to trek through the snow to see the immigrants off to Manchuria.

ISHI: Does it really hurt?

TERAMACHI (*as if to say it is really nothing*): Ach. . . .

MATSUE (*spitefully*): Who's kid are you, anyway? A real weakling, aren't you!

ISHI: Matsue! (*She glares at her.*)

MATSUE (*ignoring her*): When I was little, even in winter, your mother used to. . . .

ISHI: Cut that out! (*She stops her.*)

HIDEMATSU (*remembering*): By the way, I heard your father's been under the weather. How's he doing?

TERAMACHI: Not too well, I'm afraid. Right now we've got another problem, though. The Hokkaido government's changed its policy, and either the Mrs. or I have to quit teaching beginning with the new school year.[8]

ISHI: Why?

TERAMACHI: There are too many graduates from the teacher's college, so when a husband and wife are both working, one's got "to do the right thing" and step aside, I guess.

ISHI: That's terrible! You'll feel like a bird with one wing.

HIDEMATSU: I don't know how they can do that. They always go after the most defenseless first, don't they!

AYAKO (*weeping dramatically*): Call the doctor . . . I want my mommy!

TERAMACHI: You'll be all right. You'll be all right. You'll feel better as soon as you warm up.

AYAKO: No I won't! My mommy says to call the doctor right away when you get sick.

TERAMACHI: You'll feel better, just wait a minute.

AYAKO: I want to take a cab the rest of the way!

TERAMACHI: You see what I mean? (*Mumbling to himself*): They learn this stuff at home. Funatsu, I'm sorry to trouble you, but could you lend me one yen?

HIDEMATSU: I can lend you the money, but wouldn't it be faster to call?

TERAMACHI: Is there a phone?

HIDEMATSU: Across the street.

ISHI (*signaling with her eyes*): Psst!

HIDEMATSU: It'll be all right. It's an emergency.

TERAMACHI: That's Igarashi's mill, isn't it? Igarashi from the Igarashi farms?

AYAKO: No, please! I'll get scolded if I go there.

Sagara Tomoyoshi, foreman of the lumber mill, enters from across the road with Morita Otozo, an elderly mill worker.

SAGARA: Hello! The boss just. . . .

HIDEMATSU: Hello, Tomo!

SAGARA: The boss was watching from the window, and he noticed the girl—from Hayakawa's place, isn't she?

HIDEMATSU: That's right.

SAGARA: He said if she's in trouble to bring her over.

HIDEMATSU: That's very kind of him.

---

[8]That is, by April.

ISHI: The boss said that?

SAGARA: Yeah, well, his son's here today, too, so. . . .

TERAMACHI: Sorry to put you to the trouble. Ayako, I'm going to explain everything to your mother so you won't be scolded, all right? Let's go.

AYAKO: No! No!

ISHI: Come on, I'll give you a piggyback ride. (*She turns around for the girl to climb on.*)

SAGARA: Hah-hah-hah! That's the way!

ISHI (*finally getting Ayako on her back*): You're pretty big to be carrying like a baby! Umph!

SAGARA (*to Otozō*): Okay, Oto. No, wait a minute, I almost forgot. We already got bawled out once today. You've got the numbers, right?

OTOZŌ: Yeah.

Led by Sagara, Ishi crosses the road and exits with Ayako on her back.

OTOZŌ (*unfolding a piece of paper he has brought with him*): Let me see, there's Sagara the foreman . . . (*He looks after Sagara*): Heh-heh-heh . . . Then there's the sawyer, two at Chūmaru, and the driver, that's me. That makes thirty wreathes, ten pine boughs, and burdock festoons, er. . .

HIDEMATSU (*pointing to the ornaments on display*): Will these do?

OTOZŌ: They don't have to be that big.

Ishi returns from across the road.

ISHI: What a brat! I wouldn't think she was cute even if she were my own! (*To Matsue*): You shouldn't talk like that to a person's face.

MATSUE: Who cares about some lady landlord's kid anyway!

ISHI (*to Otozō*): Oto, everybody's sitting around inside over there. What's going on?

OTOZŌ: We're preparing the balance sheets. After all, we're managing the company together with the boss, you know. How do you like that for a new-fangled system, eh? Hah-hah-hah!

HIDEMATSU (*taking items down with a long pole*): How about these? So how did you make out the past six months?

OTOZŌ: You know, you never can tell. I had my doubts about this inexperienced young boss, but, you know, things seem to be working out all right. Take that forest up at Kitami for example: when Mitsubishi made a bid for it, the boss and Tomo jumped right in after them—said it would be a source of cheap lumber. Had their eyes peeled, all right. Me, I'm just getting too old, I guess. (*He points to his head.*) Problem's up here!

HIDEMATSU: Not enough fertilizer, eh? Hah-hah-hah!

OTOZŌ: Maybe I got too much in other places! (*Everyone bursts out laughing.*)

MATSUE: That's right! Ren's going to be in the Olympics! At least that's what it said in the newspaper.

ISHI: I think it's wonderful!

OTOZŌ (*glancing nervously across the road*): Not so wonderful. The young boss loves anything new, see, so he says he'll lend us the money to send Ren'ichi. If he wins, we don't have to pay the money back. All he's got to do is win a medal. I had a good mind to turn him down, but. . . .

MATSUE: Why?

OTOZŌ: He's sticking his nose in where it doesn't belong. Anyway, how much will that be all together?

Hidematsu picks up his abacus.

MATSUE: Will he be coming home before he leaves? Ren'ichi, I mean.

OTOZŌ: He said he would.

MATSUE: Let me know when he gets here, all right?

ISHI: Ah, to be young again!

HIDEMATSU: Four yen and . . . make it fifty sen even.

OTOZŌ: Thanks. (*He pays.*)

Miyake Tetsuya comes back from across the road.

MIYAKE: Hasn't anyone shown up from the paper yet?

MATSUE: Not yet.

MIYAKE: Damn. Well. . . .

HIDEMATSU: Matsue, help him carry these things.

MATSUE: My pleasure!

ISHI: Will you listen to that? She could change the weather when she talks like that!

Fyodor Kovankov, a Russian who operates a hard cider bar in the vicinity, appears at the entrance to the stall.

KOVANKOV: Pardon me.

ISHI: Yessir! (*Looking at the sky*): I'll be, it really is clouding up!

OTOZŌ: You think it's going to snow again? (*He and Matsue exit with his purchases.*)

MIYAKE: Mr. Kovankov!

KOVANKOV: No! No! I am Japanese. My name No-bu-go-rō. You see? Ah-hah-hah! Please, you give me new year's ornaments. This and this and that. . . .

MIYAKE: Do you put this sort of thing up in your bar?

KOVANKOV: There's a saying, no? When in a country, do like that country, yes? I say it right? Man without country honors customs of others. Like this. (*To Ishi*): That one good.

MIYAKE: Then what about Christmas? I heard you had some trouble over at your place.

KOVANKOV: You know well. Who are you? Students get drunk on cider. Knock down Christmas tree with skis. Big mess.

Something seems to be happening at the end of the road. Two or three people can be seen running in that direction.

HIDEMATSU: What's going on? Look at all the people!

ISHI (*looking*): It's a snowplow! But what a strange looking snowplow!

MATSUE (*running from across the road, to Miyake*): That's the tractor, the one from the beet farm!

MIYAKE (*looking*): You're right! What do you know!

MATSUE: What are you so impressed about?

MIYAKE: I was wondering what the town was going to do with it. Somehow it seems like a waste.

MATSUE: That one there's called OT-25. I've had a ride on it. Look, see how it pulls to the left? See? See? Now what's happening? People are running away! Ah-hah-hah! Mother, I'll be right back. (*She runs off.*)

MIYAKE (*to Kovankov*): What's wrong?

Kovankov is staring wordlessly down the road.

MIYAKE: Look at that! Ah-hah-hah! Look at Kovankov with his mouth hanging open! Hah-hah-hah! Don't worry, Kovankov, it's American—"Made in U.S.A."!

KOVANKOV (*to the stallkeepers*): Please wrap up for me. I come back, later. Good-bye. (*He strides off through the snow.*)

ISHI (*suspiciously*): What's wrong with him? Did you make fun of him?

MIYAKE: Hah-hah-hah, he takes the cake! Listen, when they come from the paper. . . .

There is the sound of a car driving up and coming to a halt.

KAWABE'S VOICE: Miyake? So it is you. Come on, we're running late.

MIYAKE: What? But I don't have an arm band or anything.

KAWABE'S VOICE: I brought an extra one with me! See? You finish?

MIYAKE: Yes. I have to add some things, but. . . .

KAWABE'S VOICE: What are you standing there for? Hurry up and get in!

Miyake runs off, grumbling. The car pulls away. The roar of the tractor also fades into the distance.

ISHI: Papa, it's time to eat. (*She goes out in front of the stall and calls*):
Matsue! Matsue!

*Matsue comes back. The three of them sit around the pot on the stove
and begin to eat their noon meal.*

*A cloud passes before the sun, and the snow on the streets takes on a
bluish cast. The area falls silent.*

A shabbily dressed, middle-aged man appears at the stall.

ISHI (*noticing him after a few moments*): Welcome! (*Wiping her
mouth*): Sorry to keep you waiting.

The Man looks as if he wants to say something but remains silent.

MATSUE (*whispering in Hidematsu's ear*): He's the one who was
yelling out of the train before!

ISHI: I know you! You're. . . .

HIDEMATSU (*coming out*): Well! If it isn't old Kametarō!

ISHI: That's it! Well, well!

HIDEMATSU: Come in, come in! Don't just stand there! (*He guides him
into the stall and has him sit down.*) Let me just finish this, all right?
Have you eaten?

KAMETARŌ (*shaking his head*): All the way here, I sat looking out the
window of the train . . . the wheat and oats are still stacked in the
fields, and it looks as if insects have infested the soybeans. Nothing's
been harvested as far as I could see.

HIDEMATSU (*while he's eating*): It's the weather. It really got to us this
year. At my place, too.

KAMETARŌ: Listen, you might laugh, but didn't my Hidema walk by
here a little while ago?

ISHI (*eating*): Yeah, did you meet him? He's one of the children
chosen to represent the school. Fine boy. He went to the depot to see
off the immigrants to Manchuria.

KAMETARŌ: Then it was him! I really thought to call to him, but, well,
if a man can't recognize his own son. . . .

MATSUE (*to Ishi in a low voice*): He's Jirō's father, isn't he?

ISHI: Don't point at people with your chopsticks!

HIDEMATSU: I've been hearing rumors about you. What happened?
I've been jealous. From what I hear, you're off in Otaru running a
little restaurant for sailors. You here by yourself?

KAMETARŌ (*nodding*): I was sitting there watching the fields go by,
you know, and I was trying to figure out what to say, to Jirō
especially. Five years is a long time, you know. And then I seen this
stall here, and without thinking, I. . . . Stupid, there's no way you
could have heard me over all that racket.

Yoshimitsu Yosaburō, a charcoal burner from the marshes, appears at the entrance to the stall.

YOSABURŌ: Excuse me! Did somebody come by here before to take your order for charcoal?

HIDEMATSU: Yeah.

YOSABURŌ: He'll be by in a little while with your order. How many bags did you want? Oak, right?

HIDEMATSU: Since we don't have to settle up until new year's eve, we told him to leave five bags. *(To Ishi):* Right?

ISHI: Er, right. Darned good charcoal it was, too. I told him so.

YOSABURŌ: That's funny. I thought all orders were supposed to be cash in advance.

Komai Tsuta, mistress of absentee landlord Hayakawa Sentarō, enters from across the road with her older brother Nenokichi. She is wearing an old-fashioned hood of silk crepe and a wrap with a fur collar. Nenokichi, raised as a poor peasant, wears an overcoat over ill-fitting Western-style winter clothes.

TSUTA *(entering the stall without ceremony):* Thanks for looking out for Ayako.

HIDEMATSU *(bowing low):* Why, Miss Komai, how nice to see you!

ISHI: We really couldn't do anything for her. But please, do come in. Matsue, get out of the way.

TSUTA: Hidematsu, I really do have to thank you. You didn't have to take her over to Igarashi's personally.

Yosaburō had been hesitating, but now he makes a run for it.

TSUTA *(watching him):* Who? . . . *(Recognizing him):* Hey, it's Yosaburō! Yo, wait a minute! *(Turning around):* Nenokichi, go after him.

Moving faster than the dim-witted Nenokichi, Hidematsu grabs Yosaburō.

HIDEMATSU: Hold on there, you!

YOSABURŌ *(his arms pinned by Hidematsu and Nenokichi):* Hey, take it easy! Let me go! Let me go!

TSUTA: What are you doing around here, anyway?

HIDEMATSU: There was another one by before. They want us to buy charcoal from the marshes, cash in advance.

TSUTA *(shocked):* What! *(Pushing Yosaburō around):* You bastard, who told you you could go around selling charcoal?

YOSABURŌ: I . . . I don't know anything about it. Jirō said he'd cleared the whole thing with you, so. . . .

TSUTA: Jirō said that? The bastard thinks he can get away with murder just because I'm a woman. The boss just left! You bastards start making trouble the minute you think the coast is clear!

YOSABURŌ: I'm sorry! I didn't know!

TSUTA: Neno! Don't just stand there. Why do you think he's struggling? He thinks you're too weak to hold him. Go call a car. A car!

NENOKICHI: Mr. Funatsu, where can I call from?

HIDEMATSU: Matsue, go call a car.

MATSUE: Right!

ISHI: Hurry up!

Matsue runs off. A light snow begins to fall.

TSUTA (*recognizing Kametarō*): Aren't you Izumi Kametarō?

KAMETARŌ: Yes.

TSUTA: Neno, hold on to him now! (*To Kametarō*): When did you get back?

Kametarō is silent.

ISHI: He showed up out of the blue a few minutes ago.

TSUTA: Is that so? While you've been away, that boy Jirō of yours has turned into a real menace!

Kametarō is silent.

TSUTA: I couldn't handle him so I had to take him to court.

KAMETARŌ (*taken by surprise*): Court?

TSUTA: In the first place, you haven't got a formal contract for your land. As head of the household, you'll eventually have to. . . . Wait a minute, what happened to that woman you were with?

Kametarō does not answer.

TSUTA: Heh, I'll bet she turned out to be a real ball-buster!

Kametarō is still silent.

TSUTA: Hah-hah-hah! Her pimp probably milked you for all you had! And at your age, too! Shame on you! Hah-hah-hah! Anyway, that Jirō did nothing but accumulate debts, and if a person said something to him, he'd raise a stink, so I got to the point where it was more trouble than it was worth, and I decided it would be best for all concerned just to have him get off the land. It's only been a few days since I sent him the eviction notice by registered mail. And now look at this new trouble the good-for-nothing's caused!

MATSUE (*returning at a run*): Papa, they said there's not a single car available.

HIDEMATSU: It's always like that when you need them!

The snow continues to fall. Sleigh bells are ringing in the distance, and over them, a band can be heard playing.

MATSUE (*looking toward the bridge*): Look, there's Jirō now!

There is the sound of the approaching sleigh bells, their musical accompaniment, and, from a different direction, the sound of a train.

TSUTA: Damn him! (*She rushes out into the street.*)

NENOKICHI: Where are you going? Mr. Funatsu, stop her. Stop!

HIDEMATSU: Miss Komai, wait a minute.

Momentarily released, Yosaburō darts away like a frightened hare.

ISHI: Kame, go after him! Matsue, call Jirō!

The crossing gate closes. The sound of the bells and the music stops suddenly. In this vacuum, the sound of the approaching train resounds like thunder. From both sides of the tracks voices shout, "Banzai! Banzai!" Then there is the shrill whistle of the train and a trail of smoke.

TSUTA (*struggling*): Stop him! Let me go!

HIDEMATSU: It's dangerous! Watch out!

The crossing gate reopens, and once again there is the sound of sleigh bells and the band.

TSUTA: Stop! Wait!

NENOKICHI: Cut it out! You're going to get yourself run over!

ISHI: Kame, come out where he can see you.

MATSUE: Jirō! Oh, look, he's riding in the first sleigh . . . He's flicking the reins!

ISHI: Jirō!

MATSUE: You're father's back! He'll never hear us!

TSUTA: Damn him! Damn him! Stop! Wait, I said!

HIDEMATSU: It's dangerous! Watch out!

In the steadily falling snow, the sounds of the bells and the band reach a crescendo.

Curtain.

Act Two: A New Year's Party

Here, the title is projected without music before the lights come up:
ACT TWO: A NEW YEAR'S PARTY.
*A clock strikes five. Then it strikes six. As it is striking seven, the title
fades and the stage lights come up.*
*Standing on a stepladder designed for taking books from high shelves,
Amamiya Reiko is setting the   clock on   the wall. She is dressed in   a
countrified school uniform.*
REIKO: Shino! Look at the clock in the living room. How many
    minutes after seven is it exactly?
*It is a simple, Western-style   room that might be taken for either a
sitting room or a library in the home of Amamiya Akira, director of the
local agricultural station. The   house   is located   within   the station
compound, not far from the foot of the bridge where the last act took
place. The white walls of the room are punctuated by   straight, plain
pillars   and doors of varnished wood. The double storm windows and
steadily falling snow virtually soundproof the room, so after the clock
has finished striking seven, there is silence. Only the whispering sound
of the coal-burning stove remains.*
   *There is a sturdy writing table covered with files and stationery, and
among   them a telephone that   links the house   with   the   station's
laboratory. Tomes with impressive-looking titles, presumably about
agricultural theory, fill the bookshelves. Lining the wall are a radio,
phonograph, sofa, and the like.*
   *Luxuriant new year's   ornaments hang from   the ceiling, and
beneath them several tables have been put together for a modest dinner
party. The white tablecloth reflects the diffuse light of a frosted- glass
chandelier and the red glow of the stove.*

The room has three doors.   Door A leads to the foyer and entrance to the house; Door B to the   family dining room; and Door C to the kitchen.

TERUKO (*only her face visible at Door A*): Do you have to shout so!

REIKO (*from the stepladder*): You want the clock to tell the right time, don't you? (*Striking a comical pose, she imitates the radio call letters*): "This is J.O. . . ."

TERUKO (*into the foyer*): Come in!

Amamiya Teruko, wearing   an apron over her house clothes, escorts Tsuji Shohei, a senior worker at the station, into the room.

REIKO: Oh! (*She hurriedly descends from the stepladder.*)

Tsuji watches her and laughs.

TERUKO (*offering him a chair*): I stopped the clock on purpose.

REIKO: Why?

TERUKO: I'm going to have our guests listen to some records after dinner.

Reiko does not understand.

TERUKO: Don't you see?   The sound of the pendulum would be so distracting.

REIKO: Oh.

TERUKO: I don't know what I shall do with you, Reiko, you're such a bumpkin! (*She looks back at Tsuji and laughs.*) Go find something to do.

REIKO: Mother, you know that Debussy Prel— or whatever you call it, the one you brought back from Tokyo?

TERUKO: Don't   worry!   Tōru's over borrowing records from Mr. Shimura right now, ones that everyone will enjoy.

REIKO: Mother. . . .   (*Thinking better of it*): I guess I'd better not—I'll just get scolded again.   (*She exits through Door C, leaving Tsuji laughing behind her.*)

TERUKO (*sitting opposite him*): Have you spoken to my husband?

TSUJI: Not yet. He's been so busy these past few days, I haven't had a chance.

TERUKO: No, I suppose not.

TSUJI: I have to hand it to him, though. It probably has something to do with the   kind of paper he's writing, but he certainly is single-minded about his work!

TERUKO: Totally absorbed, isn't he?

TSUJI: Yes. By the way, I understand you've been a big help behind the scenes in getting us the Neubauer apparatus.[1]

TERUKO: Now who's been spreading rumors like that?

TSUJI: It reminds me of the story about the clock tower in Sapporo. The bell sounds so sweet, they say, because when the school of agriculture was being built the ladies of the town melted down their rings to make it. They wanted to do their part in pioneering this new land. I wonder what the Neubauer would sound like if you struck it?

TERUKO: How appalling! Where do such rumors start? I do hope you won't strike the Neubauer, though—you'll surely break the glass!
They both laugh.

TSUJI: Well, how about it? Of course, I wouldn't ask you to stop in the middle of the preparations for your party, but how about a compromise? You could excuse yourself early, and. . .

TERUKO: Oh, but that would spoil everything!

TSUJI: Why?

TERUKO: I don't like to say it, Mr. Tsuji, but I think you lack a certain sensitivity toward your subordinates. Perhaps it's because you're second in command here, but those working at the lower echelons of the station—don't like to bring up the subject of money, but—well, they only make forty or fifty yen at the most . . . Aoki and the others like him. . . .

TSUJI: I understand your point.

TERUKO: But that's not all. Once a year I like us to get together as families. Why, just yesterday I discussed the idea in our magazine group, and everyone agreed that it was a fine custom to establish. It's wonderful to get together beneath the new year's decorations. . . . (*She looks up.*) I love it! I do! Perhaps it's because I was raised in Tokyo, but. . . .

TSUJI: Mrs. Amamiya, I don't like to have to say this, but, well, I'm afraid I just can't keep quiet any longer. You see, compared to the previous director, our people seem somehow constrained under your husband. If this continues, well. . . . The point is some of the men don't have the slightest inclination to sit around drinking with their old ladies in the room.

TERUKO: You sound as if you're describing yourself!

---

[1] The Neubauer seedling method is a method developed in 1923 by H. Neubauer, a German botanist, to grow plant seedlings in petri dishes or beakers under controlled conditions to determine the uptake of soil nutrients. The Neubauer apparatus referred to here is the incubator necessary to maintain the steady temperatures required by the method.

TSUJI: Do I? Anyway, the director's stoicism . . . that is, his diligence is admirable, but perhaps if he'd, how shall I put it, if he'd view the station more within its social context, then, well. . . . For example, if he'd leave the routine tests to us and concentrate on getting his doctorate. . . .

TERUKO: But. . . .

TSUJI: It certainly isn't my place to speculate, but I wonder if Professor Takimoto might not wish the same thing for the man who married his daughter?

TERUKO: No, you're wrong there. My husband's the kind of man who leads the female hands out the minute the snow melts and gets covered with mud working beside them. Why, when I was in Sapporo, Father said the very same thing: that it's at least as important for Akira to apply his work to the actual lives of the farmers as it is for him to follow in Father's footsteps as a scholar.

Aoki Yoshie, a young technician at the station, appears through Door A carrying several folding chairs. Amamiya Tōru follws him, dressed in his university uniform and carrying a stack of record albums.

AOKI: Seven wasn't it?

TERUKO: Yes, thank you very much. What's been keeping you, Tōru?

TŌRU: Er . . . I was busy. (*He seems ill at ease.*)

TERUKO: You got involved talking to Mr. Aoki, didn't you? The laboratory is not a place for you to amuse yourself, you know. Let me see what you've brought.

TŌRU: The Unfinished Symphony. (*He hands her an album.*)

TSUJI: I don't know what you have in common, but you and Aoki really seem to hit it off, don't you, Tōru?

TERUKO: Didn't Mr. Shimura say anything?

Tōru is thinking about something else. Aoki attracts his attention.

TŌRU: Oh, yes, he said Shōji Tarō[2] would be good for this sort of party.

TERUKO: Heavens! Look at this! He's left them in their albums, and they're all warped! Shoji Taro indeed!

TSUJI: I'll be going, then. . . .

TERUKO: Oh, aren't you going to stay to hear the broadcast?

TSUJI: I have some, er, business to attend to. I'll be near a radio. . . .

TERUKO: Eight o'clock, then, don't forget!

TSUJI: Of course, I should be finished by that time. I opposed his theory, so I of all people. . . .

---

[2]A popular male vocalist (1898-1972). His songs would not have been in keeping with the high cultural level of Teruko's party.

Teruko sees him out through Door A. The doorbell rings.[3]

TŌRU: That's the man. I'm sure it was him!

AOKI: Do you really think you remember him?

TŌRU: I've seen him before.

AOKI: But what would he be doing just standing there, staring at the fields?

TŌRU: You've got me.

AOKI (*peeking out through a   corner of the curtain*): I don't see anybody coming.

Teruko returns.

TERUKO: Mr. Aoki, I have a favor to ask your wife tonight. I'd like her to step back to the days when she was employed in the marketing department at the sugar company—back to the days when you were engaged!

AOKI: Ma'am?

TERUKO: The   reason "The Beet Song"[4] was such a hit at the exposition was that beauties like Michiko played the records.

AOKI: Yes, but, well, I already mentioned this to your husband, but actually. . . .

TERUKO: You don't mean she's not coming?

AOKI: She's not feeling well, and. . . .

TERUKO: Not expecting, is she?

AOKI: No, it's not that sort of thing. She just hasn't wanted to mix with people recently. . . .

TERUKO: Now, Mr. Aoki, you mustn't keep her all to yourself! Hah-hah-hah!

TŌRU: Mother, you don't mind if I con't come tonight, do you? It's my last night before I go back to Sapporo.

TERUKO: Absolutely not! Don't be silly! (*She exits through Door C.*)

AOKI: Tōru. . . .

TŌRU: I remember. I promised to be as cheerful as I can tonight. Would you like to see the book of paintings I was talking about? The one that made me decide to be a painter?

AOKI: Please.

---

[3]The bell is attached to the sliding door to the house and rings every time the door is opened and someone enters or leaves the foyer.

[4]"Tokachi kouta," lyrics by Hayashi Hōshū, music by Komatsu Kyōsuke.

TŌRU: I found it here a while ago. They took it away from me before. (*He drags the stepladder over and speaks as he ascends it.*) It was around here someplace. (*He searches the shelves.*)

AOKI: Won't you get scolded again?

TŌRU: Who cares! Oh, here it is. Catch! The testament to my defeat!

AOKI (*opening the book*): Pretty gruesome, aren't they?

TŌRU (*descending*): Yeah, that's the one where the blind are leading the blind. The blindman on the end looks like he's going to fall in the water.

AOKI: I see.

TŌRU: Look ahead a few pages.

AOKI (*turning the pages*): Say, here's a snow scene!

TŌRU: You see all the peasants working, fanned out in the snow? (*Looking over his shoulder*): What do you think? This farmer's hut, for example, and the way the birds are flying over the bare trees?

AOKI: I'm afraid I don't know anything about painting.

TŌRU: No, I mean, don't you think it looks like the winters around here?

AOKI: I see.

TŌRU: And then . . . here, let me see that. (*He takes the book, and speaks as he turns the pages.*) There's one in here of a peasant wedding. Everyone's drinking and dancing. (*Finding it*): Here it is!

AOKI: I don't understand these things too well, but they seem different, you know, from the farmers around here.

TŌRU: I should think so. This was painted four hundred years ago by an artist from Flanders!

AOKI: They don't look like they're bothered by frost or crop failures. Tonight your father's going to talk about depletion farming, and that's.
    . . .

TŌRU: Rape! That's it!

AOKI: What?

TŌRU: Remember, I couldn't think how your wife came up in conversation last night. That was it!

AOKI (*concerned that someone inside the house might overhear*): I see.

TŌRU: I wonder why my old man talked to me like that? He was all excited and kept rambling on about rape and "jus primae noctis." . . . You don't mind, do you? It helps me to talk things out. . . . Anyway, he said they were barbaric, outdated customs; and he wanted to know what I thought about what old Shimura had done, even though · he was manager at the sugar company.

AOKI: Don't you think we'd better talk about this someplace else?

TŌRU: But it really bothered me. Talking about rape and all that. I'm afraid he knows everything.

AOKI: I doubt it. Ah, but maybe that's why you mistook that fellow before?

Tōru nods.

AOKI: Tōru, as far as Michiko's concerned, it was all my fault. I didn't have the guts to stand up for her, that's all. As for you—now, don't get me wrong—but farm girls just don't take these things that seriously. Not so's you should suffer like this anyway.

TŌRU (*without replying, staring at the paintings*): Did you ever meet Sugai? He was two or three years ahead of me in school. Used to come around here a lot to paint.

AOKI: I don't recall. Listen, Tōru, I didn't mean to speak out of turn, but. . . .

TŌRU: Never mind. Anyway, Sugai's the one who sent me this book. He'd already gotten into art school, and so. . . . He was the youngest and most committed member of that artists' cell. You know, he still hasn't been able to get anything shown.

AOKI: That's why your father is so opposed to the idea of your. . .

Reiko enters through Door C.

REIKO: I'm beat! (*She adjusts the stove. To Tōru as he goes to the book shelves*): What are you looking for?

TŌRU: Something in German.

REIKO: You'd better not mess them up or you'll catch it for sure. Mr. Aoki, you know what? At our class party, everyone was telling what they wanted in the new year, and you know what I said?

AOKI: No, what?

REIKO: A bicycle!

Aoki laughs.

REIKO: A third of the girls in my class already ride to school on bicycles during the summer. Tōru, what do you think?

TŌRU: A bicycle? You really have turned into a country bumpkin!

REIKO: You sound just like mother!

Behind Door C—in the kitchen—there is the sound of plates breaking.

REIKO: Uh-oh, Shino's broken something. She says she doesn't feel well. Tōru, in England women go touring on bicycles! It's the most up-to-date thing. What's wrong?

AOKI: Miss Reiko. . . .

REIKO: Oh, I see! I've been all tense since this morning, too. After all, when Daddy tries to talk in formal situations, he always twists everything around. Why, Mr. Aoki, at your wedding, Daddy kept saying "flax company" instead of "sugar company" even though he was your go-between. I thought I would die!

AOKI: I remember.

REIKO: He was *so* nervous! Tōru, you know, when he left, I gave him some good advice. I told him that he mustn't cough next to the microphone. (*She gestures with her hands.*) It makes this big, ugly noise, and. . . .

TŌRU: Shut up, Reiko.

REIKO: I wonder if he'll be all right. (*Mimicking*): Eh . . . as you will notice in walking through the fields in this area, there are places where the soil is black and places where it is red.

AOKI: What's that supposed to be?

REIKO: Daddy's so funny! Last night he was talking and walking around like this. . . . (*She imitates him*): The black soil is peat bog, and the red soil is volcanic ash. . . .

Aoki smiles.

REIKO: Don't you think it's funny?

AOKI: You've got it backwards. The peat is red.

REIKO: Oh . . . and the black part's volcanic ash?

Teruko peers through Door C.

TERUKO: Would you all come into the dining room, please?

REIKO: You want us to get out of here?

TERUKO: Yes. Shino's brother's here. (*She disappears momentarily.*)

Tōru flees to Door A.

REIKO (*on her way to Door B, looking back at her brother*): Where are you going?

TŌRU: I'll be back. (*Exits.*)

Aoki starts after Tōru, but Teruko ushers Henmi Shōsaku into the room, and he exits with Reiko through Door B instead.

SHŌSAKU (*looking at the table*): Sorry to interrupt. You must be busy.

TERUKO: Now this is better, isn't it? Far from the kitchen. Please. (*She offers him a chair.*)

SHŌSAKU: Thank you for the gift you sent.

TERUKO: Gift?

SHŌSAKU: A . . . you know, a little one of these. (*He points to the ornamental bough suspended from the ceiling.*)

TERUKO: Oh, that! Not at all. Now, there is something I've been wanting to discuss with you, but unfortunately today as you can see. . . .

SHŌSAKU: I guess I did come at a bad time. . . .

TERUKO: To put it in a nutshell—in a minute I'll show you the figures—but I belong to a little group that supports a magazine called

Women in Society. I suppose it sounds a little pretentious to talk about "the salvation of farm girls," but, well, that's what we're involved in. Wait here just a minute. (*She exits through Door B.*)

Henmi Shino brings tea in through Door C.

SHINO: Tea?

SHŌSAKU: Don't bother about me. (*Shino does not withdraw.*) What's wrong?

SHINO: Shōsaku, help me! I don't want to stay here any longer. Don't let Mrs. Amamiya change the subject. She's a real smooth talker.

Examining a notebook, Teruko returns through Door B. Shino exits through Door C.

TERUKO: The number of girls sold into prostitution is tremendous, isn't it? They say there are actually brokers who handle them. Do you have such a person in your village?

SHŌSAKU: Yes, ma'am.

TERUKO: You see, that's what I can't tolerate. Here you have a person, a farmer, too mind you, taking money to corrupt the daughters of other farmers. They actually expedite the process! And to make matters worse, they say the brokers are usually women! Well, in our group, the ladies have a great many ideas, but when it comes to putting them into action. . . . So I decided that charity begins at home, and well, I hope you don't mind, but I began to think about Shino.

SHŌSAKU: Now, hold on. I was wondering what you were getting at. I'd never sell my sister like that, no matter how difficult things got!

TERUKO: No, of course you wouldn't. I'd never suggest such a thing. But let's suppose for a moment that I let her go. Even with a dependable brother like you, in the final analysis, I can't help feeling she'd succumb to the same fate.

SHŌSAKU: But. . . .

TERUKO: Excuse me, but in our magazine—it might take some time to explain this, but—we like to talk about the "Kingdom of God." Let me see, is there time today? (*She looks at the clock on the wall.*) I'll just have to make it brief. The point is, we think that the only way the world will improve is if each individual—you and I—when each of us raises himself or herself to the exalted status of God. Now in the case of Shino, well, she's still young and totally innocent, and if I were to just let her go, well. . . .

SHŌSAKU: Yes, we're grateful for all you've done. It's just that she's written time after time, and, well. . . .

TERUKO: My! Has she written that often?

SHŌSAKU: Yes, I mean, let me see, there was a letter after we'd harvest the late beans, and then there was one at the end of the year, and. . . .

TERUKO: What did she say?

SHŌSAKU: Recently she's been saying how she wanted to come home. To be honest, if she came home right now, I'd be in a fix, but, well, she's so insistent, so I've been moonlighting at the sugar factory since last fall, washing down the beets, in order to put together a little extra, you know. . . .

TERUKO: Is that so? She's such a quiet girl, it's hard to tell what she's thinking. Actually, the other day I had to scold her. I'd been away for some time, and the day I returned, I took her out with me to shop for the new year. Well, she said she wanted to do some shopping of her own, so we separated. And do you know she didn't come back until all hours of the night!

REIKO (*poking her head out through Door B*): Mother, it's almost time.

TERUKO: Yes, I'll be done in a minute.

Reiko disappears.

TERUKO: Well, if she insists on going home, I'll speak with Miss Komai of the Hayakawa farm, who recommended her in the first place, but . . . has she talked to you about being dissatisfied here?

SHŌSAKU: Well, perhaps once.

TERUKO: What was the problem?

SHŌSAKU: Ma'am, the agricultural station here must be thirty hectares. On my way over I got lost and wound up wandering around in the fields. It certainly gets dark in these parts.

TERUKO: Yes?

SHŌSAKU: Well, Shino was saying how one night you had guests and sent her out on an errand real late and how she never was so scared in all her life.

TERUKO: Ah, that was last fall. My father was here, you see, and the men got into a deep academic discussion.   The discussion got so involved that they needed more data, so they decided to call in our Mr. Aoki. I tried to stop them, but they sent Shino out after him anyway. It's really quite distressing, the way they get so engrossed in their research! . . . Well, thank you for coming today. . . .

Reiko rushes in through Door B. She is followed by Aoki.

REIKO: Mother! What are you doing? It's started! (*She turns on the radio.*)

TERUKO: Oh, dear!

RADIO (*in midsentence*):   . . . the third day of programs celebrating its establishment. We'll begin our program this evening with an address by Amamiya Akira, director of the Agricultural Experiment Station, who will speak to us on the subject of "The Management of Volcanic Ash Soil."

SHŌSAKU (*getting to his feet*): I'll be going, then. . . .

TERUKO: Please stay and listen, if you'd like.

SHŌSAKU: Yes, ma'am.

Everyone takes a seat and listens attentively.

RADIO: Um, Amamiya is my name. . . . Um . . . If you walk through the fields of this district you will notice that there are places where the soil is red and places where the soil is black. . . . Um . . . The red soil is your peat, and . . . the black is your volcanic ash soil.

REIKO: See! (*She glances around the room.*) Where's Tōru?

RADIO: Er . . . both of these are unique types of soil, and . . . consequently . . . soil management in this district . . . um . . . must also be unique. . . . Um. . . . As you know, in chemical fertilizer . . . the three basic nutrients are . . . um . . . N, P, and K. If any one of these three nutrients—nitrogen, phosphorous, or potassium—is not present in sufficient quantity, . . . the soil will be depleted, and there will be a steady diminution in yields—that is, after a while you won't be able to grow anything anymore. It follows that, in order to preserve the soil, it is necessary to constantly replenish—er . . . make up for—this by supplying these three elements in precise amounts in a predetermined ratio. However, . . . er . . . it has been the accepted theory among agronomists that . . . um . . . because the soil of Japan is rich in potassium . . . or, rather, is insensitive to an insufficiency of potassium . . . there is no particular need to apply fertilizers containing potassium. . . .

REIKO: How is it, Mother?

TERUKO: Shhh! Listen.

RADIO: Um . . . this theory is wrong . . . I'm sorry, I mean, it seems to me that this theory might be mistaken. At least insofar as cultivation in volcanic ash soil is concerned, the replenishment of potassium is absolutely indispensable . . . it seems . . . and I am of the belief that the tragic consequences of the crop failures of recent years might in large measure be mitigated by an understanding of this fact . . . Um . . . . Let me see, . . . I guess I should have said this first. Er . . . living at the agricultural station, I spend each day in an intense dialogue with the land. . . . Now, we . . . or I should say I . . . can lie to people. But I can't lie to the earth. If you lie to the earth, it will throw that lie right back in your face. And it seems to me that our theory of agriculture still contains such lies—surprising number of them, in fact. Now, when we go out into the fields and advise the farmers on the basis of our experiments, even if a lie seems insignificant at first . . . it has far-reaching consequences that are eventually reflected in the lives of the farmers. And this, I submit, is criminal. Criminal! . . .

SHŌSAKU (*who has been listening attentively*): Ma'am?

TERUKO: Hm?

SHŌSAKU: If you'll pardon me, the fields around the station are so. . . .

REIKO (*annoyed*): Be quiet! (*Realizing she's been rude*): Sorry.

RADIO: Er . . . um . . . There is something known as "depletion farming." That is, we deplete the soil, raping it of its riches, pillaging it for whatever we can get, without a thought to whether it is being weakened, whether yields are diminishing; and even if we haphazardly throw some fertilizer on the ground. . . . we never give a thought to returning to the soil a scientifically appropriate mixture of the three basic nutrients. It is because this way of doing things is so primitive, thoughtless, and barbaric that we can refer to it as . . . er, reaping the land. . . .

REIKO (*scandalized*): Oh, no! He did it again!

RADIO: Er . . . Consider, for example, the fact that several years ago, when a flax competition was held in our town, almost all the entries had been grown with only a small amount of pure phosphorous fertilizer. Another example is the premixed fertilizer provided by the flax company: hardly any consideration has been given to this, er, the need for potassium. Er . . . um . . . um . . . Now I . . . the problem that has been plaguing me night and day is . . . er . . . as I stated earlier . . . the web of lies that envelops the farmers. It is these lies that I would like to see rooted out. . . . Er . . . no matter how diligently they labor, plagued by frosts and . . . floods and . . . crop failures . . . the majority of farmers languish in the depths of inescapable poverty, and even though I am a man of meager talents, I would like to do something, anything to ensure that the power of knowledge is applied to bring happiness to these farmers—all of them. . . . I have to do something . . . night and day, I have racked my brains. . . . (*He breaks off in midsentence.*)

A confusion of barely audible voices can be heard in the vicinity of the microphone. After a few moments, the mike goes dead.

Teruko, Reiko, and Aoki react simultaneously.

TERUKO: Heavens!

REIKO: What happened?

AOKI: Mrs. Amamiya! . . .

Short pause.

RADIO: Uh . . .   our lecture presentation . . . one moment, please. . . .
   Short pause.
AOKI: Mrs. Amamiya, would you like to call?
   Teruko nods.
RADIO: Uh . . . our lecturer has suddenly fallen ill, and we will be unable
   to continue this evening's   presentation. Unforeseen . . . uh . . .
   unavoidable as these circumstances are, we still apologize to our
   listeners   for this   inconvenience. Our next program   will   be   a
   performance,   also   to   commemorate   the establishment of our
   broadcasting station, and it will begin in approximately nineteen
   minutes forty-one seconds. We beg your indulgence in   the interim.
   The time is now   seven forty and twenty seconds. J. . . .
   Teruko switches off the radio.   Aoki picks up the telephone.
TERUKO (*wrenching the receiver from his hand*): Hello! Hello! Isn't
   there anyone in the laboratory?   . . .   Hello! Hello! Oh, is this the
   maintenance man? Yes, connect me to the radio station. (*Pursing her
   lips*): Mrs. Amamiya!
   *Shōsaku whispers something to Reiko.   Reiko nods. Shōsaku stands
   and starts toward Door C.*
TERUKO: Oh, wait a minute, will you? (*Into the telephone*): Is this the
   radio station? I'd like to speak to Mr. Nishikata in public   affairs. Yes
   . . . yes. . . . (*To Shōsaku, who has stopped in his tracks*): Never
   mind. I'll speak to you later.
   Shōsaku bows at the waist and exits through Door C.
TERUKO: Ah, hello . . . I just heard the announcement on the radio. .
   . . Yes . . . yes. . . .   What? Dizzy? Yes . . . yes. . . .   I'm terribly
   sorry to put you to all this trouble. . . .   No . . . yes, I'll   leave here
   right. . . . What? . . . But. . . . Yes, I see. . . . Well, in that case . . . yes .
   . . . Thank you very much. (*She hangs   up.*) They said he's just taken
   a little wine.
REIKO: You're going right away, aren't you?
TERUKO: Well, they said they'd send him home in a car, but. . . .
REIKO: But, Mother! . . .
AOKI: I wonder if it's all right for him to be moved?
TERUKO: If we go, we're liable to miss them. Perhaps we had better
   wait here.
AOKI: Shall I go? (*Teruko nods. Aoki picks up the telephone.*)
   Hello? Hello? ˙ Yes, send a car around to   the house. . . . Yes, right
   away.
REIKO: Well, I guess. . . . (*Into the house*): Shino! Never mind,
   never mind, I'll spread it. . . . (*She exits through Door B.*)

AOKI: He's been overworked, that's for sure.   Ever since that fellow
from the public affairs department came to see him, he's spent every
spare moment reading in his office. He was going to destory the
theories of   Professor Takimoto and Mr.   Saegusa at the main
laboratory, so he wanted to be absolutely sure of what he was going to
say. . . .

TERUKO: Mr. Aoki, how can you say such a thing? Akira wouldn't
"destroy" what my father has done. He might supplement some of the
deficiencies, or. . . .

*Beyond Door A, the doorbell rings. Aoki goes to answer it. Reiko peeks
in through Door B. Karasawa Katsumi, manager of the flax mill enters,
ushered in by Aoki.*

 AOKI: It's Mr. Karasawa from the flax company.

*Reiko looks disappointed. She signals to Aoki with her eyes, and they
exit together through Door B.*

KARASAWA: Sorry not to have stayed in touch. Allow me to wish you
a belated happy new year.

TERUKO: You're looking well.

KARASAWA: I've been so busy since the end of the year, I could hardly
think straight.   The holiday season's all but over, and I'm   just
beginning to   make   my courtesy calls! Our parent company's been
flooded with orders for airplane wings, so we've had to step up
production at our mill, too. We've had so much work, I almost feel like
apologizing to   other companies, but, as they say,   the increased
demand for military supplies   will eventually stimulate the whole
economy, so I'll suppress the urge! Hah-hah-hah!

TERUKO: I'm happy to hear that.

KARASAWA: By the way, I received a new year's card from your
father. He said he hoped Amamiya wouldn't spend all his time getting
covered with   mud this year and would finally get to work on his
dissertation. He wanted to know if there was any sign of his getting
down to business.

TERUKO: I see.

KARASAWA: Amamiya and I grew up in the same town and left the
nest together. I guess Professor Takimoto feels he can write things to
me that he can't discuss with anyone else.

TERUKO: Perhaps you're right. (*She looks down, embarrassed.*)

KARASAWA: I heard the broadcast.   Tōru and I listened to it
together.

TERUKO: Really? Where?

KARASAWA: You know where you come out of that row of acacias—the snow is really awful around here, isn't it?—there's a little cafe?

TERUKO: Yes.

KARASAWA: I'd been out all day, you see, and I needed a bite to eat, so I had my driver drop me off. I went inside, and there was Tōru.

TERUKO: Really!

KARASAWA: The boy can really hold his liquor, can't he? Not like his father. I only had a couple of drinks, and look at me! (*He rubs his cheeks.*) It doesn't show on him at all. I don't mean to blame Tōru for my showing up after such a long time in this condition, but. . . . Ah-hah-hah!

Outside, the sound of a car. Teruko starts to get up.

AOKI (*entering through Door B*): It must be ours. I'll be on my way then.

TERUKO: Thank you.

KARASAWA: You must be very concerned.

REIKO (*following Aoki through Door B*): Here. (*She hands him a small package.*)

AOKI: Oh, yes. (*He takes it.*)

TERUKO: What's that?

AOKI: Something to calm him down, she said.

TERUKO (*to Reiko*): Silly, it's Calmotion, isn't it? (*Calling Aoki, who is on his way out of Door A*): Just a minute. (*She rises and goes to him.*) On your way. . . .

KARASAWA: Pardon me, but if it's Tōru, I think you'll be too late.

TERUKO: What?

KARASAWA: He's probably well on his way to the neon lights in town by this time. Hah-hah-hah!

TERUKO: No, I want you to call on Dr. Nakaide, our family physician, and. . . . (*They exit through Door A, leaving Karasawa.*) *The doorbell rings, and then there is the sound of a car driving off.*

Karasawa notices the partially completed essay on the writing table and is about to stand up when the doorbell rings again. Teruko, Reiko, and Miyake Tetsuya enter through Door A. Reiko proceeds to Door B.

MIYAKE: I have to write something today or else. Company orders. They won't let me off as easily as they did with that article on the new year's market. (*To Karasawa*): Haven't seen you for a while.

KARASAWA: Hello! You know, that Russian really got hot under the collar.

MIYAKE: That's the first I've heard of it.

KARASAWA: He wanted to know who wrote that malicious piece of trash about him.

MIYAKE: I didn't know the good, upstanding people of the flax company frequented his log cabin. Do you shout "Good Evening!" in Russian as you go in? Maybe the culprit was none other than Karasawa Katsumi, manager of the mill!

KARASAWA: Don't look at me! Some of the young people in the office took me there—over my objections. . . .

MIYAKE: I'm only kidding. Kovankov mentioned me by name in the letter he wrote to the paper. I didn't even think he knew who I was.

KARASAWA: What's that? As disreputable as you are? Give yourself credit! There's hardly a man, woman, or child in this town who doesn't know you. Hah-hah-hah!

MIYAKE (*to Teruko*): Is this the first time Mr. Amamiya's been on the radio?

TERUKO: Yes.

MIYAKE: Then I suppose it can't be helped. Anybody'd be nervous.

TERUKO: You seem to know what it's like.

MIYAKE: I was on the radio myself once, a long time ago. "Our speaker tonight is Miyake So-and-So. Mr. Miyake has distinguished himself recently on Lake Matsubara as a member of the Meiji University skating club." Just sit there and have somebody introduce you like that—anybody'd get butterflies in their stomach!

The headlights of an automobile flash across the window.

REIKO (*going from Door B to Door A*): This time it must be Father.

Teruko also goes to Door A. There is the sound of the doorbell. Karasawa gets up and walks to the writing table.

MIYAKE: Do you mind if I ask you a sensitive question?

KARASAWA: What is it? (*He picks up the unfinished manuscript.*)

MIYAKE: How do you think the flax mill will react to today's broadcast?

KARASAWA: I don't think we'll have any reaction at all. It's irrelevant, really.

Amamiya Akira, director of the agricultural station, enters. He wears a black suit and tie. His face is grey with fatigue.

MIYAKE: How are you feeling, sir?

AMAMIYA: Sorry to cause all this commotion. It's nothing really. Ah, Mr. Miyake, there was something I've been meaning to tell you. What was it now? (*He strides purposefully up to Karasawa.*) Please keep your eyes to yourself—this isn't finished. (*He takes the manuscript away.*)

The telephone rings.

TERUKO (*picking up the receiver*): Yes . . . yes, just now. Thank you. No, he looks much better than one might have thought from. . . . I don't really know. Let me ask. (*She puts her hand over the mouthpiece and speaks to Amamiya.*) You're not going to cancel it are you?

AMAMIYA (*sardonically*): They won't let me off the hook that easily.

TERUKO: Not that.

AMAMIYA (*displaying the manuscript he has in his hand*): This? Of course not.

TERUKO: No, the party.

AMAMIYA: What? Oh, I don't know. Here let me talk. (*Into the receiver*): Hello? Amamiya here. Thank you very much. Yes . . . yes, it really is strange. . . . Perhaps we should make it some other time. . .

TERUKO: Akira! . . .

AMAMIYA (*into the receiver*): All right, please do. Sorry for the trouble.

TERUKO: Wait a minute, please.

AMAMIYA: He hung up. He's going to have the maintenance man call everyone.

Teruko is speechless.

AMAMIYA: The Neubauer, that was it! (*To Miyake*): Are you familiar with the Neubauer *in vitro* method?

MIYAKE: *In vitro*?

AMAMIYA: It means "in a test tube."

MIYAKE: I see.

AMAMIYA: It's been my hope for years . . . you know, to install an apparatus so we could use it here.

MIYAKE: Pardon me, but just now I'd really like to ask you some questions about today's broadcast.

AMAMIYA: Well, hear me out. You put a hundred grams of soil in a petri dish and spread quartz over it. Then you plant a hundred oat sprouts in there—of course in Germany they use rye. If you set a number of those dishes in a glass case and maintain a constant temperature of 22 to 23 degrees centigrade for a period of 17 to 18 days, the plants will sprout and the roots will absorb all the nutrients in the soil, right?

MIYAKE: Does this have something to do with today's talk?

AMAMIYA: I should say it does! Look, if you exclude the nutrients inherent in the plants themselves and analyze what they have aborbed from the soil—do you see?—you can calculate the results to within a few ten-thousandths!

KARASAWA: I see. So that's what "Neubauer" refers to?

AMAMIYA: Yes.

KARASAWA: Must have cost the station a pretty penny! Hah-hah-hah! The way I hear it, you owe a lot to Mrs. Amamiya's maneuvering behind the scenes.

TERUKO: That's not true! That rumor is causing me no end of grief.

KARASAWA: It's a good match for that story about the clock tower in Sapporo! What do you say, Amamiya? Hah-hah-hah!

During this interval, Reiko enters with a change of clothes for her father.

AMAMIYA: Excuse me, will you? (*He begins to change his clothes.*)[5] The point is, Miyake, until now we've been analyzing soil samples simply by dissolving them in hydrochloric acid. But with that kind of analysis, you don't know exactly what the plants actually absorb from the soil; you don't know the extent of the absorption; and the percentages you do come up with are nothing more than rough estimates. Let me tell you, I shed many a tear trying to get this equipment into our laboratory!

Reiko giggles.

AMAMIYA: What's so funny?

REIKO: It doesn't seem right for you to say you "shed many a tear," that's all.

AMAMIYA: I learned it from you, you know. I thought you said that you had to "shed many a tear" to get a bicycle out of your father! Hah-hah-hah!

REIKO: That's right. Will you buy me one?

TERUKO: Reiko! This is hardly the time! You come with me this instant! (*They exit through Door B.*)

MIYAKE: What were you planning to say in the rest of your talk? (*To Karasawa*): Let me take care of this first, will you? Here's the evening edition, if you haven't seen it yet. (*He takes a newspaper from his pocket and hands it to him.*)

AMAMIYA: Have you ever been up to the "bucket land"?

MIYAKE: I can't say that I have.

---

[5] Amamiya is changing from Western clothes into Japanese. It is only slightly unusual for him to change in front of guests. He would drape his kimono over his shoulders and remove his pants beneath its cover.

AMAMIYA: You'd understand if you went up there. They picked a good name for it, that's for sure. You see, those are high paddy fields, but the topsoil is so porous, they won't hold water. They leak, just like a leaky bucket.

MIYAKE: I see, but . . . actually, I haven't got much time, so. . . .

AMAMIYA: That's why I'm trying to explain this to you. That land originally belonged to the Igarashi farm, but it was divided into plots for independent farmers under the government's development plant.

MIYAKE: I see.

AMAMIYA: I'll tell you, these past two or three years have been terrible. Even when the rice plants grew, they didn't produce any grain.

The doorbell rings. Aoki enters through Door A.

AOKI: I went to pick you up. I must have just missed you.

AMAMIYA: Yes, I heard. Thanks. Aoki, remember those paddy fields on the bucket land we inspected year before last? As I recall, they were only getting two bags of unhulled rice from seven hectares of land. Isn't that right?

AOKI: Yes. If memory serves, they only had about fifty liters left once it was polished. How are you feeling?

AMAMIYA: Thank you, I'm all right now. (*To Miyake*): Some of the farmers sold their harvests, stalks and all, for hog and cattle feed. Others converted their paddies to dry fields. But eventually most of them defaulted on their loans and lost their land to the development bank.

MIYAKE: I see.

AMAMIYA: They called me in, and I tried to do something to help. I had a power winch installed and four-and-a-half tons of earth hauled up there. We graded the land, and things improved, but then what do you think happened?

MIYAKE: Hayakawa bought that land as I recall.

AMAMIYA: Exactly! A new landlord bought the land from the bank and raised the tenants' rent sky high. The farmers want to grow rice if they can. Even though they know the soil's not right for it, they still want to grow rice.

MIYAKE: They want to "Japanize" Hokkaido, isn't that it?

AMAMIYA: I suppose you could put it that way. The point is, the system traps the farmers with their own psychological needs. Here the land was finally taking on the semblance of real paddy fields, and. . . . It breaks my heart!

MIYAKE: I see. So?

AMAMIYA: Well, for example, I work out a new compound of the three basic soil nutrients. I devise a whole variety of tests and install a Neubauer apparatus. On the radio, I mentioned. . . . No, I guess this is the part that got cut off. Well, let's assume that I'll publish it in *The Journal of the Agronomy Association*. . . . This sort of thing makes a coward of you, you know what I mean?

MIYAKE: Sort of, but. . . .

AMAMIYA: The point is, my findings conflict with the theories of the established scholars at Sapporo University and at the main agricultural station. At the same time, they have implications for Karasawa's flax company and the fertilizer they're peddling, too. Right, Karasawa?

KARASAWA *(reading the evening edition)*: Hm? I guess so.

AMAMIYA: If there's some friction in academic circles, well, that can't be helped—and I'm not in the least afraid of that. What I am afraid of is that because of that friction my findings won't be communicated to the farmers or that they'll get perverted beyond recognition. I begin to wonder if there's any point. Now, as to who's going to do the perverting. . . . Well, perhaps I'd better leave that unsaid.

AOKI: Mr. Amamiya, perhaps you should excuse yourself and get some rest.

AMAMIYA: You're right, you're right. *(To Miyake)*: Will that do for now?

MIYAKE: Yes. Er, thank you very much.

KARASAWA *(from behind the newspaper)*: Would you include Professor Takimoto in the "established scholars" you just mentioned?

AMAMIYA: I wouldn't exclude him.

KARASAWA *(putting the paper down)*: I think you should reconsider publishing your article.

AMAMIYA: What? Why?

KARASAWA: Why? Don't you understand? Look, forget the whole thing right now, for your own good. You're so damned shortsighted! That article doesn't amount to a hill of beans. You're just wasting your breath, don't you see that?

AMAMIYA: What do you mean I'm shortsighted?

Teruko enters through Door C, carrying a tray of coffee.

KARASAWA: If you want to write something, write your dissertation! You've got Professor Takimoto's backing and everything. What are you afraid of, that it would look bad if you flunked?

AMAMIYA: You wouldn't understand.

TERUKO: My word, what seems to be the problem, dear?

KARASAWA: Finish your Ph.D. and get yourself promoted to a real agricultural station in Manchuria or someplace. There are lots of men who'd give their right arm to trade places with you. Manchuria's the land of opportunity—Hitler's placed a mountain of orders for soybeans for explosives[6] . . . and I dare say Professor Takimoto would rest easier, too.

AMAMIYA: I wonder.

KARASAWA: Don't you even understand that much? Consider how your wife must feel!

AMAMIYA: I don't think I need you to worry about my wife!

TERUKO: Akira, what's gotten into you? Please, excuse yourself and rest. You're not well today.

AMAMIYA: Karasawa, why don't you say what's really on your mind?

KARASAWA: What's that?

AMAMIYA: That you're upset because I impugned your company's fertilizer. Just who in the hell do you think you are, presuming to speak for Professor Takimoto!

AOKI: Sir!

KARASAWA: Say that again!

MIYAKE: Karasawa, take it easy!

KARASAWA (*poking Miyake in the chest with the newspaper*): You! What's this article supposed to mean? When did the company ever "fall into disarray" over some new theory the agricultural station cooked up. Amamiya gets a fat head because you write crap like this. There's a Ph.D. or two working for the company, too, you know! (*To Amamiya*): You're not the only scholar around here, so don't be so damned smug!

AMAMIYA: Get out!

AOKI: Sir!

KARASAWA: I wouldn't stay if you asked me! Mrs. Amamiya.

TERUKO: Please wait. I still have something to. . . .

Karasawa and Teruko go through Door A.

MIYAKE: Well, I guess I'll be going, too. (*To Aoki*): What time did Karasawa get here?

AOKI: As soon as the broadcast was over.

MIYAKE: Well, well! You know that bastard showed up at the radio station about noon today, too? (*Exits.*)

---

[6]Nazi Germany planned to use soybean oil instead of petroleum in the manufacture of plastic explosives.

During this interval, Amamiya sits down at the writing table and gazes at his unfinished manuscript.   Looking pale, Teruko returns through Door A.

AOKI (*to Amamiya after whispering something to Teruko*): Well, I guess I'll. . . .

AMAMIYA: Stay a while, won't you?

AOKI: Yes, but my. . . .

AMAMIYA: Of course. I hope she's feeling better soon.

AOKI: Thank you. (*He exits through Door A.*)

Pause. Quietly, music begins.

TERUKO (sitting opposite her husband at the writing table): I have something I'd like to discuss with you.

Amamiya looks up without speaking.

TERUKO: It's about the money for the Neubauer apparatus. Actually . . . it came from my father.

AMAMIYA (*startled*): What?

TERUKO: I. . . .

AMAMIYA: I thought it came out of your savings.

TERUKO: That money's for the children. Amamiya is silent.

TERUKO: Won't you reconsider? I took it for granted that you'd . .you'd follow in Father's footsteps. . . . (*She weeps.*)

Reiko enters through Door B.

REIKO: Would you like to eat now, Father? (*Noticing her mother*): What's wrong?

AMAMIYA: I'm not hungry right now.

REIKO: Mother, what happened?

Teruko remains silent, her eyes downcast.

AMAMIYA: I don't think your mother will want dinner either. You go ahead . . . in the other room . . . with your brother. He's here, isn't he?

REIKO: Father, in class today, . . .

TERUKO: Reiko, this isn't the time. . . .

REIKO: No, you don't understand. Everyone promised to listen to Father's broadcast. What should I say when I see them?

With his eyes, Amamiya orders her to leave the room.

REIKO: What are we going to do with leftovers for fifteen people? (*She exits through Door B.*)

There is a pause in the music and in the distance the sound of a train whistle.

TERUKO: Please, won't you consider Father's feelings? These days, every time I hear a train whistle in the night, I. . .

The music resumes.

TERUKO: I jump up in bed and feel like rushing back to Sapporo. . . . I don't know why Mother committed suicide. I was only a child. We moved to Sapporo suddenly after she died. Father's been alone ever since. His only pleasure in life is training his students. He hasn't any money really, but I begged him to give me some . . . to arm his enemy! (She groans in anguish.)

Amamiya is silent.

TERUKO: Please . . . please, let me tear this up! (She reaches for the manuscript on the table.)

AMAMIYA: What are you doing! (He grabs his wife's arm.)

TERUKO (her wrist in her husband's grasp): In your heart . . . you know you're hurting him. You know it's wrong. That's why today. . . . If you go on, your health will suffer, I know it will!

AMAMIYA (slowly releasing her hand): What am I supposed to do? If this were just an academic dispute it would be different. But lie to the farmers? I can't do that.

The two of them stand motionless for a few moments. Then Teruko silently withdraws.

AMAMIYA: Where are you going?

Teruko exits through Door B without responding.

Pause. Amamiya presses the creases out of his manuscript, then gazes into space. Shino enters through Door B.

AMAMIYA (*still gazing off into space*): I'll return the money. I'll get it somehow.

SHINO (*confused*): Sir?

AMAMIYA (*turning around*): Oh, Shino. What is it?

From the time Amamiya noticed Shino, the music has changed. Shōsaku enters through Door C.

SHŌSAKU: Excuse me. . . .

SHINO: Um . . . Mrs. Amamiya told me to take down the decorations. . . .

SHŌSAKU (*intervening for his sister*): I'll do it. You're not feeling well. (*He removes the tablecloth and climbs up on the table.*) Here, I'll hand them to you.

Brother and sister begin to take down the ornaments.

SHŌSAKU: Mr. Amamiya, sir? Sure are big, though, aren't they, the fields here at the station?

AMAMIYA: Yes.

SHŌSAKU: I was out there before, just staring at them. Not a hint of crop failure, is there?

AMAMIYA: What do you mean?

SHŌSAKU: No heaps of soybean pods, no mounds of potatoes. . . .

AMAMIYA: No, we don't leave them here.

SHŌSAKU: Sir,   do   you   really   think crops do better with more potassium?

AMAMIYA: You were listening?   (*His face brightening*): Come   over here and sit down for a minute.   You can take care of that later. *Curtain.*

Act Three: Inspection at the Kilns

The music and narration commence in the darkness.

NARRATOR: What they call "marshes" in this region/ Are really the gently hollowed valleys/ That lie nestled in the mountains/ That shape this land./ In order to reach them,/ You cross the national highway that runs from the village center/ And slog ankle-deep in mud down a road/ In the rubber boots/ That people wear here both summer and winter.

At the entrance to the marshes,/ There are pastures cleared of timber,/ And the skyline soars high overhead./ You continue on beneath arches of trees/ That flourish in the wet ground—Poplar, ash, and spring elms—A snowscape for the theatre./ Then you follow the stream that flows through the valley,/ Your boots kneading the red soil of the bog,/ Through stands of mugwort, reeds, and bamboo grass,/ Until suddenly,/ Through one of the arches,/ You come upon a clearing./ It is in places like this/ That the grass-enveloped huts of the charcoal burners stand,/ Always at the edge of a stream,/ Where one can stand on a board laid across the flow/ And draw the water of life.

Above these huts grown thick with pigweed,/ On terraces carved into the mountainside,/ Stand charcoal kilns of hardened clay facing the slopes./ Beside them,/ In windbreaks,/ Their limbs lashed numb by an unseen whip,/ Crouch the burners who will fire the kilns today and again tomorrow,/ The joy of their work and the curse of their life/ Bound up with the kindling they cut down from the peaks.

It takes two or three years to clear a mountain,/ To incinerate its wood./ In the pastures that are left/ Glisten the coats of horses prancing free./ And so it is that the coal burners are driven from one mountain to the next.

The music continues.   And a slide is shown: ACT THREE: INSPECTION AT THE KILNS

As the final bars of the music fade into the real sound of the wind, the title disappears and the stage lights come up.

Close to the proscenium, a clump of snow sprung from the branch of a large tree near the edge of the stream falls to the ground in a flurry. Then, once again, there is the sound of the wind.

Just as the audience is concluding that the stage is deserted, Izumi Jirō and his younger brother Hidema emerge from the mouth of the kiln.

JIRŌ (*looking back at Hidema*): See, it'll get in through that hole. Look, here on the side of the windbreak, it comes through right under here. There's even more water in winter, 'cause the snow melts when we fire the kiln. If we don't dig out a trench around here, we'll never get a good fire. (*He crouches near the windbreak for a moment. Receiving no answer, he looks around.*) You got that?

HIDEMA: Yeah. (*He is thinking about something else.*)

JIRŌ (*trying to encourage him*):   Come on, one more layer and we're through!

The two of them walk to a nearby lean-to and return with firewood.

HIDEMA: How much more? I'm tired!

They enter the kiln.

The kiln, which is about four meters wide, six meters deep, and two meters high, is built out of cubes of soil piled up like hewn stones. The domed roof is supported by pieces of wood embedded in it and hung by wires from the cantilevered windbreak that extends it. Clay wings splayed to the left and right of the mouth of the kiln also protect it from the wind.

The kiln sits relatively high on the stage. A slope constructed of flats descends toward the proscenium, and the kiln sits on a plateau about half-way up. The lean-to where the firewood and bags of charcoal are stored stands at the edge of the same plateau.

Again there is the sound of the wind blowing across the mountain. The withered stalks of the reeds and mugwort along the stream in the foreground spring up, freed from their caps of snow.

The brothers come out of the kiln.

JIRŌ: You just don't understand, do you? I told you, you can't count on Pa. Ma's too frail, and. . . . What'll we do if you don't learn to fire the kiln?

HIDEMA: But. . . .

JIRŌ: Damn it! Ever since Pa came back, you ain't listened to a thing I say! Put all kinds of fancy ideas in your head, didn't he?

HIDEMA: Like what?

JIRŌ: He told you not to tell me, didn't he?

HIDEMA: I don't know what you're talking about.

JIRŌ: Forget it then.   Come on, let's finish up.   (*He goes toward the lean-to.*)

HIDEMA (*sluggishly*): But I'll have to quit school then.

JIRŌ: So what?

HIDEMA: But I'm different from the other kids.

JIRŌ: What's so different about you?

HIDEMA: Jirō! I'm the best of the boys, and Komai Ayako's the best of the girls.   I can't let a girl beat me! Mr. Teramachi said so.

JIRŌ: Never mind about her.   Who cares about some lady landlord's kid anyway?

HIDEMA: That wasn't all he said.

JIRŌ: Yeah, what else?

HIDEMA: He said if I, if I keep up like this to the sixth grade, I could get a scholarship and go to high school!

JIRŌ: High school?

HIDEMA: But I told him I might as well forget it as long as you're around.

JIRŌ (*throwing aside the bundle of wood he's carried from the lean-to*): You damned fool! (*He slaps him across the face.*)

HIDEMA (*trying not to cry*): What'd you do that for?

JIRŌ: Pa's been gone, so I go easy on you and don't make you do no chores, and first thing I know you're talking high school! Look at me! Look! When I was your age. . . .

HIDEMA: I don't want to hear! (*He starts to run away.*)

JIRŌ (*stopping him*): Wait a minute! Okay, I'm sorry. I bet that hurt. You all right? Look, pretty soon I'm going up to Kamikawa,[1] see? Who knows when I'll be back! Try to learn. It's fun!

HIDEMA: I already learned all that stuff by watching.

JIRŌ: You can't learn the real tricks unless you do it yourself. When you get through piling the wood up crisscross, see, it's tough to . . . I mean, it's fun to lay them twigs around the top and light the fire. Come on, I'll show you! (*He goes ahead into the kiln.*)

Hidema reluctantly picks up the bundle of wood. Then he sets it down again and tries to run away. Jirō emerges from the kiln, drags him back, and strikes him.

---

[1]Kamikawa is the area of Hokkaido around Asahikawa, where the Seventh Division of the Imperial Army was headquartered. Jirō is going to join the army.

JIRŌ: You son-of-a-bitch!

HIDEMA: Ouch! (*He begins to cry.*)

JIRŌ: Why're you running away! Damn you! (*He hits him.*)

HIDEMA (*bawling*): Pa said . . . Pa said! . . .

JIRŌ: Yeah, what?

HIDEMA: That you're the one who causes all the trouble!

JIRŌ: So what?

HIDEMA: He said if you weren't here we could get money from the charcoal concession. We could move to the city, and I could transfer to the city school.

ICHIHASHI: Hey! Hey! Cut that out! (*He stops Jirō. To Hidema*): Fine brother you've got, beating up on little kids! I'll get back at him for you. Watch! (*He claps his hands together near Jiro's face, pretending to strike him. To Jirō*): They haven't shown up from the charcoal concession yet, have they? What's keeping them?

JIRŌ: How the hell should I know? (*He picks up the wood that Hidema left.*) It's their business if they want to traipse all the way up here. (*He goes into the kiln.*)

ICHIHASHI: What'd you do to get him so angry? He's good to you.

HIDEMA: I hate him! He can drop dead!

ICHIHASHI: Hah-hah-hah! You just don't appreciate him! When your pa took off, why Jirō . . . let me see, it was just after I came here from Nemuro, so he couldn't have been much older than you are now, but he was already burning charcoal on his own, yessir. Why, he taught me! . . . Whew, it's cold! At least the kiln over at my place is fired up.

Jirō comes out of the kiln.

ICHIHASHI: Wasn't this the day your case was supposed to come up in court? Now that the lessee of record's back, everything should be all right.

JIRŌ: Every goddamn thing's got to happen at once! If the lease for this land wasn't in his name, I wouldn't let that old man into the house, the bastard! (*He goes toward the lean-to.*)

ICHIHASHI: Hey, that's no way to talk! (*To Hidema*): I remember something! It was summer, see, and your mother was sick in bed. You were a little baby, so Jirō strapped you to his back here . . . no, wait a minute, it wasn't here. The kiln was over near the entrance to the marshes then—you know, the part that's pasture now. There was a lean-to just like this near the kiln, see, and since you were heavy and a bother on his back, Jirō got this idea. (*To Jirō, who has stopped working and is looking down toward the entrance to the marshes.*) They here?

JIRŌ: No. Don't pay him no mind. You'll just spoil him worse. (*He goes back to work.*)

ICHIHASHI (*to Hidema*): So he got this rope, see, and he took a length of it and tied one end to the lean-to and the other end to you, and he let you crawl around. Well, pretty soon you started bawling, so I came running over, shouting, "What happened?   What happened?" just like I did just now, and what do you think?   There's Jirō stripping you stark naked and picking all these ants off you like they were lice, and I'll be damned if he didn't have tears big as this pouring down his face!

HIDEMA: Jirō cried?

ICHIHASHI: Hard to imagine, huh?

Hidema starts to laugh.

ICHIHASHI: But Jirō's smart, you know, burning charcoal and all. Let me see, who's smarter, you or Jirō?   Yeah, you must be smarter for sure!

HIDEMA (*with childlike wariness*): You just want to get me to work, that's all.

ICHIHASHI: Hah-hah-hah! Really are a smart little rascal, aren't you? I guess you deserve to be number one in school.

HIDEMA: Jirō, I'm going.

JIRŌ: Good riddance!

HIDEMA: Humph.   (*Running as far as the foot of the bridge in the foreground*): Jirō's a beggar! A shit-eating beggar! (*He runs away.*)

JIRŌ (*watching him go*): I can't do a thing with him. Pa spoils him rotten.

ICHIHASHI: Listen, you think that lady landlord's going to inspect every kiln personally?

JIRŌ: Maybe. Who knows. Anyway, people ain't that scared of her. You don't think they're coming up a different way, do you?

ICHIHASHI: Over the mountain, you mean? A sleigh wouldn't make it.

JIRŌ: I guess you're right.

ICHIHASHI (*spying someone in the distance*): Over here! Over here! What's she looking at?

JIRŌ (*looking*): Who is it?

ICHIHASHI: Adachi Kimi, can't you see?

JIRŌ: I don't have much use for her. Too damned straightforward for a woman if you ask me.

ICHIHASHI: You get that way when you've been in the movement for a while. (*To the approaching figure*): Hey, I moved my kiln up here!

KIMI'S VOICE: I was beginning to think you'd sent me on a wild goose chase!

Wearing a shawl over a tattered coat, Adachi Kimi enters along the stream. She slips on the snowy incline and almost falls.

ICHIHASHI: Watch your step!

KIMI: That's all I need right now! . . . Hello!

ICHIHASHI: Still aren't yourself, are you?

KIMI: Nope. Six months I spent in bed, for all the good it did me!

JIRŌ: What'd you come for? You here to cheer us on?

KIMI: Not exactly. I just came to see what's happening. Things have changed while I was sick. Everybody acts so innocent down in the village. They don't even gossip about the marshes. If they say anything, it's bad.

ICHIHASHI: Nothing new about that! Hah-hah-hah!

KIMI: Aren't they here yet?

ICHIHASHI: No. When they arrive, first we're gonna impress them with Jiro's place. That means my place'll be next. We figure if if we can get through our two first, the rest'll come out all right.

JIRŌ: It doesn't matter where they start. Don't worry.

KIMI: You two are lucky. At least you've got something to keep you occupied. I don't know what to do with myself. I've been working as a secretary at the beet farm, but it's only made things worse. I don't know anything about farming, and everybody keeps their distance from me, so. . .

ICHIHASHI: And you aren't woman enough to be a barmaid in town, either, is that it? Ah-hah-hah!

KIMI: No kidding! It makes me think I ought to just give up and get you to marry me or something!

ICHIHASHI: What do you mean "or something"? Hah-hah-hah! Take a look: I'm undernourished, bald, scar-faced, and have three eyebrows to boot! If I'm good enough for you, help yourself! Just get permission from that tractor driver first, will you?

KIMI: Here we go again!

JIRŌ: Hey, cut it out. You can flirt some other time. (*He starts for the lean-to.*)

KIMI: You don't have to get upset. I heard Shino's on her way here.

JIRŌ: She is?

KIMI: Get a load of that look on his face! Hah-hah-hah! She got some time off. She's over at her brother's place today.

JIRŌ: Yeah?

KIMI: She says she's got something to talk to you about.

JIRŌ: Yeah? (*He goes toward the lean-to and continues his work.*)

KIMI: I may really have to move away from here.

ICHIHASHI: How come?

KIMI: Listen, you said there'd be a job starting in April, and, well, I've been putting my folks off, but lately they're as much as telling me to get out—not that I blame them. Here. (*She hands him a postcard.*)

ICHIHASHI (*taking it from her*): What's this? Oh, from Mr. Teramachi. What does he want all of a sudden?

KIMI: My folks found that and read it. . . . Apparently either Teramachi or his wife are going to be laid off at the beginning of the year. Overstaffed, you know. So they're running scared.

ICHIHASHI: All right, I'll go speak to them. We can't have you leaving now.

KIMI: If I were working at the station, I'd be through by sundown. It'd be like getting paid to study farming!

ICHIHASHI: I'll be your guarantor, that's no problem. If there's any trouble, they can always say they didn't know anything about you, they just hired you because Ichihashi asked them.

KIMI: Yeah, then they'll be in real trouble! Hah-hah-hah!

ICHIHASHI: Ah-hah-hah!

Jirō carries a bundle of kindling to the kiln.

ICHIHASHI (*whispering*): What's this about Jirō's girl?

KIMI (*keeping an eye on the entrance to the kiln*): I'll tell you later. It's not the sort of problem anybody can solve for them. They're going to have to work it out for themselves.

Yoshimitsu Yosaburō, another charcoal burner, appears across the bridge.

YOSABURŌ: Ichihashi, I've been looking all over for you.

ICHIHASHI: Had a bit of tough luck, eh, Yoshimitsu? Ah-hah-hah!

YOSABURŌ: I thought I was going to croak! That lady landlord grabbed me by the shirt and drilled her eyes right through me!

Ichihashi is laughing.

YOSABURŌ: It ain't funny! Listen, I've got to talk to you.

KIMI: Mind if I stick around?

ICHIHASHI: Why don't you wait for me over by my kiln?

Kimi exits along the stream.

YOSABURŌ: Ichihashi, things weren't like you said at all.

ICHIHASHI: What're you talking about?

YOSABURŌ: When you send out a horse and sleigh . . . Oh, that's right, you were worried about sales and went on ahead to take orders. . . .

Anyway, I cleared the whole thing with Jirō, and he said it was okay. I just feel like I got the wool pulled over my eyes.

ICHIHASHI: Wool pulled over your eyes?

YOSABURŌ: You know what I mean. It's different from the way we usually do things. It used to be that you needed the go-ahead from the charcoal concession before you could send out a horse and sleigh like that.

Jirō, who has been out of the kiln and listening for some time, strides forward.

JIRŌ: I don't remember saying anything like that.

YOSABURŌ: See what I mean! You drive me crazy! You told me I shouldn't worry because they were going to let us sell a certain number of bags of charcoal in order to clear our debts.[2]

ICHIHASHI: Didn't Jirō just say that so you'd know what to tell customers when you went into town? You've got everything mixed up.

YOSABURŌ: I do not! He said so!

JIRŌ: Asshole! If I said I didn't say it, I didn't say it!

YOSABURŌ: There's . . . there's no use talking to you! Ichihashi, I been thinking, and it don't make sense for them to cancel our debts for stuff we sold without permission. And on top of that, with prices down, this ain't no time to be demanding the original rate. So, I. . . .

JIRŌ: Want to pull out, right? Why don't you just say so? Don't be blaming others 'cause you're chicken!

ICHIHASHI: Hold on a minute, Jirō. (*To Yosaburō*): Listen. . .

KIMI'S VOICE: Hey! The inspection's already started!

ICHIHASHI: What!

KIMI'S VOICE: They came up the back way!

JIRŌ: Oh, no!

KIMI'S VOICE: Hurry up!

ICHIHASHI: Damn them all to hell!

Ichihashi and Jirō run off along the stream.

YOSABURŌ: Hey, wait for me! What am I supposed to do? (*He runs after them.*)

Izumi Kametarō and his wife Toku enter across the bridge. He is wearing his best clothes; she wears everyday attire and snowshoes.

TOKU (*looking around from the kiln to the lean-to*): I wonder where he went? (*To Kametarō, who is still standing at the foot of the bridge*): Don't just stand there. Jirō's not going to eat you! Hah-hah-hah!

---

[2]Payment for the charcoal was usually made in kind, which made the burners especially vulnerable to inflation, since the price of charcoal was fixed.

KAMETARŌ: I'm not afraid of him. I've just walked so much today. . . .
(*He climbs up toward the kiln.*) I'm more interested in what you think
than Jirō.

TOKU: Look, just talk to him and see, all right?

KAMETARŌ: Does that mean you don't want to settle out of court
either?

TOKU: Well . . . it wouldn't be easy to leave this land, not for Jirō
anyway. You probably wouldn't understand that, but. . .

KAMETARŌ: But they said if we vacate the land they'll give us five
hundred yen. With that much money, we could. . . .   I've still got the
touch, you know. . . .

TOKU: You're a little touched, that's what I think!

KAMETARŌ: I'm not talking about going back to Otaru. I couldn't go
back there if my life depended on it.   We could go to Nemuro or
Kushiro. . . .

TOKU: A likely story.   You wouldn't feel right anyplace but Otaru.
And knowing you, if you hired a barmaid, it'd turn out to be one of
your old girlfriends!

KAMETARŌ: Hey, cut it out! You're a disgrace!

TOKU: Is that so?   Which one of us is the disgrace? I know all about
you!

KAMETARŌ: What?

TOKU: Never mind what.

KAMETARŌ: No, I won't never mind. What do you know?

TOKU: Everything will be all right if I just hold my peace.

KAMETARŌ: Come on, out with it.

TOKU: You asked Ichihashi to write a letter for you, didn't you? Who was
it to?

KAMETARŌ: Letter? I don't know what you're talking about.

TOKU: Hidema says he saw you. He says you told him not to tell his ma
and you even gave him money to keep quiet! Hah-hah-hah!
Kametarō is silent.

TOKU: You ought to be ashamed. I thought this time you'd really turned
over a new leaf.

KAMETARŌ: It weren't to no woman in Otaru. Look, I owe this
person, and . . . well, my handwriting's no good, so. . . .

TOKU: Then why couldn't you ask Jirō? Any letter Jirō couldn't write
couldn't have been on the up-and-up. (*She shoots him an icy glance.*)
Even if you never did pay him no mind, Jirō can still read and write!

KAMETARŌ: All right, I tell you. I . . . I ran into a streak of bad luck, and . . . well, if I didn't do something they were going to turn me over to the cops.

TOKU: The cops? This ought to be a good one!

KAMETARŌ: Honest! I couldn't admit that I had to shut down the restaurant 'cause a woman ran off with all the money, could I? So, I said I didn't have the fare to come home, and, well, . . . I hadn't eaten anything for three days, so finally, there was this sea otter coat hanging in the entranceway, and. . . .

TOKU: Did you steal it? Where was this?

KAMETARŌ: I think the name was Satake. Look, do me a favor, don't tell Jirō about this, please. It seems this Satake was the vice-chairman of the Chamber of Commerce. . . .

TOKU: Hah-hah-hah! This one takes the cake! How're you going to mail a letter if you don't even know the name and address!

KAMETARŌ: If I went to the house. . . .

Charcoal burner Nose Kiyoji enters over the bridge. Kametarō and Toku cut their conversation short.

KIYOJI: Ain't Jirō here?

TOKU: What do you want him for?

KIYOJI: Old man, if you weren't around, I'd skin that bastard alive.

KAMETARŌ: I don't know what's been going on, and I don't know why you're all riled up, but . . . leave him be, will you? He won't be around much longer.

KIYOJI: That's just the point. That bastard may get a guaranteed meal ticket for himself when he goes up to Asahikawa, but. . . . By the way, how's your case going?

KAMETARŌ: As a matter of fact, we were just. . . .

TOKU: Stop right there. (*To Kiyoji*): Ask Jirō, will you? It's all too complicated for us.

KIYOJI: Look, you're about to lose your land and Jiro's leaving anyhow, so he can make all the trouble he likes—what's he got to lose? What I don't like is his dragging other people into it. I been off working on the dredging project, in water so cold the whole lower half of my body went numb—and I didn't make a single grain of rice out of it neither—and when I finally got home, Jirō tells me not to hand over any charcoal the next time there's an inspection, and he won't listen to anything I say. Shit! I had a good mind to put my fist in his face a couple of times . . . but, well, you're here, and. . . . What's all this about now, demanding that they raise the price of charcoal?

Looking upset, Jirō returns.

JIRŌ: Nose, you fink! You're going to spoil everything!

KIYOJI: What's that?

JIRŌ: They know you ain't got no guts, so they started the inspection with you. You turn my stomach! You'd think you'd have learned at your age.

TOKU: He said he was going to put his fist in your face, too.

JIRŌ (*jumping on him*): If you think you're man enough, go ahead and try!

KIYOJI: Hey, take it easy!

JIRŌ: All right, now go and apologize to Ichihashi. Go on, what are you waiting for? The lady landlord didn't come in a sleigh this time, so they're going to have to come back for the coal. Don't give them any, you understand?

KIYOJI: I think you guys are nuts, deciding something like this behind a person's back.

JIRŌ: Yeah? Who was it fixed things so you could go work on the project? It was Ichihashi, head of the guild. He's the one said you were the worst off and overrode the others' objections. He's the one made them agree to pay off your rice levy and reduce your share of the debt. Now go on, apologize!

KIYOJI: All right, I'm going, I'm going!

Kiyoji slinks off.

JIRŌ: How'd it go, Pa?

KAMETARŌ: Yeah, well. . . .

JIRŌ: Don't tell me you agreed to settle!

KAMETARŌ: Well, see, they say we don't have a leg to stand on. If we don't have a written contract. . . .

JIRŌ: You old fool! Don't you understand yet, even after I spent all that time explaining it to you? (*He grabs Kametaro by the scruff of the neck.*) Come over here, come on!

KAMETARŌ (*as he is being dragged along*): Hey, take it easy!

JIRŌ: I remember exactly what happened. When you rented this land, the lady landlord had Nenokichi bring you out here to take a look. Remember? He stood here and pointed over that way. . . (*He points toward the audience.*) See that big ash? From there south. . . . (*Moving his finger*): We cut them down already, but from there to the two big oaks that used to stand at the edge of the buckwheat field: he told you they'd lease you all this land. Right?

KAMETARŌ: You're hurting me. (*Vaguely*): I guess so.

JIRŌ (*turning around*): Ma, you must remember?

TOKU: Sure, sure, that's just the way it happened.

JIRŌ: That's not all, either. Pa, you listening? When we put our house up, they came to the roof raising, the lady landlord and Nenokichi, the both of them. They gave us a whole bottle of shochu,[3] so you're bound to remember. They brought us food stacked in lacquer boxes and made a speech congratulating us. Remember? I was just a kid, so I even remember what was in the boxes: red rice,[4] and fried bean curd, and burdock cooked with potatoes in soy sauce. . . .

TOKU: That's right, that's right, I remember, too!

JIRŌ: See! Even if we don't have a written contract, we still leased this land with their agreement and consent. They're the ones said we didn't need nothing in writing 'cause it was a deal between us and them. Pa, don't you see, you've got to stick to your guns!

KAMETARŌ: Now listen. I didn't just cave in. I said I could understand how they could sign a lease with someone else if the original lessee failed to renew, but that since I'm the original lessee and I'm back wanting to renew, that eviction notice they sent you ought to be considered invalid. I told them off just like you said.

TOKU: Then why didn't you say so in the first place?

JIRŌ: It doesn't amount to a hill of beans if you agree to settle though.

KAMETARŌ: At least wait till I'm finished before you get sore. I haven't agreed to anything yet. It's just that I. . . .

JIRŌ: Oh, what's the point? According to Ichihashi, members of the family can appear during oral arguments. But today was the inspection, and the next time there's a hearing, I'll be. . . . So when will the court hand down its decision?

KAMETARŌ: They send us a written verdict a month or two after the judge makes his decision. That's when they tell us we've got so-and-so many days to vacate the house and get off the land.

JIRŌ: Damn it! Nobody knows that's what they'll decide!

KAMETARŌ: I asked you to hear me out. Anyway, at that point, even if we appeal —the way I understand it, the period for appealing is . . . er. . . . Now see, you got so angry you made me forget!

JIRŌ: A week.

KAMETARŌ: That's right! We've got a week. But they say we should think twice before we appeal, because appealing in cases like this is, you know, hopeless.

---

[3] A strong-tasting distilled liquor considered inferior to sake.

[4] Okowa, glutinous rice cooked with red adzuki beans and served on special occasions. Also called sekihan.

JIRŌ: What kind of a fool believes everything he's told? Anyway then what happened?

KAMETARŌ: Well, see. . . .

TOKU: Pa told me before that he'd get five hundred yen. . . .

JIRŌ (*shaking his head*): I want to hear it from him. What's this about five hundred yen?

KAMETARŌ: Yeah, well, they said they'd give us five hundred yen cash on the barrelhead if we'd get out. And I thought, you know, we'd be better off if we settled out of court.

JIRŌ: You just don't understand, do you? It's not just us. If we set a bad example, we'll cause trouble for everyone who comes after us. I don't care if they offer five hundred yen or a thousand!

Ichihashi appears along the stream.

ICHIHASHI (*from a distance*): Jirō!

JIRŌ: What?

ICHIHASHI: Come here a minute.

JIRŌ: What is it? (*He approaches and speaks to Ichihashi in a low voice.*) Yeah . . . yeah . . . yeah. . . . (*Suddenly very loud*): But if we hadn't said that, they'd've been afraid to let us have the horse and sleigh! (*Restrained by Ichihashi*): All right . . . yeah. . . .

KAMETARŌ (*who has been talking to Toku*): No!

TOKU: Just ask him!

JIRŌ (*to Ichihashi*): Hey, come on! If you start talking like that, it's the end of everything!

TOKU (*approaching*): Ichihashi?

ICHIHASHI: Yes?

TOKU: You wrote a letter for my old man, didn't you?

ICHIHASHI: Letter? I don't know what you're talking about.

TOKU: Don't try to hide it. He's already confessed.

ICHIHASHI: Hah-hah-hah! Well, in that case. . . . A real romantic letter it was, too!

TOKU (*to Kametarō*): See!

KAMETARŌ: Hey, I'm in enough trouble as it is!

ICHIHASHI: Hah-hah-hah! All right, all right! As a matter of fact, it was a thank you note to someone in Otaru.

TOKU: Are you sure? A thank you note for what?

JIRŌ: Get out of the way, Ma. This is no time for that. Ichihashi, if that's what you want, so be it. I'll just go ahead on my own.

ICHIHASHI: Don't be such a hothead! People just aren't ready to take action like they used to. It'd be pointless to go ahead on your own. At this point it's more important to. . .

JIRŌ: Talk! I trusted you! I discussed everything with you! But you're just like all the rest! Well, I'm through with you, see! Go to hell!

TOKU: Jirō! Ichihashi's stood by you all the time Pa was away, . . .

JIRŌ: Damn you all! You're driving me crazy! You can all go to hell!

ICHIHASHI: Come on, Jirō, don't get so excited.

JIRŌ: Where do you get off, acting so high and mighty? I can't stand the sight of you. Get the hell out of here!

TOKU: Jirō!

ICHIHASHI: Hah-hah-hah! You're a hard man, Izumi Jirō!

Komai Tsuta, dressed lightly in a hood, pants, and boots, enters over the bridge accompanied by Tashirogi Ryoichi and two or three other big men. Tashirogi carries a large balance scale.

TSUTA (*pleasantly*): Sorry to bother you. We're here to take a look at your charcoal. (*She starts for the lean-to.*)

JIRŌ (*standing in her path*): Wait a minute. Hasn't Nenokichi told you?

The men with Tsuta tense for trouble.

TSUTA: He hasn't told me anything. He came back late last night, and today he left at the crack of dawn for the courthouse in town. (*To Kametarō*): Ah, Kametarō, back already? How did things turn out? I gave Nenokichi very firm instructions. Did you come to an agreement?

KAMETARŌ: Not exactly, but. . . .

JIRŌ: Shut up! If Nenokichi didn't tell you, then I'll tell you myself. . . .

TSUTA: First things first. Hold the small talk until we've inspected the charcoal.

ICHIHASHI: Jirō. (*He signals him with his eyes.*)

TSUTA: Ah, Ichihashi, you here too? Your place is going to be last. Sorry for the wait. We'll be over as soon as we're done here.

ICHIHASHI: I'll be ready.

TSUTA: All right, let's see here, is it is, or is it ain't? Ah-hah-hah!

Ichihashi exits, laughing.

TSUTA (*to Tashirogi*): Take down the bags.

The men begin opening the bags of coal stacked in the lean-to.

TSUTA (*peering in at the coal*): Jirō, you really know what you're doing, don't you? You've got the temperature just right so there're no cracks; the color's good. . . .

TASHIROGI (*hefting the bags*): Now, there won't be any problem with the weight, will there?

Giving the end of a log to one of the men, Tashirogi places a bag on the scale, then he picks up the other end of the log and adjusts the counterweights.

TSUTA: Jirō wouldn't do anything so underhanded. (*To Toku*): Would he?

TOKU: No, ma'am.

TSUTA (*looking at Tashirogi*): Man stands like he's farting in the wind!

TASHIROGI (*as he weighs the coal*): This ain't the army, you know! I don't have to stand at attention, do I? (*Looking at the counterweights*): Right on the nose! (*Taking the bag down*): You don't think he wetted it down, do you?

TSUTA: You're the one who's wet—behind the ears! If he wetted it down in weather like this, it'd freeze and crack, wouldn't it?

TASHIROGI: I guess so.

TSUTA: Little Mother, you can be proud: Jirō's the best burner in the marshes, hands down.

TOKU: Yes, ma'am. Thank you very much, ma'am.

JIRŌ (*no longer able to contain himself*): Get out of here! I ain't giving you spit!

TSUTA: Why Jirō, what's come over you?

JIRŌ: I said get out!

TOKU: Jirō!

TSUTA: Don't talk nonsense. You burned this charcoal for me from trees you cut down on my land. Why shouldn't I take it? (*To Tashirogi*): You don't have to weigh them all. You can trust the Izumis. Just count the bags.

The men place markers on the bags to show that they've been inspected.

TASHIROGI: Ten, twenty, thirty . . . forty-two all told.

TSUTA: You're a real worker, Jirō. You must've fired the kiln twice already this year. Kametarō, let me have the chit book. (*She holds out her hand.*)

KAMETARŌ: Sorry, I, er. . . .

TSUTA: You're supposed to have the chit book ready for these inspections.

KAMETARŌ: I'll get it right away. (*He starts off hurriedly to get the book.*)

JIRŌ (*stopping him*): Wait, Pa, you don't have to get it.

TSUTA: Hah-hah-hah! Until I raise the price, is that it? (*Suddenly, in a shrill voice*): Come on, I haven't got all day! You going to hand over the coal or not?

JIRŌ: Get out!

TASHIROGI: Hey, who do you think you're talking to?

JIRŌ: You want to make something of it?

TOKU: Sorry, ma'am. Pa, hurry and get the chit book for Miss Komai.

KAMETARŌ: Right. (*He starts to go.*)

JIRŌ: Wait! I said wait! (*He yanks him back.*)

TOKU (*while Kametarō and Jiro are struggling, toward the house*): Hidema! Hidema!

HIDEMA'S VOICE (*from inside the house*): What?

TOKU: Be a good boy and bring the chit book. It's hanging by the partition!

HIDEMA'S VOICE: All right!

JIRŌ: Ma, don't!

TOKU: I . . . I . . . I've never gone against you before, Jiro. But you're going to Kamikawa, and I have to stay back here with your father and Hidema to take care of. What else am I supposed to do?

TSUTA: You people! Kametarō, give me a light, will you? (*She sits down on a bag of charcoal and takes out a cigarette.*)

KAMETARŌ: Yes, ma'am. (*He nervously strikes a match and lights her cigarette.*)

Jiro glares at them. Hidema runs across the bridge with the chit book.

HIDEMA: Here it is! (*He holds it out to Jiro, who does not take it.*)

TOKU: Here, give it to me. (*She takes it away from them.*)

HIDEMA: Hah! (*Going as far as the bridge*): Jiro's a beggar, a shit-eating beggar! (*He runs off.*)

TSUTA (*taking the chit book from Toku*): You really know how to put a person out. Let me see here now. (*She takes out a portable case containing brushes and ink.*) Credits are . . . it's all oak, right?

TASHIROGI: Right.

TSUTA (*writing*): Oak, forty-kilogram bags, first class . . . let's see, that was forty-two bags. Jiro, you really out-did yourself. That's forty-two times twenty-four sen. What does that come to?

TASHIROGI (*working a small abacus*): Ten yen eight sen.

TSUTA (*writing in the chit book*): Credit: ten yen eight sen. Oh, I almost forgot! There's the little matter of that charcoal you sold at the end of the year. I have no way of knowing how many bags you sold, so I'll do what I've been doing with everybody else: I'll just enter a debit here in the same amount as your credit for today. That'll be all right, won't it? (*She writes*): Debit: ten yen eight sen.

TASHIROGI: It just doesn't pay to be a working man these days, does it? Hah-hah-hah!

The men laugh together.

TASHIROGI: I'll take over from here.

TSUTA: You think you can handle it? (*She hands him the brush and ink.*)

TASHIROGI: Sure! (*To Toku*): What would you like?

TOKU: Some rice, please. A couple of liters would be plenty.

TASHIROGI: Rice? You must be doing better than I thought. Buckwheat and millet not good enough for you anymore?

TOKU: Jirō's going to Kamikawa. I want to feed him some rice before he goes.

JIRŌ: You're just wasting your money, Ma.

TSUTA: I'm not going to be responsible come fall if your account doesn't balance, you know.

TASHIROGI: Anything else?

TOKU: Yes. A knit shirt and a pair of children's work gloves.

TASHIROGI: Children's work gloves? Is Hidema going to help you with the kiln, then?

TOKU: Yes. That'll be all, if you don't mind.

Tashirogi makes notations in the book and returns it.

TSUTA (*getting to her feet*): All right, let's go. Ichihashi's still waiting. Sorry for the inconvenience!

Tsuta, Tashirogi, and the men march away along the stream.

JIRŌ: Damn! Damn! I don't care! You can all go to hell! (*He collapses, splayed out in the snow.*)

TOKU: Jirō, get up! You're going to catch your death! Pa, help me get him up.

JIRŌ (*weeping*): Leave me alone!

TOKU: I tell you you'll get sick.

JIRŌ (*shaking her off*): Get your hands off me! Both of you, go away! Go away, I said!

Tōku and Kametarō look at each other, then exit in silence.

The wind has died down, and the long icicles that hang from the windbreak over the kiln turn opaque as a cloud conceals the sun.

Gentle music flows over Jiro's defeated figure. After a while, Jiro sits up and stares into space. Then he wipes his tears and walks toward the lean-to. He carries a bundle of twigs into the kiln and lights the fire. In a moment, the mouth of the kiln glows red, and white smoke rises gently from the chimney.

Clenching her shawl tightly to her breast, trying to contain her overflowing heart, Henmi Shino walks nervously over the bridge. The music continues.

Shino stands silently behind Jiro, who is crouched down before the kiln. Jiro stares into the flames. Shino does not speak.

Pause.

JIRŌ (*after a few moments, without moving*): When did you get here?

SHINO: Before.

Again Jirō is silent.

SHINO: I have to talk to you.

JIRŌ: What about?

SHINO: I want to leave the Amamiya's.

JIRŌ: Again? But you promised you'd stay there until I got back.

SHINO: I have to get away from there.

JIRŌ: Did something happen?

SHINO: Not really.

JIRŌ: Then what's wrong?

Pause. Music. Shino moves away from the kiln toward the stream.

JIRŌ: Shino, I can't talk to you right now, okay? Everything's gone wrong today.

SHINO (*stopping for a moment*): All right. It's not that important. (*She walks to the edge of the stream and stands there.*)

Pause. Music.

SHINO: I. . . .

JIRŌ (*still in front of the kiln*): What?

SHINO: I remember this bend in the stream. There didn't used to be a kiln here, did there? Before, I mean.

JIRŌ: Of course not. Charcoal burners clear a section of forest, then move deeper and deeper into the mountain. When I was a kid, there was nothing here but bamboo.

SHINO: I wonder why I never recognized it before? We used to come here as children to play in the stream. Somehow I thought it was much farther up. . . .

JIRŌ: We did?

SHINO: You've forgotten, haven't you? That's a man for you! (*As she turns around, their eyes meet.*) You're smiling! You do remember! You stretched a net across the stream here at this bend and waited. "Chase the fish! Chase the fish!" you shouted. And if the way I was chasing them wasn't just right, you'd get so angry! You were always nasty, even as a child! Do you remember the time you put a caterpillar down my neck and made me cry? (*She touches her collar.*)

JIRŌ: Yes.

SHINO: When you took up the net, we'd make a fire and cook the crayfish and the little trout we'd caught. The crabshells would get bright red, and when you split them open they'd snap and the white meat would bulge out.

Caught up in the story, Jirō walks toward the stream.

JIRŌ: You sure talk a lot, don't you?

SHINO: Mrs. Amamiya says she can't tell what I'm thinking because I'm so quiet. But I don't have anything to say around them.

JIRŌ: I suppose not.

The two of them crouch beside the stream. Music.

SHINO (*caught up in her memories*): Playing by the stream—even then you were the leader.

JIRŌ: I might have been a leader then. Now I'm nothing.

SHINO: No, you're still the leader!

JIRŌ: How would you know?

SHINO: I saw you with my own eyes.

JIRŌ: Saw what?

SHINO: Just before new year's, a whole bunch of you went into town to sell charcoal. You were standing in front of the labor office and telling everybody what to do. "You, work East Nijo Street. You, go over to the railroad dormitory."

JIRŌ: Then you saw what a fool I've been.

SHINO: I told Mrs. Amamiya I had to do some shopping and went off on my own. I don't know, I just had to see you that day. I walked half-way to the village, but . . . well, I turned back because I didn't want to get scolded.

JIRŌ: I see.

SHINO (*suppressing the feelings of love that fill her breast, as if she feels unworthy of them*): Jirō, . . . I love you . . . very much.

Pause. Music.

JIRŌ: Get up! You'll catch cold crouching down like that.

SHINO: Oh! (*She emits a short cry and gets to her feet.*)

JIRŌ (*after looking at her for a few moments*): What you wanted to talk to me about—it wasn't about leaving the Amamiyas'—as it?

Shino does not answer.

JIRŌ: You're going to have a baby, aren't you? My baby.

Shino begins to weep. She clings to Jirō.

JIRŌ: What are you crying for? There's nothing to cry about! So that's why you want to quit your job!

Shino weeps even more desperately.

JIRŌ: All right. Come on, let's tell Ma and Pa.

SHINO (*shrinking back*): No. Please, no, . . . I. . . .

JIRŌ: There's nothing to be ashamed of.

SHINO: No! Jirō, please, don't tell anybody. All right? Don't tell anyone.

JIRŌ: Why not? If we don't tell them, . . . I'm leaving. What'll you do while I'm gone?

SHINO: I know, but I just don't want you to say anything. Just wait a little longer.

JIRŌ: I don't undertand you at all!

SHINO: I . . . I guess I will stay at the Amamiya's a little longer. Wait, all right? I'll think of something before it's noticeable. All right? Please!

JIRŌ: All right, if that's the way you feel. (*He looks into her eyes.*) Look at you, you're white as a sheet! Let's go in the house.

SHINO: No! I don't want to meet your people. Come on, it's warm by the kiln. (*She walks unsteadily toward the kiln, supported by Jiro. Exhausted, she seats herself on one of the windbreaks.*) Let's stay here. I want to stay with you like this forever, just the two of us.
Red light from the kiln plays across their faces.
The white smoke rises gently. Music.
Curtain.

Act Four: The Experimental Fields

Before the lights come up, a woman's voice is heard singing.
VOICE:
Sapporo Ag School,
On old Ezo Isle,
Imposing alma mater
In the land where bears do dwell!
Oh, how pleasant
Beneath the elms
To expound upon the truth!
Oh, how pleasant
Beneath the elms
To expound upon the truth!
Over this first voice is the voice of a second woman, reading a novel.
SECOND VOICE: "'We are now divorced and you are again Agnes
Smedley.[1] As I sit here with these red and gold autumn leaves falling
about me, I am very sad. I have loved you dearly. You were the first
love in my life and I think you will perhaps be the last. Our marriage
has been a failure, some way or other such a useless failure.   There
were always things between us that I did not understand.   Perhaps I
was too ignorant. Now perhaps we can be friends, and at all times I
shall be ready to help you. If you are in need, let me know and I
shall help you.'
"I did not like to read the letter...."
A title appears: ACT FOUR: THE EXPERIMENTAL FIELDS

---

[1]This quotation and those that follow are from Agnes Smedley, *Daughter of Earth*, 2nd ed.
(Old Westbury, NY: The Feminist Press, 1976), pp. 210-211. In this autobiographical novel,
first published in 1929, Smedley uses the name Marie Rogers, but Kubo has replaced the
pseudonym with Smedley's real name.

As the novel is being read, the title fades and the stage lights come up.

In the foreground, a group of female Workers from the agricultural station are taking their three o'clock break. Dressed in white work clothes with white kerchiefs over their heads, they are lounging near a hedge bordering a field where the sprouts of sugar beets are just beginning to appear. Worker 1 is lying on a mat, gazing at the high, blue sky; Worker 2 is absorbed in knitting; and a third (Funatsu Matsue) is singing. Several others (Workers 3, 4, 5, etc.) have formed a semicircle and are listening to the woman who is reading: Adachi Kimi.

A portion of an old-fashioned laboratory is visible behind the hedge. The carved eaves cast a clear shadow against the building's peeling green siding, and the windows reflect the violet color of the high May sky, which still secrets a vein of winter chill. Several tables and chairs, racks filled with test tubes, the pale blue flame of a Bunsen burner, shelves lined with specimens, statistical wall charts, the sweating glass of the Neubauer apparatus and its glistening black motor give a chaotic impression through the windows; and in the vicinity where, when the windows are open, the strange odor of chemicals pierces the nose, a door with a plaque reading "Laboratory" can be seen through a break in the hedge. The building is surrounded by a wooden fence like those used on ranches; a bell used to announce the hour hangs from the high branches of an elm tree; in the red barn a beautiful, brindled cow moves in and out of sight; and painted white signs mark off sections of the experimental fields. In short, there are many reminders of the legacy left by the American experts hired in the distant days of early Meiji to help develop Hokkaido.

Heat waves rise from the moist earth, and Adachi Kimi reads on in her novel.

KIMI (*reading*):   "I glanced over it quickly, that it might not awaken something in my heart, that I might not wish for love. For love is an enemy of woman."

WORKER 3: You really think that's true?

KIMI (*reading*):   "Then my mind that worked so tyrannically over my spirit began to draw that veil of suppression and forgetfulness down over the desire for love and the need for tenderness between man and woman. Somewhere there was loneliness, uncertainty, sadness. Yet I tossed my head—such things are for the weak."

MATSUE: Oh, how pleasant/ Beneath the elms/ To expound upon the truth!/ Oh, how pleasant. . . .

WORKER 4 (*turning around*): Pipe down, will you!

MATSUE: Look who's talking!   Aaaa! (*She yawns. To Worker 2*):
You're so dumb! What do you want to knit gloves now for?

WORKER 2: Mind your own business! (*She continues knitting.*)

KIMI (*reading*):   "I was   a   free   person again,   my name was Agnes
Smedley, the world was my home and the wind my companion."

WORKER 3:   You mean   they got divorced? But, Kimi, the story has a
happy ending, doesn't it?

WORKER 4:   You're really thick, aren't you? The book doesn't have a
happy ending! Does it, Kimi?

WORKER 5:   I really understand how she felt,   though, you know?   I
mean, where she says how   if you're a whore   and some man tells you to
give back   the dress he bought you, you   can tell him to go to hell, or if
he hits you, you can call   the cops, but once you're   married,   you're at
his mercy.   Nobody   should get married if you ask me.

KIMI: I don't think you should go that far.

WORKER 5: Why not?   Don't you agree with Smedley?

KIMI: There are places where I don't agree with her, no.

WOMAN 5:   Where exactly?

KIMI: She says that marriage is hell for a woman—she's beaten; forced to
slave in the kitchen;   if she has a child, she's done for;   and she has   to
obey her husband's every command. I love the   way she   evokes   male
violence   and the way she protests against   a society that accepts such
violence as perfectly natural.   But if you accept   the idea that to   love is
to be enslaved, then. . . .   (*To Worker 3*): No, the book doesn't have a
happy ending.   No matter   how many   men she lives with, she splits up
with them all, just like she split up with this one.

WORKER 3:   She must really have had her sights set high.

KIMI: Maybe she was   a   little too uncompromising in   her resistance.
Do you see what I   mean?   Look, in order for us to break out of   this
hell. . . .   (*To Worker 5*): If you found the right man, you'd marry him,
wouldn't you?

WORKER 5: I just said I wouldn't!

KIMI (*to Worker 4*): How about you   then? Once you were married, you'd
do everything you could   to see that the marriage worked, wouldn't you?
I know   from experience   what it's   like. . . . Can't you   listen without
laughing? . . .   Sure you're bound to be disappointed   when Mr. Right
turns out to   be a real feudal taskmaster.   But   unless   the   two   of you
work   together to gradually. . . . See, in   my case, I forgot   that part of
the responsibility   might   be   mine,   that there   were   bound to   be
elements in me that   nurtured those characteristics in him. I just began
to hate him, and in the end, we didn't make it.

MATSUE: Don't sit there with that dumb look on your face, listening to that romantic mush. Let me tell you something about Kimi. When she was over at the beet farm, she got hooked up with a tractor driver, and now that she's here, she's got her eye on Aoki.

KIMI: Don't be ridiculous!

MATSUE: Yeah? Well, I saw you hand him a book through the window!

WORKER 3: She did?

MATSUE: That's why she's reading you that dirty book: so you'll be on her side.

KIMI: Hah-hah-hah! Matsue, you're about the only person in the world who believes Agnes Smedley writes dirty books! If you don't believe me, come over here and listen for yourself.

WORKER 1 (*still lying down*): Hey cut it out. Take a look at the sky!

WORKER 2 (*knitting*): I don't think it's a dirty book—but maybe you'd better not read it all the same. It's a little on the pink side, isn't it?

WORKER 4: You think so?

Tsuji Shohei appears from the entrance of the laboratory carrying some papers. The women fall silent.

TSUJI: Is there somebody here by the name of Adachi Kimi?

KIMI: I'm Kimi.

TSUJI (*looking at the papers*): Let's see, your guarantor is . . . (*He points to a spot in the documents.*) Him, right?

KIMI: That's right.

TSUJI: Hmmm. That's strange. . . . (*He spies the book.*) What have you got there?

KIMI: It's a novel. From America.

TSUJI: Let me have a look. (*Kimi gives it to him.*) Daughter of Earth?

Aoki Yoshie opens the window to the laboratory and sticks his head out.

AOKI: Hey, Tsuji, do you know where Mr. Amamiya is?

TSUJI: How should I know? (*To Kimi*): Anyway, come with me for a minute, will you?

KIMI: What's the problem?

TSUJI: If you come with me you'll find out. (*He goes ahead toward the door.*)

AOKI: Tsuji, the motor's gone out again.

TSUJI: Again? Terrific. All right, you'd better find Amamiya and tell him right away.

AOKI: Yes, sir. (*His head disappears from the window.*)

TSUJI (*ushering Kimi*): Come along, then. (*The two of them go through the door and exit.*)

WORKER 2: See, I told you! Right, Matsue?

MATSUE: What's wrong, I wonder?

WORKER 4: You think we're all in for it?

WORKER 5: Stop worrying!

Amamiya Akira, director of the agricultural station, enters from the beet field. He is wearing ill-fitting, white work clothes that look more like a gown on him. Though it is still early in the season, his cheeks are already tanned by the sun.

AMAMIYA (*looking over his shoulder*): Terrible! (*To the Workers*): Hey, you there!

AOKI (*from the entrance to the laboratory*): Ah, Mr. Amamiya, the Neubauer apparatus has broken down again.

AMAMIYA: All right. (*He hurries inside. Aoki follows him.*)

WORKER 2: What do you suppose they want with Kimi?

MATSUE (*without replying, to Worker 1*): I heard on the weather report that it's supposed to rain today.

WORKER 1 (*lying back again on her mat*): Not likely. Look at that sky! Oh, I'm so sleepy!

The Maintenance Man appears out of the shadow of the building. He yanks the long rope hanging from a branch of the elm. The clear sound of the bell peals through air.

WORKER 5: Back to work, huh?

The Workers rise from their places and go to retrieve their tools from the work shed behind the hedge.

Behind the windows of the laboratory, Amamiya and Aoki are working on the motor.

AMAMIYA (*forcing a smile*): Wouldn't you know it? No sooner do we get the laboratory mechanized than the damned machine has to break down. We're going to be running all our frost damage and crop rotation experiments with electricity soon, but at this rate. . . .

AOKI: You want me to call somebody from the plant?

Amamiya nods. Aoki goes to the neighboring room, which is not visible from the stage. There is the sound of a telephone being dialed.

Each carrying her tools, the Workers pass the windows of the laboratory on their way into the fields.

AMAMIYA (*over the sill*): Hey!

MATSUE: Yes, sir? (*She stops.*)

AMAMIYA: I want you people to be careful. I just had to yell at somebody who was urinating in the field.

MATSUE: Sir!

The Workers burst into laughter.

AMAMIYA (*again serious after a brief smile*): It's no laughing matter. If we have people urinating all over a controlled experiment like that, it'll ruin the results of our fertilizer tests. I don't care if it's a dog, if you see somebody pulling a stunt like that, chase them away. Do you understand?

MATSUE: Yes, sir!

Biting their lips, the Workers exit to the fields. As soon as they are out of sight, they dissolve into torrents of laughter Amamiya sits down at a table and gazes at a chart on the wall.

AOKI (*reappearing*): They said they can't send anyone right away, but as soon as someone's free. . . .

AMAMIYA: I see. I wonder if we'll have to start all over from scratch?

AOKI (*bringing two or three test tubes, rack and all, from a table in the corner*): It's about this agar culture of Rhizobium japonicum. . . .[2]

AMAMIYA: Is it ready? (*Examining the test tubes*): Why do they have to be like that?

AOKI: Are you talking about Tsuji?

AMAMIYA: Tsuji?

AOKI: Yes . . . I mean. . . .

AMAMIYA: No. I was just thinking about the researchers at the main station. The minute they hear that in Germany common vetch is considered the best green manure crop, they assume that it's best here, too. They don't have the decency to consult the soil. No respect, you know? (*Indicating the wall with his chin*): You put the figures up, I see. It's going to look like you did it for Professor Takimoto's visit. Hah-hah-hah!

AOKI: No, sir, that's not the reason. I've just been procrastinating, and. . . .

AMAMIYA (*tracing the figures with his eyes*): The results on this chart bear me out. In contrast to an index figure of 100 for land treated with the flax company's fertilizer, the figure for land where red clover was plowed back into the soil is 118. That's in the column where 38 kilograms of potassium were applied. Now, the index for common vetch is one-zero-? . . . (*He stops.*)

AOKI: Is there something wrong?

---

[2]*Rhizobium japonicum* (Kirchner) Buchanan. These bacteria form nodules on legume roots and fix atmospheric nitrogen. If the plants are plowed back as green manure, they increase the nitrogen available in the soil for the next crop.

AMAMIYA: I'm sure it was 106, not five.

AOKI: I'll check it right away.

AMAMIYA: It's not like you to make mistakes. I remember at last year's conference of station directors, the only way Saegusa could deal with your statistics was to ignore them. "Probably trumped up anyway," he said. Remember? Hah-hah-hah!

AOKI: Won't the conference this September be a repeat performance?

AMAMIYA: I suppose it will. (*Picking up one of the test tubes*): This is the red clover, right?

AOKI: Yes, sir.

Amamiya goes to the window and looks at the test tube in the light.

AMAMIYA (*to the test tube*): I'm depending on you.

Dr. Nakaide enters, cutting across the experimental fields from the Amamiya's house.

AMAMIYA (*catching sight of him, through the window*): Ah, Doctor, I thought you'd already left.

NAKAIDE: Yes, well, the patient refused to be examined. She wouldn't let me get near her at first.

AMAMIYA: And?

NAKAIDE (*indicating Aoki*): May I?

AMAMIYA: Yes, it's all right.

NAKAIDE: It's already moving.

AMAMIYA (*nodding*): I see. And about the request I made earlier?

NAKAIDE: Don't worry. As a doctor, I'll honor it, naturally. Well, if you'll excuse me.

AMAMIYA: Thank you for coming. I hope you don't mind if I don't see you to the gate.

Nakaide goes along the hedge and exits through the rear gate. Amamiya is silent.

AOKI (*warming a test tube over a Bunsen burner at his own work bench*): Sir?

AMAMIYA: Yes?

AOKI: If you don't mind, I'd like to meet Tōru at the station.

AMAMIYA: Thank you. He's supposed to arrive at 4:35, but. . . .

AOKI: Of course I wouldn't go if the time coincided with Professor Takimoto's visit.

AMAMIYA: Let's wait and see.

AOKI: Yes, sir.

The two men continue working.

AMAMIYA: Aoki, do you think I was wrong?

AOKI: I couldn't say, sir.

AMAMIYA: No, I mean about your marriage.

Aoki looks at him questioningly.

AMAMIYA: Or that I stuck my nose in where it didn't belong?

AOKI: Oh, not at all. Without you as go-between. . . .

AMAMIYA: I'm just afraid that, you know, because I got involved you weren't able to act as you wished.

AOKI: No, sir.

AMAMIYA: I was shocked when I heard about this mess Tōru's gotten himself into, but I was even more disappointed to learn that even though you knew everything. . . .

AOKI: I'm sorry.

AMAMIYA: No, don't say that. Even though you knew everything, you kept it from me and my wife and, well, felt you had to shield Tōru from us.

AOKI: Yes, sir.

AMAMIYA: I wonder if you didn't feel that way because you're still suffering from your own affair.

AOKI: Yes, sir. I mean . . . actually, as far as that's concerned, I have a favor to ask.

AMAMIYA: What is it?

AOKI: I suppose I should have asked you before the end of the fiscal year, but do you think I could be transferred to some other work?

AMAMIYA: Other work?

AOKI: Well, from now on sugar beets, like flax, are going to become an important industrial crop and, well, that's all the more reason why I'd like to work on the statistics for these experiments, but, . . .

AMAMIYA: Yes?

AOKI: Well, I'm sure that the farming methods of the sugar company could be improved . . . but if I get involved in the research, it'll just make people all the more hostile . . . and I thought that it wouldn't be right for me to. . . .

AMAMIYA (*nodding*): I'll consider it.

They continue working. Pause.

AMAMIYA: Aoki?

AOKI: Yes?

AMAMIYA: I was thinking about the phrase "to rape the land."

AOKI: Sir?

AMAMIYA: Maybe it's not enough to understand the phenomenon simply as man robbing nature of its wealth.

AOKI: I don't understand.

AMAMIYA: The point is, if some people didn't have advantages—social advantages, that is—over other people, then it wouldn't be possible to exploit the land, would it? Everything . . . everything the phrase implies suggests. . . .

Dressed in her school uniform, Reiko enters on a bicycle. She stops beside the elm from which the bell is hung and leans against its trunk.

REIKO (*to the window*): Daddy! Look!

AMAMIYA: Reiko? (*He sticks his head out the window.*)

REIKO: I borrowed it from the Shimuras. I'm on my way to the station.

AMAMIYA: To meet Tōru?

REIKO: Oh, is Tōru coming home today? But it's not vacation.

AMAMIYA: Yes, well. . . . Who did you say you were going to meet?

REIKO: Isn't Grandpa Takimoto supposed to arrive on the 4:30 or whenever it is?

AMAMIYA: Silly, he's already arrived. He's dropping in at the municipal office first. He'll come here after that.

REIKO: Why didn't somebody tell me! What about Tōru, then?

Amamiya Teruko enters through the fields. She wears everyday clothes and an apron.

TERUKO (*sighting Reiko on the bicycle, from a distance*): Reiko! What are you doing?

REIKO: Mother, the Shimuras. . . .

TERUKO: Return it this instant!

REIKO: But. . . .

TERUKO: I told you you're not allowed.

REIKO: Tsk, nobody lets me do anything! (*She lets go of the tree and reluctantly pedals away.*)

TERUKO (*standing beneath the window*): Akira, come out for a minute, will you?

AMAMIYA (*from the window*): What is it?

TERUKO: I'd prefer to speak to you out here.

Amamiya goes around to the door.

TERUKO (*remembering the magazine still in its wrapper in the pocket of her apron*): Oh, here, this just came.

AOKI: Thank you. (*He takes it from her through the window.*)

TERUKO: The mailman was livid. Apparently someone scolded him in the fields.

AMAMIYA (*coming out*): What is it?

TERUKO (*stepping away from the window and lowering her voice*): It's about. . . .

AMAMIYA: Yes, I heard. I spoke to Dr. Nakaide.

TERUKO: Oh . . . well, I do hope you won't scold Tōru the minute you see him. He will have dinner with Father and us?

AMAMIYA: I suppose. . . .

TERUKO: What shall we tell Father? On second thought, never mind. I'll think of something. Shall we call Shino's brother?

AMAMIYA: Perhaps we'd better discuss it with Miss Komai.

TERUKO: Do you really think so? It's so unpleasant when someone like that gets involved.

AOKI (*through the window, indicating the newly arrived magazine*): Pardon me. Do you mind if I take a look at this?

AMAMIYA (*turning around*): What? Oh, it's *The Journal of the Agronomy Association*. Be my guest. (*To Teruko*): It's just the way things are done.

TERUKO: We can discuss it more later. (*She starts to go.*)

AMAMIYA: Teruko, buy her a bike, will you? We can't keep blaming it on Herr Neubauer forever.

TERUKO: Absolutely not.

AMAMIYA: If you don't, it'll get like Tōru's painting—although there's a difference, I suppose.

TERUKO: All right, I'll explain it to you. I really wish you didn't make me do this. You are a scientist, after all. You see, a growing girl . . . they say the saddle isn't good for a growing girl.

AMAMIYA: Is that it! I had no idea you had such a specific reason. Why didn't you tell me?

TERUKO: It's so embarrassing. . . . You should have understood.

AMAMIYA: There's nothing to be embarrassed about it. I am a scientist after all!

TERUKO: Well! (*She makes a face and exits.*)

　　Adachi Kimi appears. She has removed her work clothes and is ready to go home.

AOKI (*turning the pages of the magazine, from the window*): Sir, it's not here.

AMAMIYA (*noncommittally*): Hmm.

　　Kimi bows silently to Amamiya and is about to pass him.

AMAMIYA: Going home early? Are you ill?

KIMI: No, sir. Mr. Tsuji just called me to the reception room and told me I was fired.

AMAMIYA: Did you do something wrong?

KIMI: Not that I know of. I was about to ask for an explanation when somebody named Karasawa from the the flax company arrived, and. . .

AMAMIYA: Karasawa? (*Toward the window*): Aoki, is Karasawa here?

AOKI: I don't know. I'll go and see. (*He exits.*)

AMAMIYA (*to Kimi*): If I remember correctly, you were. . . . No, Funatsu's the one who used to be at the beet farm, right?

KIMI: I was there, too.

AMAMIYA: Is that so? I've been wanting to ask someone about what happened, but. . . . In any event, I'll ask Mr. Tsuji about you, all right?

KIMI: Thank you, sir.

Amamiya starts back into the laboratory.

KIMI: Sir, do you know a man named Watari from the Igarashi farm?

AMAMIYA: Watari? No, I can't say that I do. What about him?

KIMI: Never mind then. . . . Sir, please don't put yourself out on my account. I've decided to reconsider working here in any case.

AMAMIYA: I see.

Kimi bows and exits.

Amamiya sees her off briefly, then goes through the door. He reappears in the window and picks up the magazine.

Aoki returns.

AOKI: Karasawa's here all right. He said he'll come to see you as soon as Professor Takimoto arrives.

AMAMIYA: I see.

AOKI: Do you think someone tried to squelch it?

AMAMIYA: What?

AOKI: The continuation of your article. It's not there.

AMAMIYA: No, I put it off. I knew you'd scold me, but . . . I just can't seem to get the conclusion right.

AOKI: Isn't the conclusion the most important part?

AMAMIYA: I suppose it is. What about that woman who was just here?

AOKI: You mean Adachi? Actually, someone tipped us off.

AMAMIYA: Tipped us off?

AOKI: We got an anonymous card saying she used to work for the Hokkaido Council.[3]

---

[3]*Hokuhyō*, presumably a left-wing labor organization. There was such an organization active in Tokachi at this time called *Zenkoku nōmin kumiai Hokkaido rengōkai*, the abbreviation for which would have been *Hokuren*.

AMAMIYA: I see.

AOKI: The funny thing is. . . . (*He opens a drawer at one corner of the desk.*) Tsuji must have taken it with him. Anyway, it was in the same handwriting as her work application.

AMAMIYA: That is strange.

AOKI: Why did you put off publishing your article?

AMAMIYA: Well, take the problem of green manure crops: which is better, common vetch or red clover, for example.

AOKI: Yes?

AMAMIYA: Of course it's an important problem, and I have to see it through to come kind of conclusion, but somehow it's begun to strike me as, you know, too narrow.

AOKI: What do you mean "narrow"?

AMAMIYA: Well, if nitrogen's the issue, then instead of worrying about the absorption activity of Rhizobium japonicum, why not run a strong electrical current through the earth to attract the free nitrogen in the air like the Germans did during the Great War?

AOKI: But that's. . . .

AMAMIYA: Impossible? (*He nods vigorously.*) Of course it would be impossible for agriculture alone. In the German case, they needed the help of the military. But if. . .

AOKI: Yes?

AMAMIYA (*taking the magazine in his hand*): What about Saegusa's rebuttal?

AOKI: It's not there either. There was a rumor he was going to write it immediately, too.

AMAMIYA: Look here. Professor Takimoto's writing about predicting cold damage. What I was just saying applies to this, too. I don't know what he says in this article, but let's suppose that the cause lies in the midsummer temperature of the Kurile current.

AOKI: Of course you're oversimplifying.

AMAMIYA: Of course. The current moves south at approximately ten nautical miles per day, right? That means that conditions in the waters around northern Chishima, seven or eight hundred nautical miles away, will show up here seventy or eighty days later. If we could survey oceanic conditions in the north in February or March, we'd know immediately whether we were going to have trouble with cold during the summer. But at the marine experimental station, they don't even have a ship set up for surveying those conditions. When they're not busy doing experiments for the fishing industry, they just dabble with the problem in their spare time.

AOKI: They seem to be as strapped for money as we are.

AMAMIYA: On the basis of some skimpy meteorological data, we're supposed to make these prophecies—the prognosis for this year's harvest is. . . ."—it's if we were fortune-tellers. I often dream about. . . . But never mind. Get back to work.

AOKI: What do you dream about, sir?

AMAMIYA: Hah-hah-hah . . . first, we'd send a sea-going laboratory fitted out with all the latest equipment up to northern Chishima, and we'd have it notify us of the temperature of the Kurile current by radio at regular intervals. (*As he is talking, he closes the window gently with one hand.*) Of course, unless our farm here was much, much bigger, we'd never be able to hire a ship like that, much less buy one. But, you see, if we knew in advance that there was a potential for cold damage, we could increase the proportion of root crops like sugar beets that are resistant to the cold. As for the paddies and the flax, we could put together some fast-acting fertilizer, in large quantities to minimize the expense, plant early and harvest early. Then the soybeans: you know it's tremendously time-consuming for a man to apply Bordeaux mixture[4] manually. I wonder if we couldn't mechanize the process, or, better yet, spray from airplanes?

AOKI: I see. You know, if I closed my eyes, . . . hah-hah-hah, I'd swear I was listening to a socialist!

AMAMIYA (*unamused*): Aoki, that's the whole point! If my thinking leads to that sort of conclusion—the same conclusion as the socialists—then there must be some mistake in my reasoning. I must have gone wrong somewhere. You see?

AOKI: I suppose. . . .

AMAMIYA: And if that's the case, then I lose confidence. That's what happened on the radio, and that's why I put off publishing my article. There's no point in promoting one lie in order to avoid another.

AOKI (*cautioning him*): Someone's coming, sir.

Outside the window, Henmi Shōsaku is bowing and smiling. Behind him is another man who also appears to be a farmer: Watari Junzō.

AMAMIYA (*opening the window*): You two, wait a minute. (*He goes around to the entrance.*)

Shōsaku and Junzō are discussing something between themselves.

AMAMIYA (*coming out*): Did my wife call you? I didn't realize. . . .

---

[4] A fungicide made from copper sulfate, lime, and water.

SHŌSAKU (*surprised*): No, sir. Actually, we had a favor to ask. Oh, this here's Watari Junzō. He's from the east two cooperative, same as me.

JUNZŌ: Glad to make your acquaintance. (*He bows.*)

AMAMIYA: Watari? I see.

SHŌSAKU: We should've dropped by Miss Komai's first and then swung by here, but we figured there wouldn't be no point till we knew what you had to say, so. . . .

AMAMIYA: So you haven't spoken to Miss Komai yet?

SHŌSAKU: No, sir.

AMAMIYA (*to the window*): Aoki, is the reception room available? I'm having them copy the Sagino[5] materials in my office just now.

AOKI: I'll see. (*He exits.*)

SHŌSAKU: Er . . . that article you wrote? Well, there's this school teacher, Teramachi, and, well, it's too hard for us, so we had him explain it to us, but. . . .

AMAMIYA (*understanding*): I see, you're here about my article?

SHŌSAKU: Yes, sir. You see, we wanted to. . . .

JUNZŌ: We're having trouble following Mr. Teramachi, too. See, I don't know if it's true what it says here—that no matter how much we grow, it won't do us no good —but it sounds just like. . . .

Shōsaku restrains him with his eyes.

AMAMIYA: Like what?

JUNZŌ (*glancing at Shōsaku*): Just like . . . you know . . . what the Communists say. Anyway, there's this man from the marshes . . . . . (*To Shōsaku*): I can tell him, can't I?

SHŌSAKU (*uncomfortable*): Since you've said that much already.

JUNZŌ: Anyway, there's this man from the marshes—what's his name, the one with the scar through his eyebrow?

Shōsaku can't remember either.

JUNZŌ: Anyway, these charcoal burners from the marshes came, see, and two of them stopped us.

AMAMIYA: What do you mean, "stopped you"?

SHŌSAKU: Actually . . . you see, we was going to ask you if you'd speak to Miss Komai and, you know, tell her that we needed to borrow some money. . . .

AMAMIYA: Money?

---

[5]Sagino is a variety of flax from Japan entered into the United States Department of Agriculture collection in 1929. It is possible that this is the same as Saginaw, a variety from Michigan entered into the collection in 1928. Both are fiber varieties of flax used for linen and fine paper production.

SHŌSAKU: Yes,   sir.   Last year, all my flax went down on the stalk, and, the way I figure it, like you say, there was too much nitrogen in the company fertilizer, and that's why the plants grew too high. So, you see . . . er, I spoke to you about this the last time I was here, but, well, this year, I could use fertilizer in the proportions you wrote about and increase the potassium, and that way. . . .

AMAMIYA: I see. But won't the agricultural committee lend you the money at low interest?

JUNZŌ (*vehemently*): That'll be the day! They have a deal with the industrial union and the ammonium sulphate company. Either we use the fertilizer they've concocted, or they tell us to get it from the flax company.

Tsuji Shōhei appears in the doorway. Aoki returns to his seat inside the window.

TSUJI: Sorry to keep you waiting. The reception room's all yours, sir. We're a little strapped for space, so I was wondering if you'd let me use the laboratory until Professor Takimoto arrives?

AMAMIYA: Be my guest.

Tsuji exits.

SHŌSAKU: Sorry to bother you like this.

AMAMIYA: Not at all. As a matter of fact, I have to see Miss Komai anyway, . . . I'm just afraid things might backfire if I intervene. But let's go inside and discuss it.

Amamiya leads the two men through the door.

In the   meantime, Tsuji   and Karasawa   appear at the window.
Karasawa and Aoki greet each other with obvious distaste.

KARASAWA (*looking at the Neubauer apparatus*):   What's wrong? The seeds are just germinating, why did you turn it off?

TSUJI: It keeps breaking down.

KARASAWA: There must be somebody around who knows something about electricity?

TSUJI: That's just it, there isn't.

KARASAWA: Well, for heaven's sake, man, why didn't you say something. I'd have sent one of our electricians over right away.

TSUJI: Thank you, but you and Mr. Amamiya haven't been getting along too well, and. . . .

KARASAWA: Hah-hah-hah! We're not children. In the first place, this motor's an antique! I don't know who put this together for you, but they really stuck you good.   They must have known there was nobody out here who knew about electricity and figured they could get away with murder. Aoki, how's your beet research coming?

AOKI: Fine. (*He continues to work in silence.*)

KARASAWA: Tsuji, you know I've never had the pleasure, but I understand Aoki's wife is very *charmante*.

TSUJI: *Charmante*?

KARASAWA: I don't know what it means either, but that's what old "Diversified Farming" from the sugar company said. Ah-hah-hah!

TSUJI: What's "diversified farming"?

KARASAWA: Just what it sounds like. For example, if you grow only soybeans, then when the crop's bad you're in trouble, so you diversify. You plant some flax here and some sugar beets there. They're especially encouraging farmers to plant sugar beets because the greens can be fed to livestock, which means further diversification. The animals produce manure, and so forth and so on. The head of the administration gave a speech on the subject the other day. It was just in the paper, didn't you see it? That's a bad lapse for someone who works in an agricultural station! Ah-hah-hah!

TSUJI: Hah-hah-hah! I suppose you're right.   That reminds me, how have things been going at the mill since you changed your incentive policy?

KARASAWA: It's a tremendous relief, let me tell you.   In the first place, it's a lot less work for me personally. On the other hand, it's causing all kinds of little tragicomedies. Take this man Seki, for instance. You're probably not aware, but he's a hold-out from the time they divided the bucket land into independent plots. Anyway, every year he's been getting subsidies on an individual basis, but beginning this year, incentive subsidies are being awarded by the group. Unfortunately there's not a single decent man in the east two cooperative, so the other day he shows up complaining that he's afraid of losing his subsidy.

Takimoto Toshiaki, doctor of agriculture, appears in the window. He has a ruddy complexion and salt-and-pepper hair. He is followed by Amamiya. The people assembled in the room greet each other.

Henmi Shōsaku and Watari Junzō come out of the laboratory. They start to go along the hedge and through the front gate.

JUNZŌ (*stopping*): Hey!

SHŌSAKU: What?

JUNZŌ: We said the two of us wanted a loan, but we didn't mention the others.

SHŌSAKU: I thought of that, but I didn't think we could ask so much.

JUNZŌ: Maybe you're right. We only started out wanting a loan for you. What should we do?

SHŌSAKU: It's too late now. Let's go and think it over.

JUNZŌ (*walking*): I can't remember the last time I made any money at my place. I suppose it's my own damned fault. I neglected my fields and went around making all that noise about how the New Farmer-Labor Party says this and the All Farmers Party says that—not that I understood what I was saying, but. . . . (*They exit.*)

The men in the laboratory appear through the door.

TAKIMOTO: It's been five years since you all got together for my sixtieth birthday and retirement. There were a lot of speeches, but the ones I found most interesting were by Satake—he's quite a bit older than you and is retired in Otaru—and then Ama....—in the order that you graduated, Amamiya and Karasawa. You two in particular. . . .

KARASAWA: Sir, I just want to tell you how sorry I am to have caused you all this concern. After all, my firm has . . . we've received inestimable benefit from this agricultural station.

TAKIMOTO: Yes, I suppose you have.

KARASAWA: For example, there was the myth that because you make compost from flax stalks and don't plow them back, flax depletes the soil. For a while we had a hard time because the farmers in this area didn't want to plant flax.

TAKIMOTO: I see.

KARASAWA: It was Amamiya here who exploded that myth. As a matter of fact, the one who promoted the idea that growing flax actually benefits the soil, because it's harvested early and can be cultivated with green manure crops, which do well in the fall, was also. . . .

TAKIMOTO: Amamiya? Hah-hah-hah! If you're so willing to recognize his accomplishments, what have you got to fight about? Tonight, let's have dinner together and let bygones be bygones. (*To Amamiya*): What do you say?

AMAMIYA: Yes, that would be fine.

TSUJI: That's very kind of you, sir. I don't know how all this got started, but here at the station we've been sifting out pure strains of Sagino Number 2 and. . . .

TAKIMOTO: Yes, of course, the one that's stronger against rust than Pernau.[6] I'm sure you've had a lot of trouble with flax rust, haven't you?

---

[6]Pernau is a variety of flax from Hungary that was not entered into the USDA collection until 1958. However, Pernau is closer to the Japanese *peruno* than any other flax variety, and Professor Kondō Yukō of Obihiro University confirms it is indeed the variety referred to here.

TSUJI: Yes. Well, as a result of our efforts, the quality of the Sagino varieties has improved, but I've been afraid that this friction between the director and Mr. Karasawa might prevent the distribution of these strains and thus jeopardize the work of the entire station.

AMAMIYA: Tsuji, I've made a point of sending all our research to the flax company. You of all people should know that!

TSUJI: Of course, if you put it that way. . . .

TAKIMOTO: All right, all right! Take a look at that row of acacias. That high ground you can see beyond them is the area we've heard so much about, isn't it?

TSUJI: Yes, sir.

TAKIMOTO: So that's the bucket land? Amamiya, that's a tribute to your work.

AMAMIYA: Sir, take a look at this field. The plants are just beginning to sprout, but from here to here is. . . .

TAKIMOTO (*approaching the field*): What I don't understand is why for no apparent reason you have to start up about this so-called shortage of potassium?

AMAMIYA: Yes, well . . . er, in the rest of Japan, there are large quantities of potassium contained in night soil, compost, and ashes. In other words, farmers have been supplementing the potassium in the soil without realizing it. It's so obvious, I don't know myself why I didn't see it sooner.

TAKIMOTO: But look here . . . no, go ahead. Let's hear you out.

AMAMIYA: On the other hand, the cultivated area per household here in Hokkaido is so large, there isn't enough night soil or compost to go around. So it seems to me that if agronomists had been paying closer attention to the need to replenish the nutrients in the soil, there wouldn't be any problem with potassium today.

TAKIMOTO: I see. So?

AMAMIYA: The reason we didn't perceive the problem is, as I wrote in my Journal article, because of depletion farming. At least that's the way it seems to me. Did you have the time to read my article?

TAKIMOTO: I saw it. Leaving aside the merits of your argument, I was most impressed with your earnestness. That's all the more reason why I must point out certain facts. Amamiya, it goes without saying that the soil of Japan differs significantly from the soil of other countries. The fact is recognized in books on the subject in Germany and America, but it is also accepted in a book you probably prefer—or, I should say, one you must have perused—from the Soviet Union. It indicates that the soil of Japan is most susceptible to a shortage of nitrogen. Even if there is an insufficiency of potassium, crop yields decline only seven percent. Just seven percent, mind you. That contrasts with 42 percent for nitrogen and 12 percent for phosphorous. It's written right there in black and white. Well, have you read it?

TSUJI: Sir, do you even keep up on the literature from Russia? You see the difference, Aoki?

AOKI (*helplessly*): Yes.

KARASAWA: I wonder, though. Do you really think it's wise to use a Russian source to support your position?

TAKIMOTO: No, Karasawa, you're wrong there. I'm not the only one who recognizes that since collectivization Soviet theory has made great strides. Everyone agrees on that. For example, Amamiya here.
. . .

AMAMIYA: Sir, aren't you referring to Popov's book?

TAKIMOTO: What? Why, yes.

AMAMIYA: I'm familiar with it. That is, one of the young workers at the station pointed it out to me, so I only know the Japanese version, but. . . .

TSUJI: Mr. Amamiya, who was this young worker? (*To Aoki*): Was it you?

AMAMIYA: It's not important who it was. The point is, the figures that you just quoted, sir, . . . er, if I remember correctly, they're from a passage that began, "In the view of a certain Japanese soil scientist." In other words, the lies that come from the weaknesses in our own research—I'm not familiar with conditions in the Soviet Union so I can't be sure—but in any case, those lies are even being repeated in books in Russia. Isn't that the point?

Takimoto is silent.

AMAMIYA: Here, look at the fields. We're doing all kinds of experiments, including experiments with crop rotation. From here to here is land where oats alone have been sown, and we've used about 34 kilograms of nitrogen per hectare of land. The land on this side is land where we've plowed back the red clover that we've rotated with the oats, and we've used 23 kilograms of nitrogen with 38 kilograms of potassium per hectare. The plants are only beginning to sprout, but as you can see. . . .

KARASAWA: Amamiya, look, let's suppose we were to concede the point. Aside from increasing the potassium, what's so novel about your theory? You seem to be keen on green manure crops, but. . . .

AMAMIYA: Of course, there's nothing new about ploughing certain plants back as natural fertilizer.   As long as anybody can remember they've been using alfalfa and the Chinese milk vetch in paddy fields in Japan. But what I . . . what I'm trying to say is that the farmers don't have the money. Money, do you understand?   Even if it's true that there is a lack of nitrogen, nitrogen fertilizer is one of the most expensive fertilizers people can buy.

AOKI (*whispering, from behind him*): Potassium, sir, potassium!

AMAMIYA: What?   Oh, yes, of course. Potassium fertilizer is one of the most expensive fertilizers people can buy. That's why, sir, that's why, you see, we should encourage people to grow red clover, which is the most effective green manure crop, so that they can save as much money as possible on nitrogen fertilizer and use the money instead to buy a mixture with a higher proportion of potassium.   Do you see what I mean?   In other words, all I'm saying is that for the same amount of money we could set up a system where the proportions in fertilizer of, say, ammonium sulfate, superphosphate, rice bran, and potassium sulfate would be scientifically appropriate. Karasawa, that's the point!

KARASAWA: In other words, you're suggesting a boycott, a boycott of ammonium sulfate, is that it?

AMAMIYA: Boycott? Well, I suppose you could look at it that way.

KARASAWA: You can't do that. Fertilizer isn't the only thing ammonium sulfate is used for.   The farmers already have a system, and it's allowed them to buy ammonium sulfate up to now. You can't just go out and upset that system.

AMAMIYA: That's an entirely different problem! Listen, you just keep out of this. Sir, to be perfectly frank. . . .

Teruko has changed her clothes and enters along the edge of the fields.

TERUKO: Oh, Father, you're here!   I've been so looking forward to your visit—this time especially!

TAKIMOTO: Hello!

TERUKO: I'm going to serve you all kinds of homemade delicacies again.   After all, you are a bachelor!   Hah-hah-hah!   Oh, Mr.Karasawa, how nice to see you!   We haven't seen you for quite some time.

KARASAWA: Sorry not to have stayed in touch.

TERUKO (*to Amamiya*):   Whenever you're ready.

AMAMIYA: Just wait!   (*To Takimoto*): To be perfectly frank, sir, the idea that there is no need to apply potassium fertilizer anywhere in

Hokkaido is, well, don't you think it simply serves to reinforce the primitive agricultural methods that have been practiced here since the island was first settled?

TAKIMOTO: Very interesting.   I've been promoting primitive, that is, depletion farming, is that it?

AMAMIYA: Actually, I think its a long-standing curse.   Today, the farmers have to use tremendous amounts of expensive chemical fertilizer just to keep their heads above water, and when there is a crop failure, their situation is simply tragic.   Sir, when things reach such a state—no, perhaps it's been this way all along—it's no longer just a problem of raping the land, we're also sacrificing the farmers themselves.   In other words, the farmers. . . .

TAKIMOTO: Amamiya, if this were just an academic debate, we could argue to our hearts' content.   But I've devoted decades of my life to agriculture, and the very idea that you would accuse me of being an enemy of the farmers is just. . .

AMAMIYA: But, sir. . . .

TSUJI: Mr. Amamiya, . . .

KARASAWA: Amamiya!

There is a momentary gap in the conversation as the men, their tempers rising, all speak at once.

TERUKO (*seeing her chance*):   Gentlemen, why don't you set aside your discussion for the moment and, please, the food is getting cold. . .

.

TSUJI: Yes, excellent idea.   Our director is too, how shall I put it. . . . Hah-hah-hah. . . .

TAKIMOTO: No, you'll have to excuse me. I have other places to visit. Teruko, you'll be hearing from me by letter. Gentlemen. (*He strides off along the hedge and exits.*)

A short pause.

KARASAWA: Amamiya, go after him and apologize!

AOKI: Sir!

TSUJI: You can't just let him leave!

TERUKO (*dashing through the men*): Father! Wait! Father! Father! (*She runs off.*)

TSUJI: Aoki, the professor left his hat and bag. . . .

Aoki nods, runs into the laboratory, grabs the items, and pursues Takimoto.

KARASAWA (*casting a steely glance at Amamiya*): Tsuji, come on, I think we'd better. . . .

They hasten off.

Left alone, Amamiya stands immobilized. He had also thought   to pursue his father-in-law   but   has reconsidered.

Gradually, the sky become overcast. From the shadow of the building, Miyake Tetsuya appears, looking as if he is searching for someone.

MIYAKE: Oh, Mr. Amamiya!

AMAMIYA: Ah, Miyake.

MIYAKE: Wasn't Professor Takimoto? . . .

AMAMIYA: He's already left.

MIYAKE: Just my luck! Where did he go?

AMAMIYA: I haven't got any idea.

MIYAKE: Er . . . there's something I wanted to ask you . . . about your article.

AMAMIYA: Listen, couldn't you put off writing about that for a while?

MIYAKE: I hope I haven't written anything. . . .

AMAMIYA: No, on the contrary, if anything you've been too kind. It's just that. . . .

MIYAKE: Then will you be cutting off the debate? Are you going to let let things stand as they are?

AMAMIYA: No, not exactly.

MIYAKE: It'd be a shame to leave things unresolved like this. But, er, the reason you originally brought up this problem was—here I go again, wanting to know everything at once, but—it had something to do with the issue of selling the tractors at the beet farm, didn't it?

AMAMIYA: Why do you think so?

MIYAKE: Am I wrong?

AMAMIYA: Miyake, what did you do before you became a reporter?

MIYAKE: Why do you ask?

AMAMIYA (*allowing a slight smile to creep across his face*): Just curious.

MIYAKE: Curious, huh? Well, I guess I'm flattered. I'm not some disillusioned leftist, if that's what you're thinking!

AMAMIYA: Then what?

MIYAKE: You knew that I was an athlete, didn't you? Well, that's how I originally joined the sports department of the Tokyo Times. The only trouble is, I got demoted.

AMAMIYA: How?

MIYAKE: It was a real smooth job. They said: at the Olympics in Berlin next year—that is, this year—they're going to try to have Tokyo designated as the site of the next games, and if they succeed, the winter Olympics will be held in Sapporo. Since you're from

Sapporo, how about going up there and beginning preparations now? That's how they put it.

AMAMIYA: Then how did you wind up here?

MIYAKE: What difference does it make? (*With self-derision*): I've made a really stunning decline, hah-hah-hah! Was I wrong about what I said before?

AMAMIYA: What was it you were saying? Oh, about the tractors?

MIYAKE: That problem's fascinated me since I got here.   When they divided the tractor farm into tenant plots,   word at the sugar company was that there's no such thing as a farmer without greed: If they work as sharecroppers, they're in the field from dawn till dusk, but the minute they're hired for wages, they do nothing but loaf. Shimura and the others. . . .

AMAMIYA: You think they're wrong?

MIYAKE: Come on, sir, don't put me on! The whole point of your thesis about the three basic nutrients is that intensive farming is the only solution since large-scale collectivization is impractical.   Oh! Is that why you don't want me to write about it? Don't worry, I'm not going to say that you're a socialist! Hah-hah-hah!

Aoki returns.

AOKI: Uh . . . Mr. Tsuji and Mrs. Amamiya talked to him for quite a while, but they couldn't convince him to stay. He and Mr. Karasawa took a taxi. . . .

MIYAKE: Is he talking about Professor Takimoto?

AMAMIYA: Yes.

MIYAKE: Hmm, if he's with Karasawa, I have a pretty good idea where they're headed. If you'll excuse me. (*He exits.*)

AMAMIYA: This is terrible.

AOKI: I'm sorry. There's nothing we could do.

AMAMIYA: Of course. But if even people like Miyake begin to suspect my ideas are. . . . Even so, that's no reason to. . . . Oh, by the way, I got this back for you. (*He hands him a postcard.*)

AOKI: Thanks. (*He takes it from him and inspects it.*) What does he think he's accomplishing? Did he think you'd praise him when you found out?

Dressed in his student uniform and carrying a basket, Tōru enters with his mother through the front gate and along the hedge.

TŌRU: Come on, you can tell me that much.

TERUKO: It will keep until you've seen your father.   Oh, dear, it's starting to rain!

A light rain begins to fall. Amamiya glares at his approaching son. After a moment, he strides toward him.

AMAMIYA: Tōru!

TŌRU: Hello, Father. (*He stops and stares at the ground.*)

AMAMIYA: What have you got to say for yourself?

Tōru does not answer.

AMAMIYA: Who do you think all this work is for? Then you go and take advantage of one of the peasant's daughters—are you trying to destroy everything I've tried to accomplish? (*He knocks him to the ground.*)

TERUKO: Akira! (*She restrains him.*) Not in public!

AOKI: Sir, please don't. . . .

AMAMIYA: Get out of my way!

TERUKO: You have to shoulder part of the blame, too. . . .

AMAMIYA: Being drunk is no excuse!

TERUKO: You've been so involved in your work, you let him go out late at night like that. . . .

AOKI: Mr. Amamiya, please. . . .

AMAMIYA: You're going to take the responsibility for what you've done. Tōru, you know what that means.

TŌRU: Yes, sir.

TERUKO (*understanding her husband for the first time*): No! You don't mean. . . .

The rain is falling hard now. A group of female Workers begin running in from the fields.

MATSUE: See, I told you it was going to rain!

AOKI (*stopping her*): Funatsu!

MATSUE: Yes?

AOKI: I want to see you later.

MATSUE: What for?

AOKI: Later, I said.

The Workers exit for their shelter.

TERUKO: Akira, I'm taking him home. . . .

AMAMIYA: All right, wait for me there.

Shielding Tōru, Teruko exits along the edge of the field.

AOKI: Sir, you're going to get wet.

AMAMIYA: All right.

The two of them go through the door. Amamiya appears inside the window. He sits at the table. Aoki comes through the door again carrying an umbrella. He starts toward the Workers' shelter.

Tsuji returns. He carries a borrowed umbrella.

TSUJI (*spying Aoki*): Hey, where're you going?

Aoki does not answer but walks away with determination.

Tsuji enters through the door.

AMAMIYA (*inside*): Tsuji?

Tsuji appears in the window.

AMAMIYA: I really don't want to get involved, but just because a person's been affiliated with the Hokkaido Council is no reason. . . .

TSUJI: No, sir, there's more to Adachi than that. Word has it when she was working at the sugar beet farm, she conspired with one of the tractor drivers to make trouble.

AMAMIYA: A tractor driver?

TSUJI: Yes, sir. At the sugar company on Taiwan, they use tractors, too. Of course, down there they grow sugar cane, not beets, but. . . . The point is, the drivers are all ex-air force men and, well. . . . You see what I mean?

AMAMIYA: Well, in that case, I'll reconsider.   But I won't have people informing on their fellow workers, and I want you to know I intend to take appropriate action.

TSUJI: Yes, sir, if that's the way you feel.

AMAMIYA: And Tsuji, see that this motor is fixed by tomorrow.

TSUJI: Yes, sir, I'll take care of it. (*Exits.*)

The Maintenance Man dashes through the rain and rings the bell on the elm tree, frequently wiping rain from his upturned face as he does so.

Aoki enters with Funatsu Matsue under his umbrella and goes through the door to the laboratory.

Having removed their work clothes and kerchiefs, Workers 3, 4 , and 5 enter, all trying to squeeze under a single waxed-paper umbrella.

WORKER 3: You think Mr. Aoki's decided to switch girlfriends? Hah-hah-hah!

WORKER 5: No, it must have something to do with Kimi.

WORKER 4: Shh!

The women pass beneath Amamiya's window, bowing summarily as they do so. Shortly, their singing voices can be heard: "Youthful dreams/ Fulfilled but once/ Let it be today!"

The singing voices fade into the distance. Henmi Shino, signs of strain showing in her face, enters along the edge of the field carrying a man's black umbrella. Catching sight of her, Amamiya opens his window.

SHINO (*coming through the hedge*): I've brought you your umbrella, sir.

(*She is about to go around to the entrance.*)

AMAMIYA: Thank you, I'll take it. (*He takes it from her through the window.*)

Shino turns to go.

AMAMIYA (*from behind her*): Try not to get sent out on these useless errands. I'll speak to my wife.

Shino nods and goes back the way she came. Amamiya watches her go, then closes the window and straightens the top of his desk. He picks up the umbrella and goes around to the doorway.

Workers 1, 2, and so forth enter under a single umbrella. They are singing: "O'er the plains of Ishikari/ From afar the ganders fly." But seeing Amamiya at the door, they fall silent.

WORKERS (*together*): Good day, sir. Good day, sir.

Amamiya responds with a silent bow. The Workers disappear in the distance. Their song: "Flocks voiceless to their shelter/ Peak of Te'ine veiled in dusk."

Amamiya has come through the hedge and is now standing in the rain, staring at the experimental sugar beet field, so recently the scene of his argument with his father-in-law and mentor.

The Mainentance Man appears inside the laboratory, locking the doors and closing the curtains. The solid white of the curtains reflects the twilight. Softly, music begins.

Reiko runs in along the hedge.

REIKO (*from a distance*): Father, make room for me! I'm soaked!

AMAMIYA: Silly girl, where've you been all this time?

REIKO: I was waiting for the rain to let up. I heard Grandpa left already.

AMAMIYA: Who told you?

REIKO: The maintenance man, by the specimen room. What's the matter? Let's go!

Amamiya is staring at the field.

REIKO: Maybe I should make a run for it. I'm already soaked anyway. Oh, Father?

AMAMIYA: Yes?

REIKO: Today in science class we heard your lecture on volcanic ash soil. You know, the one you're so proud of.

AMAMIYA: You did?

REIKO: You said that back when Mt. Asahi and Mt. Tokachi were still active volcanoes, a lot of ash fell on this plain and that it's still here on the ground.

AMAMIYA: Yes.

REIKO: That seems strange. The earth . . . (*She gestures with her hands.*) The earth is going around like this. I suppose it's funny to say "like this." I mean, the sun moves from east to west, so the earth is rotating from west to east, right?

AMAMIYA: Yes. Wait a minute. (*He hands her the umbrella and stoops down to the ground.*)

REIKO (*holding up the umbrella*): Then why didn't the ashes drift west toward Ishikari instead of over here?

AMAMIYA: Yes.

REIKO: I can't understand if you just keep saying "yes."

AMAMIYA: Well, the reason is that as the earth rotates, winds occur in the atmosphere blowing in the same direction as the earth's rotation. At least I'm pretty sure that's the reason. That's why the ashes . . . the ashes fell more on this side. . . .

REIKO: Oh, I see! It still seems strange, though. Anyway, let's go home.

AMAMIYA: Yes, let's.

They start walking toward the house.

REIKO (*holding the umbrella*): But, you know, somehow your lecture makes me feel like this might not really be rain that's falling. Maybe it's volcanic ash!

The music continues. The two figures exit through the drizzle.

Curtain.

Act One: A New Year's Market

Act Three: Inspection at the Kilns

Act Four: The Experimental Fields

Act Five: The Flax Mill

Act Six: The Festival (Day)

Act Seven: Before the Dawn

Kubo Sakae on the set of *Land of Volcanic Ash*, June 1938

Photographs of the original production of *Land of Volcanic Ash*, staged at the Tsukiji Little Theatre, Tokyo, June-July 1938, courtesy of Kubo Masa.

Part Two

Act Five: The Flax Mill

The overture for Part II is played before the lights come up. It is not the same as the overture in Act One, which introduced the work as a whole.

The title of the play is projected on the screen, followed by the insignia of the troupe.

The Narrator's voice intermingles with the music.

NARRATOR: These are the seasons of northern Japan:/ Like a half-moon,/ Most of the year is eaten away by winter,/ Leaving the remaining half to be divided between spring, summer and fall.

During summer,/ One day will be clear and cloudless./ Heat will seem to radiate/ From the range of volcanoes that roofs the plain;/ And the coats of horses urged into the field rubber-harnessed,/ Will froth as if with soap./ Another day,/ Heavy eyelids of cloud/ Will change midsummer's visage to the deathmask of winter./ Mercilessly, the overcast sky will extinguish/ The few pools of sunlight dappling the fields./ Then come the rains./ Beneath the uncertain sky,/ Farmers weed and fertilize/ And in their spare moments battle the twin menaces of insects and blight./ Only after day two-ten[1]/ Like a sigh of relief/ Does the autumn wind blow.

The autumn wind blows from the sea./ Sending red corn silk streaming from stalks taller than a man./ It is harvest time,/ And the villages are filled with excitement.

Pause. Then music, expressing the work of the harvest.

After the music has established the mood, it gradually fades into the real sounds of horses' hoofs, whips, and wagons. Once they have

---

[1]Two hundred and ten days from the traditional beginning of spring, ca. September 1. The date is a vital time in the process of rice cultivation, when certain varieties mature. It also marks the onset of the typhoon season.

suggested the arrival and departure of numberless vehicles, these sounds also fade away.

Then, the sound of two or three Roman candles exploding.

Title slide: ACT FIVE: THE FLAX MILL

The monotonous sound of hot water pouring through pipes leading from the factory shed mixes with the sound of the fireworks. The title slide fades as the stage lights come up.

The thud of the fireworks and the wisps of white smoke they leave behind are absorbed into the cloudless blue sky of an early autumn morning, crisp weather more characteristic of the Asian continent than Japan.

The women sheaving flax, bent so low over the ground they almost seem to be crawling, are called "daymen." Like the farming methods that predominate in this region, the term was imported from America and has been retained untranslated in the local vernacular. Several of them raise their perspiring faces and look up.

DAYMAN 1: Fireworks!

But the first thing that strikes the spectator's eye in this scene bathed in the clear light of an early September sun is the enormous stack of flax. Raw flax collected from surrounding villages has been piled in a brilliant yellow cone that rises high overhead. Ropes radiate out from the top, securing a canvas rain cover and dividing the stack into neat quadrants of light and dark.

This central, overwhelming mass dominates the flax mill grounds and dwarfs everthing around it. It towers over the rusting tin roof of the factory shed upstage and the four hot water tanks lined up near the proscenium, where the iron pipes leading from the shed terminate. If the office and main gate in the shadows at one side of the stage and the confusion of farm wagons in the shadows at the other seem tiny by comparison, how much more so the human beings! The Daymen resheaving the flax that has been passed by the inspector look like ants swarming at the base of the stack.

Two of the four rectangular hot-water tanks sunk in the ground are empty. Tanks one and two are already filled to overflowing with raw flax, which gradually disappears beneath the surface of the water as the tanks are filled. Laborer 1 stands at the edge of the tank with two or three of the Daymen, watching the water rise.

LABORER 1 (*toward the factory shed*): Okay! Cut it!

LABORER 2 (*shouting from the shed*): Right!

The water belching from the boiler slows to a trickle, then stops. Laborer 1 drops a thermometer into the tank.

The sound of another explosion in the autumn sky.

DAYMAN 2: What's all the commotion about?

DAYMAN 3: They're trying to make it seem like there's something to celebrate.

LABORER 1 (*jumping into empty tank number three and sweeping away the water in the bottom*): Damned drain must be stopped. (*Looking up, to one of the Daymen*): Hey, go over there and you'll find a place where you can lift off the cover and go in.

DAYMAN: Where?

LABORER 1 (*pointing offstage*): Over there, where that horse is pawing the ground, the dappled one.

DAYMAN: There are so many, I can't tell. Oh, you mean that one?

LABORER 1: Yeah, about six meters this side of it.

DAYMAN: Right! (*She exits at a run.*)

On the other side of the haystack, Seki Tamekichi, a farmer of moderate means from the village, aided by Tora, a tenant farmer, is unloading sheaves of flax from a wagon that is only half-visible on stage. One by one they present the sheaves to Tadokoro, who wears the cap and uniform of an agricultural inspector. Hatano, who sits in shirt sleeves at a table beside him, records his verdict in a ledger and issues chits.

TADOKORO (*inspecting*): All right, fifth class.

SEKI (*to Tora*): That all for you?

TORA: Yeah, but I thought I'd do better than this.

HATANO (*paging through the ledger*): Let's see here . . . anybody left from east two?

SEKI (*unloading*): Just me.

LABORER 1 (*to Tora, from inside the tank*): Hey, isn't that your village? The one where "it wasn't my fault if the fog was thick"?

TORA (*turning around*): The lady landlord, you mean. Yeah, but not my place.

LABORER 1: She's got one hell of a sharp tongue, that one! Hah-hah-hah!

HATANO (*interrupting*): What's this all about?

LABORER 1: Seems when Miss Komai went up to inspect the tenant farms, people tried to make excuses for why the flax was discolored by saying that the night fog'd been thick this year.

HATANO: And she said, "It's not my fault if the fog was thick"? Ouch! *Laughter.*

DAYMAN (*voice only, from a distance*): I don't see anything wrong!

LABORER 1 (*shouting*): All right. You know warehouse three? Take a look at the drain beyond the wall on the other side.

HATANO (*to Laborer 1*): Problems?

LABORER 1: Not really. It's that damned Karasawa. Something's always wrong as far as he's concerned. Yesterday he was complaining about how the rollers weren't engaging evenly and wearing down in the middle. Who the hell ever heard of rollers wearing down on the ends?

TADOKORO (*inspecting*): Fourth class.

Funatsu Matsue, who has come to deliver flax with her father Hidematsu, appears from the crowd of wagons. She starts toward the Daymen through the inspection area.

HATANO (*stopping her*): Hey, where do you think you're going?

MATSUE: I see someone I know.

HATANO: One of the daymen? You'll have to get permission from the office.

MATSUE: It'll only take a minute. (*She ignores him and proceeds to the area where the women are bundling flax. To one of the Daymen*): Sue?

SUE (*Dayman 1*): Matsue! You here to deliver your flax?

MATSUE: Yeah, but I just had a fight with my father.

SUE: Why?

MATSUE: I've been working away from home, you know, and now I can't go near the horses. They scare the daylights out of me!

SUE: Hah-hah-hah!

DAYMAN (*from the distance*): No water coming out here!

LABORER 1 (*shouting*): All right! (*To another of the Daymen*): Okay, never mind. Go ahead and fill it. (*He climbs out of the tank.*)

The Daymen descend into the tank and begin stacking the flax vertically inside. The Dayman who had gone to inspect the drain returns and joins them. Laborer 1 exits to the factory shed.

TADOKORO (*inspecting*): Fifth class.

SEKI (*looking away in disgust*): Damn!

SUE (*sheaving*): I'm such a sight, don't look at me! Sometimes I regret I didn't take that job. This year Ma says I have to pay my own way at the festival.

MATSUE: Same here.

SUE: But if I'd taken it, I'd have wound up like Kaneyo.

MATSUE: Did the lady landlord introduce you? Yuck!

SUE: Yeah. Waitresses don't last long at that Russian's bar. As if we didn't know why!

Another roman candle explodes in the air.

DAYMAN 2 (*looking up*): Look at that!

SUE: Why the fireworks?

MATSUE: Haven't you heard? The livestock collective's having an unveiling ceremony today.

SUE: Yeah?

MATSUE: Look. . . . (*She faces the audience.*) I guess you can't see from here. (*She climbs up on the sheaves at her feet.*) There, look, flags from all the countries. . . .

DAYMAN 3: Hey, don't step on that! Can't you see you're in the way? (*She whisks her down with the sheaf she is carrying.*)

SUE (*responding to a question from Dayman 2*): Matsue, what did they call that horse? Let me see, not ding-dong. . . .

MATSUE: Hah-hah-hah! You mean, Percheron![2]

SUE: That's it, that's it!   That Perch—or whatever you call it, some fantastic draught horse. Done a real good job in Manchuria, they say. Sired them all. . . . (*To Matsue*): What was it's name, I forget?

MATSUE: Eranay.[3]

SUE: Right! They're dedicating a bronze statue of Eranay, the stud that sired them all, right over there, in front of the industrial pavilion.

TADOKORO (*inspecting*): Fifth class.

HATANO (*recording*): Hah-hah-hah! Looks like you're not going to set any records this year, Seki!

SEKI: Maybe, but I got subsidies the last three years, . . .

HATANO (*imitating Seki's manner of speaking*): "So I ain't like the others," right? Hah-hah-hah!

SEKI: Pretty good. You've got me down pat. Well, just wait and see.

MATSUE (to Sue): You remember, it was all over the papers. They put a statue of a dog in front of some station in Tokyo.[4] I thought Tokyo people must be real jerks, but the next thing I know, they're unveiling the statue of some horse right here in the middle of town! Hah-hah-hah!

---

[2]Percheron is a breed of draught horse with a grey or black coat originally bred in the Perche district of France.

[3]A statue of this horse was actually erected in Obihiro on August 10, 1930, but was melted down at the end of World War Two. The statue was rebuilt in1964. Eranay was imported from France in 1910 and died in 1928. In his 18 years in Japan, he inseminated 1,714 mares and sired 579 offspring, of which 196 were themselves studs.   No record of the spelling of the name remains, so this spelling is an approximation. In any case, Kubo's transcription of the name (*Ereine*) differs slightly from the real horse in question (*Erenei*).

[4]A statue of a dog named Hachikō stands in front of Shibuya station in Tokyo. The dog became legendary when he continued to wait faithfully at the station for his master even after he had died. His loyalty so moved the citizenry that they erected a statue to him.

DAYMAN 3: You young ladies should take a good, long look on your way home.

DAYMAN 2: Yeah, at what?

DAYMAN 3: The statue of that stud. I'm sure they paid special attention to the details! Hah-hah-hah!

SUE: As if you knew anything about "details"! Hah-hah-hah!

Matsue and the Daymen burst out laughing.

HATANO (*turning around*): Hey, keep it down!

TADOKORO (*inspecting*): This here's a reject.

SEKI (*sullenly*): Reject? Well, listen up: I was growing flax before you knew the meaning of the word, and nothing I grew was ever got rejected. Hatano, do me a favor and call the manager.

HATANO: Oh-oh, here we go again!

SEKI: I want to ask him about these grading standards. The flax crop's bad across the board this year. That ought to be taken into account. Even if some of this might have been rejected in the past, this year it ought to be marked fifth class.

HATANO: That's a bad habit you've got, Seki. The inspection committee knows a poor harvest when it sees one. They don't need you to tell them. To begin with, Karasawa's on the committee, representing the growers. . . .

SEKI: The growers? Terrific! If Karasawa's a grower, then who the hell are we?

HATANO: Hey! I've been sitting here watching, you know. Look at this. (*He kicks some of the flax beside his table.*) This must've fallen over and you just let it lie there and rot. You call this flax? Flax's supposed to be a golden color and have some gloss. If you don't like it, step aside.

SEKI: You guys are merciless, you know that?

As soon as the lights came up, keen-eyed members of the audience must have noticed Henmi Shino working as inconspicuously as she can among the Daymen. Her condition is now obvious. The Daymen are dressed in a variety of costumes—some wear hoods while others wear old kerchiefs over their heads; most wear leggings and thick-soled workmen's socks beneath their short coats—but Shino's legs are exposed, and she wears only worn, white socks to cover her feet. Since Matsue appeared, she has retreated still further into the background, but now, suddenly dizzy, she falls to her knees, her chest heaving, no longer able to endure the work that requires her to bend, almost crawl, over the ground.

DAYMAN 2 (*noticing*): What's wrong?

SHINO: Nothing. I'm all right.

DAYMAN 3: Why don't you ask permission to go home?

SHINO: No, I'm all right, I. . . .

MATSUE (*recognizing her*): Shino? Is that you? You working here with the daymen? Where're you staying these days?

Karasawa Katsumi, manager of the mill, enters.   He is guiding Igarashi Shigeo, the young owner of the Igarashi Lumber Mill. Igarashi is dressed in a morning coat and is accompanied by Sagara Tomokichi, until recently his foreman. Catching sight of Karasawa, Matsue hastily flees the inspection area. The Daymen also redouble their efforts.

KARASAWA: Well, this really is an honor.   I'm afraid we don't have much in the way of facilities to show you, but. . . .

IGARASHI (*gazing up at the stack*): Looks even bigger from here, doesn't it, Tomo? You could see this stack right out the window of the pavilion.

SAGARA: Is that why you wanted to come by here? Sorry there wasn't something more exciting for you to see.

IGARASHI (*to Karasawa*):   The way those old men in the livestock collective go on and on, it's enough to drive you crazy. The report on infectious miscarriages among horses alone took, what, at least thirty minutes!

SAGARA: I'm the one who was going crazy! I was sure you'd run off to some restaurant or bar between the board meeting and the unveiling!

KARASAWA: Hah-hah-hah! Tomo, you're one hell of a chaperon! The next time I see Mr. Igarashi's father, I think I'll mention it! (*To Igarashi*): It's wonderful, though, how the old man's still vigorous enough to treat you like a child! He feels he has to send Sagara here to look after you!

IGARASHI: I don't know what's so wonderful about it. The point is, no matter how we try to modernize our labor policy, the relationship between the mill and the Sagara workers comes down to our personal relationship with their boss, good old Tomo here. (*He takes out a cigarette case.*)

KARASAWA: I'm afraid we don't allow smoking.

IGARASHI: Oh, sorry, sorry. (*He puts it away.*)

KARASAWA: No doubt about it, he's a fitting heir to his father's legacy. Right, Tomo? (*To Igarashi*): Your father really was something, though, in the days when he was young. Why, he'd rather play the horses than eat three square meals.

IGARASHI: I'm afraid those days are over. Looking back, I realize I should've come home sooner. Rice production was moving steadily northward, and . . . see what I mean, Karasawa? If the farms had been doing well, who'd ever have thought of getting involved in livestock.

KARASAWA: Thinking of recanting? Hah-hah-hah!

Igarashi is not amused.

HATANO (*handing a chit to Seki*): Take this to the cashier. It's for everyone in east two.

SEKI: It is, eh? Well, I'll take this and shove it up Karasawa's. . .

HATANO: Go ahead. He's standing right over there.

SEKI: In my own sweet time. (*His expression indicates that he is hesitating because of Igarashi. To Tora*): I'll give him a piece of my mind later.

TORA: Yeah, you do that!

KARASAWA (*explaining to Igarashi*): Now, where was I? Oh, yes, you see, once the flax has been inspected over there . . . what the inspectors do is classify it by grade, from one to five, according to length, color, gloss, and so forth. . .

SEKI (*still grumbling as he collects the rejected flax*): You mean to tell me this isn't good enough? Damn! Hey, Tora, don't just stand there, give me a hand!

KARASAWA: And once they've got the flax sorted by appearance. . . . (*Igarashi has asked something.*) What? Oh, he's an agricultural technician from the produce inspector's office. Anyway, we have these daymen organize it in bundles as you see. Speaking of "organizing," sounds like something you'd go in for, eh, Tomo?

SAGARA: Quit the kidding. The only organizing I do is of logs on their way to the storehouse.

KARASAWA: Is that a fact? Hah-hah-hah!

SAGARA: Cut it out, will you! You're going to give me a bad name. The fact of the matter is that the joint management of the Igarashi Lumber Mill . . . well, it comes down to the boss and us. . . .

KARASAWA: Hah-hah-hah! That's what I like about you, Tomo, you never get defensive! Hah-hah-hah!

Laughing, the three men walk toward the warm water tanks.

KARASAWA: Then, once the stems are bundled together. . . . Here, let me show you this tank. . . .

HATANO: Hey, get this wagon out of here! Next!

TORA: Yessir! Giddyap, there! Giddyap! Giddyap!

Facing into the shadows, he flourishes the long reins. There is the sound of hoofs and a horse whinnying. The wagon pulls off, taking Tora with it.

Chit in hand, Seki starts toward the office. He bows perfunctorily as he passes Igarashi and Karasawa.

KARASAWA: How's it going? Any chance your group'll get an incentive bonus?

SEKI: You kidding? Mr. Karasawa, you know better than that. Aren't you aware what's been going on in our cooperative? Maybe you heard already, but—I made a proposal the other day at the committee meeting—it's not just us in east two, but all over. It's this company fertilizer, . . .

KARASAWA (*concerned about Igarashi*): Yes, I heard, I heard. .

SEKI: As a matter of fact, there's a little something I wanted to speak to you about. . . .

KARASAWA: Fine. Wait for me in the office.

SEKI: Thank you very much. (*He starts to leave.*)

SAGARA (*calling him back*): Seki! Seki! Stop by the lumber mill before you go home. It's on your way. The old man said he wants to have a word with you. About the paddy fields on the ridge, I think.

SEKI: Okay. (*Exits.*)

TADOKORO (*to Hatano*): Who's left?

HATANO: Let me see . . . there's the remainder of sector two from yesterday, and . . . we could be finished by noon.

KARASAWA (*to Igarashi*): Inside this tank . . . the temperature's kept at, er, 32 or 33 degrees Celsius. (*He lifts the thermometer out of the tank. Clucking his tongue, he calls to the factory shed.*) Hey, Akutsu! (*There is no answer.*) Hatano, call him for me, will you? (*Looking at tanks three and four, where the Daymen are stacking the flax*): Hey, hey! You know better than to stack the next batch before the tank's been drained!

DAYMAN: Yessir. (*She stops working.*)

KARASAWA (*to Igarashi*): Sorry. Where was I? Oh yes, we leave the flax soaking here for three or four days, and . . . bacteria get in between the fiber and the xylem—you know, the core—and separate the outer covering, and. . . .

SAGARA (*picking up some scraps at his feet and testing*): I see! You can't get it apart when it's raw like this.

Hatano returns with Laborer 1.

KARASAWA (*catching sight of him*): What's the meaning of this? (*He points to the thermometer.*)

LABORER 1: Yes, sir.

KARASAWA: Well?

LABORER 1: Drainage is so bad. . . .

KARASAWA: You're going to affect the yield, you know.

LABORER 1: Perhaps we could have the drains repaired?

KARASAWA: What's that? All right, never mind. Come and see me in my office. After lunch.

LABORER 1: Yes, sir. (*He exits to the factory shed.*)

Karasawa tosses the thermometer back into the tank.

DAYMAN: Would you like us to? . . .

KARASAWA: What? Oh . . . (Thinking): Yes, go ahead. I'll have them pipe in some hot water from the boiler.

The Daymen resume stacking the flax in the tank. A wagon belonging to Funatsu Hidematsu has pulled up to the inspection area, and the flax is being graded.

TADOKORO (*inspecting*): Fourth class.

HIDEMATSU (*to Matsue*): Hurry up, will you!

Matsue unloads the flax.

KARASAWA: In Belgium, they—as you know, Belgium's famous for its flax—they use the slow flow of the rivers. Holland's right next door, and it's below sea level, so there's plenty of water. They use a framing technique—in other words, they put the flax into small frames and let it soak in the river. The problem is that the temperature of the water changes from morning to evening, and conditions differ from frame to frame, so it requires a great deal of effort and time. Even so, the framing technique is   a quaint   characteristic of the Belgian countryside.

SAGARA (*snickering*): Yes, by all means, share some of your foreign experiences with us.

KARASAWA: What? Oh, yes, well, when I was in Belgium, the president himself guided me . . . or was it the king?

IGARASHI: Karasawa, you take the cake! Hah-hah-hah!

Hidematsu greets Igarashi and Karasawa from the inspection area as they approach.

HIDEMATSU: Top of the morning to you! Warm for fall, isn't it?

TADOKORO (*inspecting*): Fif . . . fourth class.

KARASAWA: How'd things turn out at your place?

HIDEMATSU: We'll be happy if we can get by without any rejects.

KARASAWA (*to Igarashi*): Then we take it out of the tank and . . . (*indicating the other side of the yard*): dry it as you see over there. Then we store it in the warehouse for two or three months. After that —I'll show you this whole operation in a moment—we put the flax through rollers in the factory shed, and since the fiber is soft and the xylem is hard, it naturally splinters.   After that we take the rolled flax to another machine with a large fan, and . . . (*gesturing*): you hold it like this and the splintered core is blown away, leaving only the fibrous part. In the final analysis, the yield for flax is 15 . . . at most 17 or 18 percent. The farmers work hard to produce something and only 17 or 18 percent gets used, so the cost of transportation and the like is way out of proportion . . . and our company doesn't make much on it either, so. . . .

IGARASHI: Hah-hah-hah! Come on, Karasawa! Every business these days, like the chemical industry, for instance, is controlled by production quotas—even little places like our lumber mill. Flax is the one industry where you've got the whole market to yourself!

KARASAWA: That may be, but there's still a limit.

Izumi Shōsaku appears timidly in the inspection area.

SHŌSAKU: Is it going to be much longer . . . before our turn, I mean. Watari and I've been waiting quite a while already . . . since dawn, and. . . .

HATANO: You'll just have to wait.

TADOKORO: Where you from?

SHŌSAKU: East two cooperative, sir.

TADOKORO: Where've you been? I thought we already finished east two.

HATANO: No, you see, he doesn't use the company fert. . . . I mean, the same transport system, so the office put him at the end of the line.

Two or three more Roman candles explode in the sky. Suddenly, offstage, there is the clamor of horses' hoofs, shouting voices, and stampeding feet. Everyone on stage looks in the direction of the commotion.

KARASAWA (*shouting*): What's wrong? What happened?

SHŌSAKU (*shocked*): Hey, that's my horse! Watari, what're you doing! Watari! (*He exits at a run.*)

HATANO: Somebody grab that horse!

SUE (*screaming*): Watch out! He's slipping!

DAYMAN 2 (*yelling*): The horse is dragging him!

SHŌSAKU (*voice offstage*): Let go of the reins! Watari, I'll get him! Let go!

MATSUE (*shouting*): Shōsaku! Not like that! Hey, watch out! He's heading this way!

People scatter upstage like leaves in the wind. There are the sounds of approaching hoofs and snatches of words being shouted. Laborers 1 and 2 spring out of the factory shed.

LABORERS: What's going on?

KARASAWA: Hey, you two!   (*He is at a loss for words but gesticulates madly, ordering them to bring the horse under control.*) *Igarashi tears off his cutaway coat and rushes offstage toward the runaway steed.*

SAGARA: You're going to get hurt!   Come back!   (*He tries to stop him but is too late.*) Wait!

MATSUE (*pushing Hidematsu from behind*): Papa!

HIDEMATSU: Not me! Not me! (*He will not budge.*)

All of this takes place in a single moment. There is the cacophany of whinnying horses, stampeding hoofs, and people's voices. But finally, the situation is brought back under control. There is an embarrassed silence, as after a quarrel.

Igarashi and Shōsaku enter, supporting Watari between them. Watari is limping and appears to have injured his thigh when he was dragged by the horse.

JUNZŌ: Ouch! Damn!

SAGARA: Let me do that. (*He offers his shoulder in place of Igarashi's.*)

KARASAWA (*abashed*):   Thank you so much. I really don't know what we'd have done. . . .

IGARASHI (*dusting himself off and wiping his hands with a handkerchief*): Don't mention it.

KARASAWA (*to Junzō*): Scraped yourself up pretty bad, eh? You'd better be more careful.   Fireworks have been going off all morning.

SHŌSAKU: Yessir.

JUNZŌ: Owww!

IGARASHI (*as Hatano helps him on with this coat*): Karasawa, never mind about that—help him!

KARASAWA: Yes, sir. All right, take him to the office. But, I've got to hand it to you. You really know your way around horses. Doesn't he, Tomo?

IGARASHI: Not really. I belonged to the equestrian club in high school, that's all.

SAGARA (*walking and supporting Junzō on his shoulder*): And all this time I thought that business about horses was just talk!

IGARASHI: Well, now you know better.

The crowd surrounding the injured man moves toward the office.

JUNZŌ (*without warning*): Bastard!

Everyone stops, aghast. It is not clear at whom this epithet was directed.

JUNZŌ: Go ahead, take all the credit, you bastard! (*He glares at Igarashi.*)

KARASAWA: Hey, what's gotten into you?

JUNZŌ: I fell, all right, but I didn't let go of the reins . . . that's what stopped the horse!

SHŌSAKU: Watari!

KARASAWA: You'd better   watch   it!   We wouldn't   have had this trouble if you hadn't brought that wild animal here in the first place!

IGARASHI: It's all right. Never mind. Come on, let's go to the office.

SHŌSAKU: All right, Watari, walk.

Everyone exits to the office.

LABORER 1: That horse was headed straight for the office. Too bad they had to stop him, eh?

LABORER 2: Yeah, if he'd have stuck his nose through the window, Karasawa'd have peed in his pants! Right, Hatano? Hah-hah-hah!

(*He exits to the factory shed with Laborer 1.*)

HATANO (*speaking into the shadows offstage*): Hey, I don't want to see any more horses running around loose, you hear?

MATSUE (*looking toward the office*): Young Mr. Igarashi's so suave and modern! . . .

SUE: You're drooling, Matsue.

The Daymen double up with laughter.

HATANO: Why don't you go after Igarashi, too, like the lady landlord? Hah-hah-hah!

HIDEMATSU: One look in the mirror will answer that! Now come on, let's get the rest of this stuff off the wagon.

MATSUE: I only take after my parents! (*She goes to get the flax.*)

The inspection continues. Tadokoro has been looking displeased for some time.

SUE (*sniffing*): You can still smell his cologne.

DAYMAN 2: I was wondering what that was. Pretty powerful stuff!

Matsue carries in the flax.

HIDEMATSU: Real go-getter, though, isn't he, Hatano? Well beyond his years.

TADOKORO (*inspecting*): Fifth class.

HIDEMATSU: Ever since they made those changes at the Igarashi mill, all the other   mills have followed suit and   gone over to joint management by the workers and the owners. Hashimoto's the only one holding out.

HATANO (*as he writes in his ledger*): Right.

HIDEMATSU: Remember how old man Igarashi figured the price of rice was going down and turned those high paddies over to independent farmers? Igarashi thought he was really pulling a fast one. Then Miss Komai came along and bought up all that land, rolled it out all nice and flat. They say that really eats young Igarashi up. I wonder whether he'll have better luck with livestock?

HATANO (*stamping tags for the flax*): He was a real pinko in college, but now that he's back on the farm he's a regular businessman. Damn it's hot!

TADOKORO (*inspecting*): Fourth class.

Shino collapses. The work is too much for her.

SUE: Not again!

DAYMAN 3: They should've never hired someone in her condition.

DAYMAN 2: Poor thing, she's white as a sheet!

HATANO (*looking around at them*): What's going on? Someone sick?

DAYMAN 2: Yessir. (*To Shino*): I'll go get you some water. (*She exits at a run.*)

SUE: Great! One person loafs and everyone falls behind!

MATSUE (*finished unloading her family's flax*): What happened? (*Going to the sheaving area*): You're such a fool, Shino. Why do you have to suffer like this? At least get them to write you up in the paper. That's what I'd do.

HIDEMATSU: Matsue, come here.

TADOKORO (*inspecting*): Fifth class.

Seki Tamekichi returns from the office in a huff.

SEKI: Damn fool, causing all this commotion! (*Walking toward the wagons*): Tora, come on, we're going! Next year we'll plant sugar beets. This flax business's for the birds!

TORA (*voice only*): No luck, huh?

SEKI: Couldn't talk a lick of sense into him.

HIDEMATSU: This just isn't your day, is it, Seki? Hah-hah-hah!

SEKI: Bastard! (*Exits.*)

HIDEMATSU (*to Tadokoro*): Thank you very much. (*Into the shadows*): Hey, Jimpo, we're done! (*To Matsue*): Okay, let's take a break. (*They exit.*)

DAYMAN 2 (*returning with a glass of water*): Here, drink some of this.

SHINO (*supported by Dayman 2*): Thanks. If I can just get through today, I won't be any more bother. Shōsaku's selling his flax, and then I won't have to work.

Hatano casts a quick glance at Shino, as if he were about to comment, but he calls offstage instead.

HATANO: Next!

Jimpo Yasohachi enters as the Funatsus exit and begins to unload the remaining flax on the wagon.

DAYMAN 2 (*to Shino*): Never mind now, you just drink.

SHINO: Thank you. I'm so sorry to.... (*She accepts the water.*)

Karasawa appears from the office, walking beside the hot water tanks. When they hear his footsteps, the Daymen hastily return to their work. Shino also gets weakly to her feet.

YASOHACHI (*interrupting his work*): Wait a minute, will you? I have to....

HATANO: What?

YASOHACHI: I've got to pee so bad....

HATANO: Hitting the bottle again, eh?

KARASAWA (*to Tadokoro*): Sorry for the ruckus. How about a break? It's almost time anyway.

TADOKORO (*brusquely*): I'm fine. (*Looking at his watch*): We still have....

KARASAWA: I've had them prepare something cold to drink....

HATANO: Go ahead. I'm feeling a little beat myself.

TADOKORO (*to Yasohachi*): If you're going, hurry up about it. (*To Karasawa*): Anyway, let's continue until its time for the break.

Yasohachi exits at a run.

KARASAWA: Five minutes more or less isn't going to make any difference.

Tadokoro does not respond.

KARASAWA (*to the Daymen who have just finished stacking flax in the tank*): Don't run the water until I say so.

DAYMEN: Yessir.

KARASAWA (*to Hatano*): I'll see you in a few minutes. (*He starts toward his office.*)

His wound bandaged, Junzō limps onto the stage supported by Shosaku. The Daymen climb out of the tank and exit, wiping their hands and feet. Karasawa waits until the Daymen have departed.

KARASAWA (*to Junzō*): Hey, Watari, after all Mr. Igarashi did for you, don't you even know enough to say thank you?

Junzō does not answer. Shosaku looks at him, urging him to respond.

SHŌSAKU (*to Karasawa*): We appreciate everything you've done. Sorry for the trouble.

KARASAWA: Think it over. If you'd used the communal transport arranged by the cooperative, you wouldn't have had to hire that beast in the first place. You really embarrassed me, you know that? The company's even subsidizing the fare—through the cooperative, of course.

SHŌSAKU: Yessir. (*He whispers something to Watari.*)

JUNZŌ (*jerking his arm from Shōsaku's shoulder*): Go to hell! (*He limps obstinately from the stage.*)

SHŌSAKU: Watari! Hey! Sorry, I. . . . (*At a loss for words, he simply bows.*)

KARASAWA (*patting his breast pocket*): I've got some money here from Mr. Igarashi. He said the horse was riled by the fireworks from the livestock pavilion and wanted to make it up to you. That's a fine way to show your appreciation!

SHŌSAKU: Yessir.

KARASAWA: Don't "yessir" me! What if somebody got killed? Then what? You bring Watari back to apologize. You'll get the money after that. (*Spitting out these words, he exits.*)

Shōsaku watches him go, relieved. Then he, too, exits, stealing a look at the sheaving area as he goes.

DAYMAN 2 (*to Shino, who is working listlessly*): Don't bother with that, just take it easy. I'll do it.

HATANO (*yelling in the direction of the sheaving area*): Hey, hey!

Jimpo Yasohachi returns at a run.

TADOKORO: All right, let's get on with it.

YASOHACHI: Sorry for the wait. (*He begins unloading his flax.*)

The whistle from the factory shed shrieks, releasing white steam into the autumn sky.

YASOHACHI: Damn, just my luck! (*He looks up.*)

HATANO: Okay, that's it. (*He closes his ledger and begins gathering the chits.*)

The Daymen stop working. Sue and the other young Daymen throw down their bundles of flax and exit, jabbering noisily as they go. Dayman 2 shepherds Shino toward the rest area.

HATANO (*calling them back*): Hey!

SHINO: Yes, sir?

HATANO: Listen, I don't care if you are only part time. You were hired on the assumption that you'd finish the job. You really planning to quit after today?

SHINO: No, sir, I. . . .

HATANO: And besides, you're special. (*To Tadokoro, who has risen from his seat*): Please, Mr. Karasawa's waiting for you in the office. (*To Shino, as he guides Tadokoro toward the office*): A little exercise now'll make things easier for you later on! Hah-hah-hah! (*He exits with Tadokoro.*)

Dayman 2 leads Shino toward the rest area. Dayman 3 is tidying up the sheaving area.

YASOHACHI: Talk   about   timing!   The minute my   turn   comes, "peeeee"!

Dayman 3 laughs.

YASOHACHI: How about a little romp in the hay. I could fix you up just like her? What d'you say?

DAYMAN 3: If an old woman like me excites you, just say the word! Hah-hah-hah! (*She finishes tidying up and exits toward the rest area.*)

Yasohachi is left alone.   He sits down between the wagons and the stack of flax and sneaks a cigarette out of his pocket.

MATSUE (*tiptoing from among the wagons*): Shame on you!

YASOHACHI (*looking up*): Hey, you scared me!

MATSUE: Mr. Demon, you know you shouldn't. (*She sits in the chair that Tadokoro had occupied and points to the flax lined up on the ground. Mimicking*): Rejects! All rejects! Pack'em up and take'em home!

YASOHACHI: Hah-hah-hah!   Pretty good. But you sound more like Karasawa.

MATSUE: Listen here, now, if you're going to grow flax, you've got to do a better job weeding, see. You've got to stay up all night to protect it from   the fog. Otherwise you'll never get the gloss,   understand? Heh-heh, all you've been doing is drinking and rolling around with your old lady, I'll bet!

YASOHACHI (*gradually becoming serious*): Quit it now. Quit it. It's not funny.

Matsue just laughs.

YASOHACHI (*thinking*): You think it's true? It said in The Daily News that beer companies send agents up here to buy the rejects at rock-bottom prices.

MATSUE: You shouldn't believe a word you read in that rag. I'll bet that rat who showed up at our stall last year wrote it. What'd he say? "Farmers' daughters can't sit still"? . . . Hey, Demon, what's the matter?

YASOHACHI (*looking depressed*): Nothing.

MATSUE: You were full of   pep the other day.   You really gave Nenokichi hell over that government surplus rice.

YASOHACHI: That was different. Fate plays funny tricks, you know?

MATSUE: You really are acting strange today!

YASOHACHI: You know old man Igarashi? . . . Listen, you ever been to the mainland?

MATSUE: If I had a father who'd send me to the mainland, my worries would be over!

YASOHACHI: They say it's gotten better, but when I came across, I had a third-class berth that was more like a shelf for silkworms. The sea was rough, and I was feeling pretty glum, so I got to talking with this fellow in the berth next to me. Today he's the big boss of farms and a lumber mill. But look at me! Twenty years, thirty years, and I'm still—

MATSUE: Just a demon? Hah-hah-hah!

YASOHACHI: That's right. It's my only time in the sun, the festival, when they carry me around and I have to take off my mask for a fag. (*He reaches for the cigarette he had put behind his ear.*) Nobody's watching, are they?

MATSUE: Don't smoke that thing here! Listen, you want to know a secret?

YASOHACHI: What?

MATSUE: A place where nobody'll see you. They finished taking the stock out of warehouse number three this morning, so it's empty. There won't be anybody there.

YASOHACHI: Yeah?

Laborers 1 and 2 enter from the factory shed with a baseball and gloves to play catch.

MATSUE (*seeing them*): Watch out!

YASOHACHI: Oh-oh! (*He hastily conceals his cigarette and flees.*)

Matsue follows him, giggling.

LABORER 1 (*looking up at the sky*): It really cleared up beautifully. (*He sings to himself as he puts on his glove*): "Our alma mater/ Meiji University! . . . " Okay!

Laborer 2 takes his mitt and runs into the shadows upstage, behind the haystack.

LABORER 1: I hope that fellow Miyake can make it to our next game. (*He pitches the ball, which streaks into the shadows behind the haystack.*)

LABORER 2 (*offstage, the sound of the ball striking his mitt*): He's a strange bird for a newspaper reporter. (*The ball comes whizzing back.*)

LABORER 1: That's because he's an athlete. They say he was one of the best free-style skaters in Japan a few years back. Practiced up at Lake Matsubara. (*The ball streaks across the stage.*)

The game of catch continues. Adachi Kimi enters from the main gate along the row of tanks.

KIMI: Excuse me, I'm looking for someone named Henmi—I believe she's working here as a dayman.

LABORER 1 (*lowering the ball he was about to throw*): Henmi?

LABORER 2 (*voice only*): You know, the one everyone's talking about.

LABORER 1 (*toward the rest area*): If there's someone named Henmi over there, tell her she has a visitor.

Dayman 2 shouts something from the distance.

LABORER 1: Right! (*To Kimi*): She's sick.

Dayman 2 again shouts something from the distance.

LABORER 1: Okay! (*To Kimi*): They want to know who it is.

KIMI: Adachi Kimi.

LABORER 1: Name's Adachi! (*The ball streaks across the stage.*)

Kimi is about to give up and leave when Shino hastens out from the rest area.

SHINO: Kimi!

KIMI (*looking back*): So you are here! I heard you were working but couldn't believe it.

SHINO: Come back to the rest area with me.

KIMI: No, I'd rather stay here. But, perhaps you'd be more comfortable. . . .

SHINO: Don't worry about me. (*She sits beside Kimi.*)

KIMI (*diverting the conversation*): It's hard to find work these days, you. . . .

SHINO: I didn't want to work here, but. . . .

KIMI: No, I was talking about myself. You must've seen the ad they placed for a female clerk to work over at the livestock collective. I'm just on my way back from handing in my application. I thought I'd see what happens.

SHINO: I see. (*She nods sympathetically.*)

KIMI: I get turned down wherever I go. It's just a waste of shoe leather, hah-hah-hah! . . . So anyway, where are you staying these days?

SHINO: Me? What difference does it make? (*She steals a glance at Kimi, then casts her eyes downward.*) Remember that terrific snow storm we had at the end of last year?

KIMI (*uncertainly*): Yes. . . . I was still in bed half the time, so. . . . (*Remembering*): Oh, the day Jirō and Ichihashi brought the charcoal to sell!

SHINO: That's right. Don't breathe a word of this to anyone, all right? (*Pained by her memories*): I'd been begging Shōsaku to let me quit the Amamiya's and come back to live with him.

Kimi, who has been distracted by the game of catch, turns and looks at Shino, whose eyes remain fixed on the ground.

SHINO: Anyway, he said I could, and I went to work washing beets for the sugar company, but then that snow storm came, and I had to spend the night at the home of one of the regular workers, and. . . .

KIMI: So that's where you're living now?

SHINO: I have to go back to the village before the baby's born, but. . . . (*Her story is interrupted by tears.*)

KIMI: Is this fellow married? Never mind.   Do you really think it's good for you to be working like this now?   I remember what it was like—under other circumstances, that is. . . .

SHINO: I have to . . . for Shōsaku. . . .

Laborer 1 comes running to the edge of the tanks, looking for the ball, which has ricocheted off his glove. Shino and Kimi fall silent.

LABORER 1 (*picking the ball out of the tank, to Shino*): You have some tissues?

KIMI (*as if to defend Shino*): I have.   (*She takes some tissues from her kimono and gives them to him.*)

LABORER 1: Thanks!   (*Wiping the ball, he returns to his place and resumes the game of catch.*)

KIMI (*after a pause*): I saw what happened, you know—the way you ran past my house, crying. Mr. Amamiya and his son were running after you, and then the three of you came back. They were trying to calm you down. I didn't know what was going on at the time, but. . . .

SHINO: I don't want to. . . .

KIMI: It was the night after I'd been fired from the station. Now I remember!

SHINO: Let's not talk about it.

Pause. The game of catch continues.

KIMI: What do you mean you're working here for Shōsaku?

SHINO: You know, he works so hard, but he still has to pay cash for fertilizer. People use that as an excuse. They say if he's got so much money, he doesn't need any help from them, and they won't give him the time of day. He couldn't even borrow a wagon to bring his flax to the mill!

KIMI: Yeah, I heard the harvest was bad up in east two.   What about Watari?

SHINO: A lot of help he is!   All he does is complain that he should never have listened to Mr. Amamiya.   So anyway, Shōsaku went to see Miss Komai about borrowing some more money, and she refused, but she said that if he promised, she'd let me work here, so. .

KIMI: Promise what?

SHINO: That next year he'd use the company fertilizer. Otherwise, she said she couldn't do anything for him.

KIMI: I see. Of course, it would have to be that way. That's why Ichihashi tried to stop him, remember, when we met at Mr. Teramachi's house.

SHINO: Shōsaku, he cried and said he'd do anything so I wouldn't have to go out in front of people like this. . . . (*Tears well up in her eyes.*) But I told him it'd be all right. I feel so sorry for him. . . .

KIMI: I see. . . .

SHINO: He says we have to do like the agricultural station says, otherwise we'll be betraying Mr. Amamiya.

KIMI: Listen, Shino, Amamiya also said his son was going to marry you, remember? They're just playing you and Shōsaku for a couple of fools, don't you think?

SHINO: Why?

KIMI: Deceit, that's all it is, just lies. It's downright criminal! If I were you, I'd demand compensation, and. . . . (*Considering*): Well, maybe not in your condition, but. . . .

Izumi Hidema appeared a few minutes ago, sauntering in from the direction of the office. Curious about the tanks, he has been crouching beside one and looking in.

LABORER 1 (*noticing him*): Hey, kid, don't be throwing rocks in there now!

HIDEMA (*turning around*): Who says?

LABORER 1: Find someplace else to play.

HIDEMA: I'm here with Mr. Teramachi. (*Indicating the office*): He's over there.

LABORER 1: Yeah? What's he here for?

LABORER 2 (*voice only*): He's from the village school, isn't he?

LABORER 1: Yeah.

LABORER 2 (*voice only*): They come by a lot. They go around to all the offices looking for old pencil stubs.

LABORER 1: Is that so? (*The ball streaks across the stage.*)
There is the sound of the ball striking the mitt.

LABORER 2 (*voice only*): Nice throw!

SHINO: Hidema? (*She has been staring at him for some time.*) Come over here for a minute. (*She beckons to him.*)

HIDEMA: No. You crybaby! You're a grown-up, but you were crying by the side of the road. Pa saw you. He said so. (*He runs off.*)

SHINO: Wait! (*She runs after him but is too slow.*)

*Kimi runs past Shino and grabs Hidema in the shadows offstage.
They return with the clerk, Hatano, who has just emerged from the office.*

KIMI (*placing her hand on Hidema's shoulder*): You're fast! I'll bet you're the fastest boy in school!

HIDEMA: Yeah, and the smartest, too!

HATANO: Hey, kid, don't bother waiting around. Mr. Karasawa's in no mood to be charitable. (*He gesticulates, indicating rage.*)

HIDEMA: Really?

HATANO: Afraid so. (*Going to the Laborers who are playing catch*): You two, come here a minute. Karasawa wants us to check the exhaust water from the boiler. He's a real stickler. It's got to be just right.

LABORER 1 (*to Laborer 2 offstage*): I'll take care of it. You wait there. (*He follows Hatano to the factory shed.*)

HIDEMA (*as he is being led back toward the haystack*): Leave me alone! Pa'll give me a licking if I talk to her!

KIMI: Don't worry! I'm a good friend of your pa.

HIDEMA: Liar!

KIMI: Really! Anyway, you already spoke to her: you called her a crybaby, didn't you?

HIDEMA: Oh, . . .

SHINO: Hidema, listen, have you gotten any letters from Ji. . . (*She blushes.*) From your brother?

HIDEMA: How should I know?

SHINO: Has your pa said anything about me?

HIDEMA: I dunno. (*Wriggling away.*) I'm going.

Teramachi Tamaki enters along the tanks, looking for Hidema.

TERAMACHI (*finding him*): There you are, Izumi. Let's go. I'm afraid we're out of luck today. (*To Kimi and Shino*): Hello!

KIMI: Where've you been keeping yourself? Listen, it's all right for Hidema to speak to Shino, isn't it?

TERAMACHI: What? (*Understanding*): Oh, of course it is.

HIDEMA (*to Shino*): Okay, what'd you do? Is it because you were crying by the side of the road?

SHINO (*not comprehending*): What?

HIDEMA: Pa said you were bad and even if you came to our house we're not supposed to let you in.

Shino is speechless.

HIDEMA: But Ma says. . . .

TERAMACHI (*uncomfortably*): Izumi, that's enough. Let's go.

KIMI: What's this about not being able to get pencils?

TERAMACHI: Haven't you heard?   I had another fight with the principal. Word reached here before we did.

KIMI: I see.

TERMACHI: The whole thing's ridiculous. Of course, I shouldn't have gone to Komai's in the first place, but what was I supposed to do? My salary got held up, and then my father died, and. . . . By the way, I haven't told you how much we appreciated your help during that difficult time.

KIMI: Don't mention it. I caused you a lot of trouble when I got fired by the station.

TERMACHI (*smiling sardonically*): Trouble? Maybe I shouldn't take it so seriously, but the very idea that I would take it out on Ayako just because I had some difficulty with her mother—it's absurd!

KIMI: Of course it is—you hated her long before that, right?

TERAMACHI: Hah-hah-hah! I guess you've got a point. Anyway, if the village doesn't pay its taxes like it's supposed to, we don't even get our government subsidy, so. . . .

Hatano and Laborer 1 emerge from the factory shed.

TERAMACHI (*seeing them coming*): Well, excuse me. Izumi, let's go.

KIMI: Good-bye.

Shino nods a silent farewell. Teramachi and Hidema exit along the tanks toward the main gate.

LABORER 1 (*to Hatano*):   Anyway, explain the situation, will you?

HATANO: What a day! (*He exits to the office.*)

LABORER 1 (*to his partner offstage*): Heads up! (*Once more the ball sails through the air.*)

Before the ball has had a chance to return, Morita Otozō, a laborer from the Sagara Group, enters.

OTOZŌ: Hello!

LABORER 1 (*noticing him for the first time*):   What's this, the cheering section from the lumber league?

OTOZŌ: Cheering section? Here, gimme that ball. (*He takes the ball.*)

Kimi and Shino have returned to their former position near the haystack and are talking. After an elaborate wind-up, Otozō hurls the ball.

LABORER 1 (*following the ball with his eyes*): Watch out!!

LABORER 2 (*voice only*):   What the hell! . . .

OTOZŌ (*shrugging in embarrassment*): Whew, that was close!

LABORER 2 (*voice only*):   You couldn't hit the broad side of a barn! First it's a runaway horse, now this!

LABORER 1: Hah-hah-hah! Now we know why his son came in last! He's got his father's reflexes!

OTOZŌ: Hah-hah-hah! (*No longer laughing*): You want to know something I just heard? All that money young Mr. Igarashi put up for us, down the drain!

Otozō whispers something to Laborer 1, who beckons to Laborer 2 offstage, and the three of them stand together talking.

KIMI (*to Shino*): He must know. The scandal was written up in all the papers, and . . . I mean, Tōru even got suspended from college, didn't he?

SHINO (*gazing off into the distance*): I suppose. . . .

OTOZŌ (*to the two Laborers*): When they went to balance the books for the first half of the year, they found out what Tomo's been up to. For all we know, young Igarashi's in on it too.

LABORER 1: How do you like that!

KIMI (*to Shino*): But why didn't you tell him when. . . . I was sure you told him when you were talking by his kiln.

SHINO: I just. . . . (*Weeps.*)

OTOZŌ (*to Laborers*): So my guys might not be able to play. . . .

LABORER 2: That'd be a shame. We skunked the Kikumaru Department Store team, and we're ready to take on all comers.

OTOZŌ: Yeah, but our captain—you know, that guy from Hashimoto mill—he wants us over at his place.

LABORER 1: Yeah?

OTOZŌ: He's afraid if we win, everybody'll forget the whole affair.

LABORER 1: Yeah? Well, never mind, you don't have to do us any favors.

OTOZŌ: You mean it?

LABORER 1: Just make sure your captain show up to apologize.

KIMI (*looking toward the office*): Somebody's coming. I'd better. . . . (*She stands.*) I'll speak to Ichihashi . . . about getting some money out of them.

SHINO: Thank you.

KIMI: My pleasure.

Kimi objects, but Shino insists on seeing her to the main gate.

TADOKORO: No, if that's what you wanted to talk about, I don't want to hear another word. Our position just isn't identical with the company, that's all.

KARASAWA: You misunderstand. I just wanted to explain. . . . In any case, please come back to the office, won't you?

TADOKORO (*taking his seat in the inspection area*): No, thanks. I've heard all I need to.

LABORER 1 (*laughing, to the departing Otozō*): Too bad for you, but we'll win by default! . . . Listen, that shortstop of yours, what's-his-name, he works on the circular saw, right? Everytime he's up to bat, he swings his ass around the same way! (*He mimics.*) Like this! Hah-hah-hah!

OTOZŌ: Aw, shut your fat trap! (*Bowing to Karasawa*): Oh, hello! Hah-hah-hah! (*Laughing, he exits through the main gate.*)

KARASAWA (*to Laborer 1*): Akutsu, you checked the hot water in the tanks, didn't you?

LABORER 1: Yes, sir. (*He and Laborer 2 exit to the factory shed.*)

The whistle on the factory shed once again releases a whisp of white steam into the air. The sound is crisp in the clear, autumn sky. The Daymen file out toward the sheaving area. Shino follows them.

HATANO (*entering from the office, to Karasawa*): Mr. Amamiya is here to see you. He's waiting in the office.

KARASAWA: What does he want?

HATANO: Maybe he's brought the test results on the flax crop. He also said he wanted to check on how this year's inspection's going.

KARASAWA: I see. That's unusual. He must really be. . . . Well, let him wait. (*On his way to the factory shed*): Hey, Akutsu! (*Exits.*)

HATANO (*seating himself at the table and spreading out his ledger and chits*): Okay, let's see the rest of east two!

HIDEMATSU (*voice offstage*): Now where'd he go? Hey, Jimpo!

MATSUE (*similarly, voice only*): Mr. Demon!

HATANO: Isn't he here?

HIDEMATSU (*offstage*): Jimpo! Where are you?

TADOKORO (*annoyed*): All right, then. Next!

HATANO (*looking at his ledger*): Let me see . . . Watari and Henmi. (*Into the offstage shadows*): Hey, get this wagon out of here!

HIDEMATSU (*entering*): I just sent my girl to look for him. I'm sure. . .

HATANO: We can't stand around waiting for drunks.

HIDEMATSU: In that case, could you write up a receipt for just our share?

HATANO: What a nuisance. Besides, it's against regulations.

HIDEMATSU (*giving up and flourishing the reins*): Giddyap, giddyap! (*There is the sound of horses hoofs, and Hidematsu disappears with the wagon.*)

Amamiya Akira enters along the tanks. He has removed his hat in the office but still wears a light summer coat.

AMAMIYA (*to Hatano*): Is Karasawa around? Sorry, but I'm a little pressed for time.

HATANO: I'll call him right away. (*Speaking to the driver of the shabby wagon that is being backed onto the stage*): Is that the horse that went wild before? Be careful not to spook him again, understand! (*He exits to the factory shed.*)

Shōsaku stops the wagon and goes to tie the horse's legs with leather thongs. Junzō enters, limping. Shōsaku jumps up on the wagon and hands the flax down to him.

SHŌSAKU (*recognizing Amamiya from atop the wagon*): Oh, Mr. Amamiya! (*He bows respectfully.*)

Shino's surprised expression can be seen among the Daymen as she too catches sight of Amamiya smiling at her brother, and she immediately retreats into the crowd.

AMAMIYA: So, how did you do this year? (*He approaches.*)

SHŌSAKU (*smiling uncomfortably*): Well, we did the best we could. . . .

Junzō offers a sullen, grudging salutation. Hatano returns from the factory shed with Karasawa.

AMAMIYA: Hello!

KARASAWA: What's up? How's Tōru, by the way?

AMAMIYA: What? Oh, fine, thanks.

KARASAWA: Righteous indignation, that's what I've been feeling about the way this whole affair's been handled. I don't know what people think your family problems have to do with your work, but. . . .

The two men fall into an uncomfortable silence. In the meantime, the inspection of Junzō's flax has begun.

TADOKORO: Fifth class.

AMAMIYA (*pricking up his ears*): Fifth class? (*Going to the inspection*): Hmm, I see: the stalks are short and the color's dull. What did you plant in this field before this crop?

JUNZŌ: Peas.

AMAMIYA: I thought I told you the worst thing you could do was plant flax after peas.

JUNZŌ: Yeah, but flax don't like it near marsh land, neither, right?

AMAMIYA: That's true, but. . . .

JUNZŌ: My land's by a little creek. There's no place to plant except where we put the peas. (*He goes to collect more flax.*)

Shōsaku rebukes Junzō quietly as he unloads the flax.

AMAMIYA: You did sow the seeds evenly with a drop-type seeder, didn't you?

JUNZŌ: We seeded by hand. (*He spreads the flax he has carried from the wagon on the ground.*)

AMAMIYA: Surely, you could have borrowed a seeder. . . .

TADOKORO (*inspecting*): Fifth class.

AMAMIYA (*looking on*): Hmm, didn't a technician from the agricultural committee work with you? I asked them to. . . .

JUNZŌ: Yeah, well he was busy with the election.

AMAMIYA: Election? (*To Karasawa*): You see what we're up against? Those technicians are important. Why can't people understand that? From what I hear, the head of the district agricultural committee is usually the retired head of the local administration, but if he doesn't know anything about agriculture, what's the point?

KARASAWA: Hah-hah-hah! Getting a little off the subject, aren't you? Anyway, come on back to the office with me.

AMAMIYA: No, I want to stay here a while.

TADOKORO (*inspecting*): Hm, all right, fifth class.

AMAMIYA: After you seeded, you covered the seed, didn't you? With one to two centimeters of soil?

JUNZŌ (*annoyed*): Yes, sir!

AMAMIYA: And you   rolled— the cooperative does own a roller, doesn't it? Did you pack the earth down well?

JUNZŌ (*no longer able to contain himself*): How're we supposed to borrow a roller when they kicked us out of the cooperative?

AMAMIYA: Kicked you   out?   Why? Because you didn't use the company fertilizer?

KARASAWA: Hey, Amamiya, that's not funny! Since when has the company forced anyone to use our fertilizer? If the crops are good, we're more than happy to designate any plot for incentive subsidies. It doesn't matter whether farmers get their fertilizer through their cooperatives or buy it individually in cash—or for that matter use the blend we've developed here at the company after years of painstaking research. We've got better things to do than cheat them out of what's rightfully theirs. We've got responsibilities. After all, our customer is the state!

AMAMIYA: Then why were these men expelled from their cooperative?

TADOKORO (*inspecting*): Let me   see, fourth class? . . . All right, make it fourth class.

KARASAWA: Don't ask me, that's the cooperative's business. Or maybe not. You know, there's that fertilizer they concocted up at your main station, the Saegusa Blend, the one you're so opposed to?

AMAMIYA: Yes?

KARASAWA: Well, if a village agricultural committee decides that it wants to use a certain fertilizer, say the Saegusa Blend, and it okays it with the Six Districts Agricultural Committee to that effect, then all they have to do is notify the company and that's it. We wouldn't have this problem. Hah-hah-hah! The whole thing's ridiculous. Come on, let's go back to my office. We've got a lot of catching up to do.

Amamiya is lost in thought.

TADOKORO (*inspecting*): Fifth class.

KARASAWA: By the way, I've been looking forward to reading the continuation of your article. What seems to be the problem? Speaking of Saegusa, I'm sure he's as anxious as I am to read your conclusions.

AMAMIYA: Don't worry, I'll get to it. They've said if I don't finish the article in time for the next issue, they're going to discontinue it. Actually, that's one reason I'm here.

KARASAWA: You know, I really respect you, after all the grief this thing's caused you. I'll grant these people are living data—unfortunately, I'm afraid it won't support your claims. (*Speaking of Watari*): The average farmer's done a lot better than this fellow.

AMAMIYA: It's hard to believe. . . .

TADOKORO (*inspecting*): Fifth class.

KARASAWA: I'm sure you've heard, but this year I'm on the standards committee, and. . . . (*Pointing*): In the past, this would have been rejected outright.

AMAMIYA: But listen, Karasawa, these farmers are so damned. . . . (*He lowers his voice.*) At the very least, they don't have much to work with. You can't judge on the basis of their performance! According to my test results. . . .

KARASAWA: The experimental station's another world. Where on earth are you going to find farms where everthing's so picture perfect? You're just afraid to face the truth.

AMAMIYA: Afraid?

KARASAWA (*patting him on the shoulder*): Come on, don't get upset. It's fine to increase the potassium in the fertilizer, but you shouldn't go around writing that an excess of nitrogen will stimulate too much growth, so the plants fall over before they can be harvested—at least not until you've got the evidence to prove it.   Farm demand isn't the only thing that sets the price of ammonium sulphate.   You understand that much, don't you?

Amamiya is silent.

KARASAWA: Anyway, come to the office.

AMAMIYA: Yes, I. . . . (*But he remains where he is.*)

KARASAWA: What's wrong? Hah-hah-hah! Well, I've got a lot of things to do. If you'll excuse me. (*He starts for the office.*)

Laborer 1 comes from the factory shed toward the tanks.

KARASAWA (*exiting*): How's the temperature, all right?

LABORER 1: Yes, sir. . . . (*To the factory shed.*) Let her rip!

LABORER 2 (*voice from the shed*): Here goes!

Hot water starts belching from the pipes into each of the tanks.

TADOKORO (*inspecting*): Afraid that's fifth class, too.

HATANO: Is that it?

JUNZŌ: Yeah. (*Beside himself*): Damn you all to hell! Ouch, shit! (*He falls to the ground, nursing his injured leg.*)

LABORER 1 (*pulling the thermometer out of one of the tanks, to the factory shed*): Okay, cut one and two! Keep three and four coming!

LABORER 2 (*voice from the shed*): Right!

The flow of water to two of the tanks stops. Several roman candles explode in rapid succession. Nearby, there is a flourish of music. Applause.

SUE (*to Dayman 2*): Hey, they've started the unveiling!

DAYMAN 2 (*looking up*): Look at all the doves!

HATANO: Next!

SHŌSAKU: Yessir. (*Hesitantly he carries in his bundles of flax.   To Amamiya, with some trepidation*): Sir?

AMAMIYA: Yes?

SHŌSAKU: Would you mind waiting over there? I'd rather you didn't watch. I did my level best. I did! But. . . . (*He falls to his knees, the bundle of flax pressed tightly to his chest.*)

Forgetting her fear of being seen by Amamiya, Shino leaps from the crowd of Daymen to her brother's side.

SHINO: Shōsaku!

The music, applause, and cheering voices from the unveiling ceremony grow louder.

Curtain.

Act Six: The Festival (Day)

Music and narration begin before the lights come up.

NARRATOR: The festival arrives/ Amid autumn harvest breezes./ In village after village/ The festival is here!

Pause. Music. Over the festive melody of drums and flutes, the following narration is heard:

NARRATOR: Along the brook,/ Where flutes and drums resound,/ Hare's ear, smartweed, and knotweed bloom,/ As if someone had sown bright-colored beads in the grass./ And dragonflies fill the sky,/ Colliding with festive folk/ On paths between paddies,/ A dessicated flapping of wings against cheeks.

Festival time!/ Time for the autumn carnival!/ But the beauty of nature notwithstanding,/ Comrades! Farmers!/ What have you got to celebrate?

Title slide: ACT SIX: THE FESTIVAL (DAY)

The music is gradually superseded by the real sounds of flutes and drums being played on the stage, and mixed with these sounds the harsh voice of a vendor hawking his wares:

VOICE: Two for a penny! Two for a penny! Sweets for a penny! The more you buy, the cheaper they get! The more you buy, the cheaper they get!

The title fades and the lights come up as the vendor continues hawking his wares.

*A stone gate (*torii*) stands at the edge of the stage, indicating that these are the precincts of a Shinto shrine. The audience is seated behind the gate, along the path that leads to the shrine. (A runway through the audience should be used if possible.) The booths of innumerable vendors stand along the path, overflowing onto the highway that traverses the stage: an ice cream vendor shouting hoarsely as he stirs the ice in a large tub; a fruit stall with pyramids of apples and grapes piled on red* *felt; a haberdasher with coin purses, embroidered bags, mock silver chains, and other cheaply crafted notions; a toy vendor with stacks of tin goldfish, trumpets, and comic books, colors bleeding, held in place by rocks; a baker barking through a megaphone before the glass showcase mounted on the wagon behind him; and, for a burst of color, someone selling vermillion ground cherries beside a bouquet of balloons. Banners announcing that a contribution has been made to such-and-such shrine stand every few meters from one end of the village to the other and flap in the autumn breeze over the heads of the throng.*

A vacant dirt lot hemmed by sparse stands of yews and maples occupies center stage. A large scaffolding has been erected in the middle of the lot for the evening's entertainment. At the edge of the lot, the land drops off, revealing a distant view of fields and volcanic mountains. Red and white bushclover are mixed among the weeds, but at the moment they are obscured by the brightly painted scenery that stands beside the proscenium.

The cacophany of voices coagulates into a single mass swirling about the stone gate.

ICE CREAM VENDOR (*stirring the ice in his tub*): The more you buy, the cheaper it gets! The more you buy, the cheaper it gets!

BAKER (*through his megaphone*): Bread! Freshly baked bread!

CHILD (*examining a comic book, to his companion*): Look at this tank, will you! They paint 'em like this so's no planes can find 'em.

TOY DEALER: Hey, this ain't no library! Buy it or back off!

SECOND CHILD (*to the Fruit Vendor*): A penny's enough for this apple, ain't it? Ain't it? A penny's enough, ain't it? (*He sidles away from the stall as he speaks.*)

FRUIT VENDOR: I said no, didn't I? Now put it back. You'll spoil it! Hey! Trying to run away, eh! (*He leaves his stall to retrieve the apple.*)

Seizing this opportunity, a Third Child grabs an apple and flees.

FRUIT VENDOR: Stop! Thief! Thief! . . . Fast little bugger!

BALLOON SELLER (*to a pair of girls who have just bought ground cherries*): Thank you! Come again!

YOUNGER GIRL: How do you make it sound so loud?[1] Come on, show me how you put your tongue.

OLDER GIRL: Hah-hah-hah! You'll never get it like that!

---

[1] Ground cherries placed in the mouth are a traditional noisemaker.

FRUIT VENDOR (*to the remaining child*): Okay, let's see that money in your sash. It'll be four *sen*—for the apple your friend took.

CHILD: He's not my friend. I never even seen him!

FRUIT VENDOR: Never mind about that, just hand it over. Regular little con man, aren't you!

HABERDASHER (*to Fruit Vendor*): What you need's a charm against thieves. You can get one from the shrine, and I'll sell you one of these little bags to put it in!

SMALL CHILD: But I want it! If you don't buy me a toy goldfish, I'll never take a bath again!

MOTHER: Fine. Let the lice eat you alive! See if I care!

And so forth and so on. The stage is a riot of sounds punctuated by the ceremonial music that comes from the shrine: ground cherry noisemakers, tin trumpets, whistles on balloons, wooden clogs, bells on girls' sandals, laughing voices, crying voices, scolding voices, loud voices, muffled voices. Into this hubbub, the portable shrine that has been carried through the village returns. First comes a man in a formal black kimono, casting salt before him to purify the way for the shrine, then Sarutahiko, who wears wooden clogs with only one cleat and uses a halberd for a crutch. A group of Children surrounds the fool, taunting him.

CHILD (*chanting*): Yasohachi demon, Jimpo demon! Yasohachi demon, Jimpo demon!

CHILD: Off with your mask, Mr. Demon, off with your mask!

A Priest follows the Fool in the procession. Behind him are several men dressed in white, each of whom carries a ritual object from the shrine on his shoulder: a branch from the sacred sakaki tree, a large umbrella, a wooden box for offerings, and so forth. Notables from the village appear next. They are dressed formally in Western frock coats or black kimono with broad-brimmed reed hats. Sagara Tomokichi from the Igarashi Lumber Mill is visible in this group.

SAGARA (*to one of the Notables*): So out of the blue, he says to me, Tomo, why don't you try to get yourself elected to the prefectural assembly. You could've knocked me over with a feather! "I'd be glad to advance you the deposit for your candidacy." Just like that! Hah-hah-hah!

NOTABLE: Very much in character for young Mr. Igarashi, I'd say.

SAGARA: Apparently a college friend of his in Tokyo is—I suppose you'd say he's an executive in the Democratic Party—anyway, that's where the idea started, and. . . . (*He continues talking.*)

CHILD: Let's see your face, Mr. Demon!

CHILD: Off with your mask! Off your mask!

CHILD: You must be dying for a fag. How 'bout it, Mr. Demon?

NOTABLE: In the last election in Sapporo, a laborer named Masaki got more votes than anybody. It's too bad you didn't stand for election then. Why, with the farmers, the lumber union, and the renters, you'd have had a terrific base of support, and with Mr. Igarashi behind you, . . .

The procession halts momentarily near the gate to regroup before proceeding to the shrine. From the rear of the procession:

VOICES: *Wasshoi! Wasshoi!*

The shouts of young men rocking the portable shrine are heard.

CHILD: Show your face!

CHILD: Come on! We're almost to the shrine!

DEMON: Persistent little beggars, aren't you! All right, here!

He removes his mask. It is Tashirogi Ryōichi.

CHILD: Ah!!! Watch out!!!

CHILD: Hey, he's not the regular demon!

CHILD: He's from the Young Men's Association!

NOTABLE: Well, you've done your duty in the procession. Come with me up to the shrine office.

SAGARA: I'm just sorry Mr. Igarashi's not here. He's showing the stud farm to people from the local office of the Hokkaido administration. I'm really no substitute, I'm afraid. . . .

NOTABLE: You're too modest!

The head of the procession goes through the stone gate and exits along the path to the shrine. Spectators along the way clap their hands in obeisance and toss small offerings of money and rice into the offering box. Finally, the portable shrine itself passes, carried on the strong shoulders of identically clad members of the Young Men's Association.

VOICES: Wasshoi! Wasshoi!

Funatsu Matsue returns from the direction of town, looking furtively about her. Sue and Kaneyo spot her and come running out of the crowd. All three of them are dressed in kimono.

SUE: Where were you? You were supposed to meet us!

KANEYO: You're awful, Matsue.

MATSUE (*looking around*): My mother's not around, is she? I'm sorry, Sue, but she wanted me go pay my respects to the lady landlord and wouldn't take no for an answer. So, I ran away to town early this morning. Wait a minute, will you? (*She goes to the Baker's wagon.*)

Seki Tamekichi has been standing for some time next to the bus stop, which is barely visible today in the crowd. He looks dazed.

CHILD (*to Youth 1, who is passing*): How come Yasohachi's not the demon?

YOUTH 1: Don't ask questions, kid!

CHILD: Come on, tell me!

YOUTH 1: I'm busy. (*He runs off.*)

Saichi and Shinji, two tenant farmers from the Hayakawa farm, spy Seki at the bus stop.

SHINJI: Well, look who's here!

SEKI: I ain't talking to you guys.

SHINJI: A little young to be going senile, aren't you, Seki?

SEKI: I say one word, and you bastards make sure I never hear the end of it.

SHINJI: There's a festival going on here, you jerk. The bus is running on the back street to avoid the crowds! Hah-hah-hah!

SEKI: Oh, yeah! (*He starts to go.*)

SAICHI: Hold on a minute.

SHINJI: Where're you going, anyway?

SAICHI: I know! I know! (*He continues to taunt him.*)

MATSUE (*her cheeks filled with the bread she has purchased*): If you can guess what I saw in town, I'll treat you. (*Looking down the road*): Ah! It's my mother! (*To Baker*): Let me hide here, okay? (*She crouches behind his wagon.*)

SUE: Get a load of her! Hah-hah-hah!

Funatsu Ishi makes her way through the crowd and approaches Seki.

ISHI: Am I glad to see you!   Miss Komai's brother Nenokichi says he wants to see you.

SEKI: I'm in a hurry.

ISHI: Where're you going?

SAICHI (*to Ishi*): He's on his way to the bank. Seki, don't worry about a thing. I've put in the good word for you! Hah-hah-hah!

SEKI: That's . . . that's not funny! I ain't afraid of no bank. What've I got to be afraid of?

SAICHI: Sure, you've got the whole thing figured out, not like rest of us, right? Hah-hah-hah!

SEKI: Bastards! (*He shakes them off and runs.*)

ISHI (*shouting to his fleeing figure*): Seki! You'd better. . . . Well, they can't say I didn't give him the message. (*She reenters the crowd, searching for her daughter, and disappears.*)

Matsue reappears from behind the wagon.

SUE: You should go with her. I'll bet she's trying to find you a husband!

KANEYO: Yuck!

MATSUE: You're really awful, you know that!

SUE (*to Kaneyo*): Shall I tell you who the lucky man is? Tashirogi from the Young Men's Association!

KANEYO: Is that right, Matsue?

SUE: But you know what she says? Right, Matsue? No one but young Mr. Igarashi will do! Hah-hah-hah! She'd rather be his mistress than wife to anyone else!

KANEYO: Why, Matsue! Hah-hah-hah!

MATSUE (*her mouth full of bread*): Where did you. . . . Oh, I'm starving! I didn't even eat breakfast. All I had was a boiled egg in the park in town.

SUE: That's it! You went to see the baseball game between the flax company and the lumber mill!

MATSUE: Hah-hah-hah! Guess I gave myself away. Here, have some. (*She holds out the bag of rolls.*)

SAICHI (*to Shinji as they walk*): I'm telling you, when I had a little time, I went to take a look at his paddy fields.

SHINJI: Hah-hah-hah! How considerate of you!

SAICHI: By the end of August you could tell what his harvest was going to be like. Hah-hah-hah!

SHINJI: I guess that makes your sake today taste extra sweet, doesn't it? Hah-hah-hah!

SAICHI: That makes us about even. . . .

They disappear into the crowd.

MATSUE (*to Sue*): That was no baseball game. It was a regular brawl! When they had that fire over at the flax company, no one showed up from the lumber mill to lend a hand. When someone finally did pay a condolence call, they beat him to a bloody pulp. Hah-hah-hah! (*To Kaneyo*): It must have been hard for you to get permission to come today.

SUE: She didn't.

MATSUE: How come?

KANEYO (*chasing Sue, who is trying to say something*): Don't you dare! Sue, don't!

SUE (*fleeing*): You know what? You know what? Someone tried to kiss her, so she yanked his ears, that's what! (*Pulling away the hand that Kaneyo is trying to put over her mouth*): So this guy says that in the West, it's a sign of affection to pull a man's ears! Ah-hah-hah!

Matsue also laughs.

SUE: He's a regular —you know, what that woman on the dayman crew said we should go and see—not a ding-dong.

MATSUE: Percheron, Percheron! Haven't you got that straight yet? Hah-hah-hah!

KANEYO: I'm going home! (*She starts to leave.*)

Takashi and Sango, two tenants from the Igarashi farm, enter from the highway.

TAKASHI: The point is, the flax harvest was bad for everybody this year, right? So they think it must've been someone whose crop didn't pass the inspection. At least that's what the paper said.

SANGO: Wrote that, did they? You act like you've got the whole thing figured out.

TAKASHI: Listen . . . (*Secretively*): If you ask me, it was Seki, that's who.

SANGO: Couldn't be. He's Karasawa's pet.

TAKASHI: Yeah, but whereas he got subsidies for three years running, this year his crop didn't even make fifth class, so he had a big fight with Karasawa—that's what Tora said anyway. See what I mean? Suspicious, right?

SANGO: I doubt it. Anyway, fire or not, we better get paid.

Funatsu Ishi has spotted Matsue and approaches her through the sea of people.

ISHI: Matsue! You know how long I've been looking for you? Now come on, let's go. (*She takes her hand.*)

MATSUE: I don't want to! I don't want to!

ISHI: We go every year. Why are you making such a fuss? Come on, you've caused me enough trouble.

MATSUE: Go by yourself. I'd rather die first!

ISHI (*releasing her hand*): You've been acting strange ever since you quit working at the station! (*To the other girls*): I never heard anything like it. Even if Kimi was having an affair with that young man at the station, so what? If Matsue'd just kept her mouth shut, she'd never've been fired! All right, Matsue, but you're really going to get it from your father when you get home! (*Exits.*)

MATSUE (*watching her go*): My mother's so stupid! (*To Sue*): Listen, why does that lady landlord have to keep our formal clothes and chests of drawers like the tenants? You see that kimono my mother has on? Every time she wants to wear it, she has to butter up the lady landlord just to get it back!

SUE: Come on, let's go. (*She starts walking.*)

MATSUE: Wait a minute, I just remembered! On my way back, I saw Shōsaku and Shino waiting at the bus stop. The regular bus was full, but there'll be an extra one along any minute. Come on, let's go see!

KANEYO: Can't Shino come back to the village? Poor thing!

Watari Junzō and Tora, a tenant from the Igarashi farm, run out of the crowd.

TORA: Hey, Takashi, listen to this!

TAKASHI: Tora, what're you doing with him? (*He glares at Junzō.*)

TORA: Hold on a minute! Watari here says Seki got paid in full for our flax after all.

SANGO: Watari, you sure?

JUNZŌ: Sure I'm sure! I hurt my leg when I got dragged by that horse, remember? Well, while I in the office getting it bandaged, I heard Karasawa talking to Seki: "This does it for east two, then, right?" he said.

TAKASHI: Yeah? But he got paid after the fire, didn't he?

TORA: Is that what the lying bastard told you? It wasn't after! We was all the way to the pavilion before we saw the flames.

SANGO: How could that be?

TAKASHI (*to Tora*): You idiot, you were with him the whole time! How'd he fool you?

JUNZŌ: Well, look, I'm partly to blame—believe me, I'm through with Henmi—so I thought I'd get hold of Seki and, not exactly apologize, but, you know, sort of work things out for you guys.

TAKASHI: Yeah, you do that. But first let's go over to his place.

SANGO: Yeah, let's go. Come on!

The four of them exit noisily.

SUE (*chasing Matsue*): Who is it? Tell me! Who?

MATSUE: No! No, I said! People will hear! (*She flees from Sue.*)

SUE: Come on, you started to say it! What difference does it make? Come on, tell me! (*She chases her friend.*)

Youths 2 and 3 pass by.

YOUTH 2 (*halting*): Come by and see me tonight! I'll tell you!

SUE (*looking around*): What's he talking about?

YOUTH 2: A little hanky-panky, that's what! (*He continues on his way.*)

YOUTH 3 (*to Kaneyo*): You know that tall grass on the other side of the shrine? Grab hold of a bunch and pull it through your hand, all right?

KANEYO: What for?

YOUTH 3: You'll get all these little cuts, see? Then you can come over to the first aid station and let me bandage it for you. (*Pointing*): It's over there by the bus stop, okay?

(*Exits.*)

MATSUE (*looking along the highway*): Here they come!

Henmi Shōsaku and Shino enter amid the whispers and stares of the crowd.

MATSUE (*moving toward the Toy Dealer*): You're not using this cord, are you? Let me have it for a minute, okay?

TOY DEALER: What for?

MATSUE: Never mind, hurry up! (*She grabs a cord used to tie up the sleeves of a kimono.*)

The girls stand in front of the brother and sister, blocking their way.

MATSUE (*pretending to have just noticed them*): Why, if it isn't you, Shino? Welcome back!

Shino does not acknowledge this greeting but keeps her eyes fixed on the ground.

MATSUE: Last time I saw you, you weren't feeling well. Are you all right now? As a matter of fact, I do believe you've put on some weight!

Matsue can't help laughing at her own remark, and the crowd joins in.

MATSUE: Let's see, now. . . . (*She stretches the cord she has borrowed.*) Exactly how big are you? (*She moves toward Shino.*)

SHŌSAKU (*unable to contain himself*): Get away from her!

MATSUE (*knocked aside*): So high and mighty! You sold her out for a handful of fertilizer! They paid you to let the Amamiya boy off the hook. How else could you pay cash for your fertilizer?

There is laughter and whispered gossip in the crowd. Shino lifts her eyes and looks around. She wants to flee but suppresses the urge.

SHINO: That's not true, Matsue! We haven't gotten a cent from the Amamiyas.

MATSUE: A likely story!

SHINO (*flushing and shaking her head violently*): We haven't!

SUE: Maybe she's telling the truth. What do you think, Kaneyo?

Kaneyo does not answer.

SUE (to Matsue): Maybe she doesn't know which stud knocked her up! Hah-hah-hah!

The crowd roars with laughter.

KANEYO (*averting her eyes*): That's enough! Stop it!

MATSUE: Maybe it was "ding-dong" Percheron!

Laughter from the crowd.

KANEYO: Stop it, I said! You're going too far!

Shōsaku is on the verge of attacking Matsue.

SHINO: No! Please! (*She restrains him.*) Please, you go ahead. I have something to say to my friends. (*She speaks to Matsue and the others, apologetically.*) I've been feeling poorly and couldn't stop anywhere, but . . . wait a minute. . . . (*She goes to the Fruit Vendor.*) Choose half a dozen apples for me, will you please? Good ones.

FRUIT VENDOR: Coming right up!

SHŌSAKU: I'll go around the back way. . .

SHINO: I'll be all right. It's been a long time. (*Her arms overflowing with apples, she speaks to Matsue and the others*): It's not much, but. . . . (*She is overcome with emotion and covers her face. The apples spill to the ground.*)

SHŌSAKU: See! (*Embracing her, trying to protect her from the prying eyes of the crowd*): Let's go. Come on. (*They slip through the murmuring crowd and exit over the ridge.*)

MATSUE: Here's your cord back! (*She tosses it to the Toy Dealer. To the Children who are scurrying after the apples*): Stay away from those apples! They're ours! (*She gathers them up.*)

To the lively accompaniment of a shamisen and drum, the float used for dance performances is pulled in along the highway. Behind the pealing vermillion railings that surround the mobile stage, a dance teacher plays the shamisen and a girl in her teens, her hair done up in traditional style, plays the drum. A straw samurai doll with toy swords stuck in its sash and wearing a crude papier mache wig bobs in the autumn wind from atop the float. A group of elementary school pupils in grey school uniforms and saffron kerchiefs pulls the float with two heavy ropes. Izumi Eima is among them. He wears a brand new uniform, and his face is ablaze with excitement and pride.

CHILDREN (*in unison as they pull the float*): Eiiiya! Eiiiya! Eiiiya!

Funatsu Hidematsu and several younger men guide the float.

HIDEMATSU: Okay, stop! Stop!

The float halts in the middle of the highway. Two young dancing girls, their lips shining with puckers of rouge, begin to perform.

SONG: If by boat I must travel,/ Then waters deep for me. . . .

Enthusiastic voices rise from the crowd. Among them is Yoshimitsu Yosaburo, a charcoal burner from the marshes.

YOSABURŌ: Beautiful!

SONG: I climb the gangway ladder,
My heart so light and free. . . .

CHILDREN (*prematurely pulling the float*): Eiiiya!

HIDEMATSU: Not yet! Not yet!

SONG: For you alone, my love,
And not the man who waits for me. .

YOSABURŌ: You're really sexy, you know that!

Voices from the crowd shout praise, tease, and call lewd remarks.

YOSABURŌ: Come to see me when you're a little older!

SAICHI (*turning back on the path to the shrine*): Who the hell is that?

SHINJI: He's from the marshes.

Someone in the crowd hands a large bottle of sake to Hidematsu.

HIDEMATSU (*calling for attention with a pair of wooden clappers*): Thanks to the residents of the second ward for one bottle of sake!

Happy shouts rise from the crowd. One of the Young Men notes the gift on a slip of paper; another climbs up on the railing and pastes it on the float.

Izumi Kametarō and Toku, also from the marshes, elbow their way through the wall of people and approach the float. Each carries a bundle wrapped in cloth.

KAMETARŌ: Hi . . . Hidema!

HIDEMA: What do you want?

KAMETARŌ: Come on, it's time to go.

HIDEMA: I don't want to!

TOKU: Come on, you've had enough fun. We have to go into town before it gets dark.

HIDEMA: But the buses are running until ten o'clock!

TOKU: Yeah, but we have a lot of things to do in town before then. You understand? Now, come on.

HIDEMA: I don't want to, I said! I want to stay here and have a good time!

KAMETARŌ: What're we going to do?

TOKU: Hidema, if you don't come right now we're leaving without you!

CHILD: But this's our last chance to play with him!

ANOTHER CHILD: Yeah, can't he stay? Please!

KAMETARŌ: All right, but just a little longer.

TOKU: Fine! That's all we need is for you to take his side!

HIDEMATSU (*coming toward them*): Well, well, Kame! Congratulations are in order! You really pulled one off, I understand. Hah-hah-hah! Let Hidema stay a while. This is really a farewell party for him. . . . All right, pull!

CHILDREN: Eiiiya! Eiiiya! . . .

TOKU: Hidema! Hidema, I said! . . . Now what are we going to do?

HIDEMATSU: Not that way! Not that way! Pull it around toward the shrine! Toward the shrine!

The Children go up the path toward the shrine, pulling the float. With a grating sound, it turns gradually to face the shrine and comes to a halt directly before the stone gate.

Komai Tsuta appears in the crowd, dressed in a conservative, gauze crepe kimono. She is accompanied by her brother Nenokichi. She directs him to present a gift to the revelers while she stands inconspicuously in the background. Several members of the crowd quickly discover her presence, however, and approach to pay their respects.

HIDEMATSU (*striking the clappers*): Thanks to Miss Komai of the Hayakawa farm for a contribution to the entertainment fund and candies for the children!

Cheers, particularly from the Children on the ropes. The Young Men note the gifts on slips of paper and again paste them to the float.

HIDEMATSU (*raising the bag of candies over his head*): All right, everybody grab hold of the ropes. Line up in two rows. In two rows! (*He distributes the candies as quickly as he can. A forest of children's hands.*) Hey, hey! No seconds! *Funatsu Ishi returns. She goes to Matsue and begins speaking to her in earnest tones.*

HIDEMA (*his mouth filled with candy*): Mrs. Funatsu, look at me!

ISHI: Why, Hidema! What fine new clothes!

HIDEMA: I'm switching to a new school in Otaru. This is my uniform!

ISHI: How nice! You must really be happy your pa's back, and that no good broth. . . . (*Noticing Kametarō and Toku*): Well, look who's here!

TSUTA (*from a distance*): Mrs. Funatsu, if you've got a minute?

MATSUE: Ma, I'm going to the shrine. (*To Sue*): Come on.

SUE: What is it with you, all of a sudden?

KANEYO: Let's stay and watch.

Matsue ignores her and exits along the path to the shrine.

ISHI (*going to Tsuta*): Why, Miss Komai, how very nice to see you! I was just on my way to pay my respects. . . .

TSUTA: Did you look into the matter we discussed? (*In a low voice*): You know, about the haiku club.

ISHI: Oh! You know, I've been so busy, I. . . .

TSUTA: That's what I like about you, you're so dependable!

ISHI: I'll take care of it right away. (*She exits in embarrassed haste.*)

Komai Ayako appears, elegantly attired, behind the dilapidated railing of the float. She seats herself in traditional fashion, her legs tucked beneath her, places her fan on the stage, and bows respectfully toward the shrine. Once again, the shamisen plays enthusiastically.

SONG: A view that never fails to please,/ The Sumida River at twilight. . .

Teramachi Tamaki runs in. He is out of breath. He elbows his way through the crowd surrounding the float.

TERAMACHI (*to the Children*): Come on, everyone, come with me!

CHILD: Mr. Teramachi!

ANOTHER CHILD: What are you doing here, Mr. Teramachi?

TERAMACHI: Come on, let's take a field trip. I'm going to show you where the battle of Chomato was fought.

HIDEMATSU: Hey, hey, hold on there! You're going to spoil the fun!

TERAMACHI: Okay, let's get going. I've got all kinds of interesting things to tell you about history.

CHILD: I don't want to!

TERAMACHI: Come on, let's all go together. It'll be fun, a lot more fun than this!

CHILD: We don't want to.

HIDEMATSU: Teramachi, cut it out!

TERAMACHI: Listen, everybody, I. . . .

YOUNG MAN 1: Hey, you! Get the hell out of here!

YOUNG MAN 2: You're going to get knocked on your ass, understand! (*They struggle.*)

Surprised by this intruder, the performance on the float has ceased.

AYAKO (*on the verge of tears*): Mommy, what should I do?

TSUTA (*coming forward*): How thoughtless can you be, Mr. Teramachi? (*To the float*): All right, go ahead.

TERAMACHI: Wai . . . wait a moment, please! I have permission from the school principal. It's taken me all this time to convince him. . . .

HIDEMATSU: Of what?

TERAMACHI: To leave it up to the children. Listen, everyone, Chomatō is where the Ainu from this area fought the Hidaka Ainu and turned the marshes red with blood!

HIDEMATSU: Cut it out! Nobody's going anyplace!

TERAMACHI (*noticing Hidema*): Izumi! You'll come with me, won't you?

HIDEMA: I don't want to!

TERAMACHI: What's wrong? You're always such a good boy!

HIDEMATSU: I said lay off, right now!

YOUNG MAN 1: You heard the man! (*He knocks him down.*)

TSUTA (*a scornful smile on her lips*): The man's a regular chameleon. One minute he's all nervous and jittery over the prospect of his wife losing her job, and the next he's consorting with the likes of that Ichihashi. As a matter of fact, I'll bet Ichihashi's the one who put you up to this.

TERAMACHI: Don . . . don't be ridiculous! I just don't think that the atmosphere of a festival like this is healthy for innocent, young. . . .

YOUNG MAN 1: Shut up!

YOUNG MAN 2: Come on, get up! (*He grabs Termachi by the scruff of the neck and drags him off.*)

The sounds of fighting and abuse.

TSUTA: Go ahead. Don't pay any attention.

The shamisen and drum again begin to play.

SONG: A view that never fails to please,

The River Sumida at twilight.

We await the moon:

There! A boat with billowed sails!

And a gull whose very name

Reminds us of the Capital![2]

The din and bustle of the crowd around the float grows louder.

HIDEMATSU: Okay, everybody, let's bring her around one more time!

CHILDREN: Eiiiya! Eiiiya!

Its wheels screeching against the pavement, the float once more changes direction and proceeds up the highway. The crowd follows. Kametarō and Toku exchange recriminating glances, argue momentarily, then go after the float.

SHINJI (*stopping Yosaburo*): Hey, you! You're from the marshes, right?

YOSABURŌ: So?

SHINJI: So this festival's for townsfolk, see. Don't be butting in where you don't belong, understand?

YOSABURŌ: Oh, lay off!

SHINJI: No, you lay off! You're a real pain in the ass. Ever since you guys went around selling charcoal without permission, they've gotten a lot tougher. It's caused trouble for everybody, including us farmers.

YOSABURŌ: It wasn't my idea. If you've got some complaint, tell it to that idiot Jirō!

SAICHI: Leave him alone. You're just wasting your breath. (*Arguing, they leave.*)

The people around the float have begun to thin out. Tsuta and Nenokichi are standing and talking. Funatsu Ishi returns.

ISHI: Miss Komai, I just inquired at the newspaper, and they said they don't know anything about a meeting of the haiku club today.

TSUTA: Do I have to tell you everything? If they don't know, ask somewhere else. If I go around asking a lot of questions, people are going to get suspicious.

---

[2]*Miyakodori*, literally "bird of the capital."

ISHI: Yes, ma'am. I don't know what I'll be able to find out, but. . . .
(*She makes a hasty exit.*)

NENOKICHI (*having been given an errand*): No! You know he always
gives me trouble!

TSUTA: Be a man for once, will you! (*She goes up the path to the shrine.*)
Nenokichi exits along the highway.

*Aoki Yoshie and Adachi Kimi enter together from the direction of
town.*

AOKI: I mean, take a simple thing like spreading Bordeaux mixture.
No one's as conscientious as you. I've already spoken to Mr.
Amamiya. I thought maybe you'd consider coming back to the station?

KIMI: That's nice of you, but . . . I thought you said you were going to
stop working with sugar beets and do something else?

AOKI: Yes, well, actually I decided not to. I mean, . . . (*He seems
sensitive on this issue, and changes the subject.*)
Everybody seems to be having a good time, don't they?

KIMI: This is the first time you've seen our local festival, isn't it?

AOKI: Yes.

KIMI (*walking over to the Ice Cream Vendor*): Two, please.

ICECREAM VENDOR: Yes, ma'am! (*He stirs the ice in the tub.*)

KIMI: How are things going these days? At the station, I mean.

AOKI: You remember the seeds you helped select? Bozu Number 3?
Well, the rice ears are so heavy, the plants are bent way over now, and
the net we spread over them is covered with dragon- flies.

ICE CREAM VENDOR: Here you are, ma'am.

KIMI (*handing one to Aoki with a smile*): Won't you have some?
Aoki accepts but looks uncomfortable.

KIMI (*eating*): I'd like to drop by and see for myself, but. . . . You know,
the work at the station, it seems so . . . so artificial. It's like working
in a vacuum tube. To be honest, I was a little disappointed.

AOKI: I see.

KIMI: That reminds me. Mr. Amamiya really bawled me out once.
There was this one experimental plot where you were trying to grow
flax and test the fertilizer, and Mr. Tsuji told me to cover the seeds
there with four centimeters of soil. Well, Mr. Amamiya caught me
doing it, and, boy, did he give me a lecture! Hah-hah-hah!

AOKI (*attentively*): Really? I didn't hear anything about it.

KIMI: I guess if the soil's more than a centimeter deep it affects the
sprouts.
*Ichihashi Tatsuji, a coal burner from the marshes, strides in. He is
covered with grime.*

ICHIHASHI (*spying Kimi*): There you are!

KIMI: I just went to look for you and met Mr. Aoki.

ICHIHASHI: It's my fault. I was late. Still feels like summer though, doesn't it? (*Referring to the ice cream*): Hey, what about me?

KIMI (*laughing*): Be my guest! (*She goes to buy some more.*)

AOKI: Here, have mine. I haven't touched it.

ICHIHASHI: No, you go ahead.

AOKI: Please. (*He hands him the cone. To Kimi*): Well, I guess I'll. . . .

KIMI: Do you have to?

ICHIHASHI: Don't worry about me, I can wait.

AOKI: It's all right. I really didn't have anything special. . . .

KIMI (*pointing down the highway*): Okay, then just go straight down this way, and pretty soon you'll see the Adachi Rice Mill. It's half grocery, actually. That's where I live.

AOKI: I see.

KIMI: It's about a block beyond that. You'll see two signs, one for the Hayakawa farm and another for the charcoal concession.

AOKI: Thanks. (*He bows to Ichihashi and starts off in the direction he's been told, but stops.*) Oh, by the way, I've still got that book you lent me.

KIMI: Keep it. Something to remember me by! Hah-hah-hah!

AOKI: You sure you don't mind?

KIMI: No. You know he died recently, Gorki.

AOKI: I heard. Well, I guess I'd better get going. (*Exits.*)

ICHIHASHI: Who was that?

KIMI: Someone from the experimental station. He wants me to come back and work there. He must be kidding!

She tries to read his expression, but Ichihashi only make a perfunctory acknowledgement and goes on eating his ice cream.

KIMI: I'll bet you're here about Shino.

ICHIHASHI: Right. This morning old man Izumi went around to all the kilns bragging that he'd made them pay through the nose to have him move off his land. Made everybody real jealous.

KIMI: I heard they withdrew the suit.

ICHIHASHI: If Jirō knew about it, he'd break down and cry!

KIMI: I'll say!

ICHIHASHI (*licking his ice cream cone*): Damn thing melts faster than you can eat it! Boy, what I wouldn't give for a nice hot bath! It's been a long time since I've been to town. I rushed here as soon as I finished emptying the kiln.

KIMI: If you'd come a little earlier, there'd have been a bath open, but. .
. .

ICHIHASHI: Shall we take a walk up behind the shrine? I'll bet it's
beautiful.
They go through the gate and start up the path to the shrine.
ICHIHASHI: During the dancing tonight...
*Matsue and her two companions are coming down the path on their
way back from the shrine.*
KIMI: Hello!
MATSUE (*hostilely*): Hello.
They pass each other. Matsue looks back.
SUE (*pointing with her chin*): Matsue, you're drooling again!
Hah-hah-hah!
MATSUE (*angrily*): I am not!
*Morita Otozō, a laborer from the Igarashi lumber mill, knits his way
through the crowd. He is looking for someone.*
OTOZŌ: Well, if it isn't Miss Funatsu. Have you seen Tomo from the
mill around?
MATSUE: How should I know where he is?
OTOZŌ: I really need to find him. Sure you haven't seen him?
MATSUE: Ask my father. He's with the float—at his age. . . .
OTOZŌ: I'll do that. (*He starts to go.*) Listen, if you do see him—you
know that coffee shop next door to the bicycle store?—the men from
the mill are on the second floor, and since young Mr. Igarashi's not
here . . . tell him to come right away. (*He again starts to leave.*)
MATSUE: By the way, I heard Ren'ichi placed last place at the
Olympics! Hah-hah-hah!
OTOZŌ: That's why I was against his going in the first place! (*Exits.*)
SUE: Who was that?
MATSUE: You know, Morita Ren'ichi's father. I even got Ren'ichi's auto-
graph once, but I tore it up. Hah-hah-hah!
KANEYO: I really liked Saijo Yaso's song, though. Just the two of us,
Fujiwara Yoshie and me. You know, the part where they're in the
stands and fall weeping into each other's arms?[3]

---

[3]Saijō Yaso (1892-1970), poet and lyricist. Fujiwara Yoshie (1898-1976), operatic tenor and
founder of the Fujiwara Opera Company. The event referred to here is the victory by Maehata
Hideko (b. 1914) over M. Genenger, the German competitor, in the 200-meter women's
breaststroke competition at the 1936 Berlin Olympics. Maehata won by only six tenths of a
second to become Japan's first female gold medalist. Her victory electrified the Japanese and came
to symbolize the 1936 Games. After winning, Maehata embraced Fraulein Genenger in a
famous display of good sportsmanship.

The Girls exit.

Engulfed by the crowd, Jimpo Yasohachi and Nose Kiyoji, a charcoal burner, enter. Kiyoji supports Yasohachi, who is drunk.

YASOHACHI: Hah-hah-hah! Did you see that fool Tashirogi? He thinks he's hot stuff 'cause he's in the Young Men's Association. But put those clogs on him, and he's got to stick his ass out like this to keep his balance! (*Imitating*): Like this. He's going around walking like this! Hah-hah-hah!

KIYOJI: Hey, watch out with that cigarette!

YASOHACHI: Listen, Nose. I love my smokes, but you know I never had a fire, not at my place.

KIYOJI (*stopping him*): Shut up, you fool! You're really going to get in trouble. Come on, let's have a drink.

YASOHACHI: Bastard! Sure can put it away when somebody else's paying, can't you! Regular bloodsucker! . . . Listen, I work on the river dredging project during the winter, don't I? Well, you bastards have to tie ropes around your boots so you won't slip, right? (*He demonstrates and falls to the ground.*)

The crowd bursts into laughter.

KIYOJI: Come on, get up! You're more trouble than a kid!

YASOHACHI: Don't laugh! Point is, I've been wearing those one-cleat clogs at the festival every year since this land was cleared, see, so I can keep my balance no matter what! Hah-hah-hah!

A crowd of Children, noticing the excitement, come running.

CHILD: It's him! (*Chanting*): Yasohachi demon, Jimpo demon!

CHILD: Hey, how come you weren't in the procession this year?

YASOHACHI: Leave me alone! (*To the crowd*): If you think I'm lying, ask him. We froze our asses together under that bridge. Right, Nose? Hey, remember how I went to negotiate with Nenokichi? (*To the Children*): You kids learn in school about the rice Hokkaido gets from Kyushu? Hey, Nose, what'd I do wrong, eh? They're supposed to distribute that surplus rice to the villagers, right? Whoever heard of setting the deadline at the first of October?

KIYOJI: Damn fool, if you'd asked my help in the first place, we could've taken care of that weasel right then and there! It was the end of the year. Damn that water was cold!

YASOHACHI: Cold? Drink a little while you haul gravel, and you get plenty warm! (*To a Child being led by its Mother*): Hey, kid, let me have that balloon for a minute.

CHILD: What're you gonna do?

YASOHACHI: Let me have it, and I'll turn it into two balloons. (*He takes the balloon.*)

MOTHER: Leave that alone!

YASOHACHI: Watch, kid, this is magic, see? Hey, there's something painted on this balloon.

KIYOJI (*looking*): Some kind of design.

YASOHACHI: This is swell! Nenokichi's face's on the balloon! I put a little pressure on the bastard, and he goes behind my back! Fixes it so I can't play the demon at the festival! Son of a bitch! Take that! (*He releases the balloon, which floats up into the sky.*) Hah-hah-hah!
Laughter and jostling in the crowd.

CHILD: Mommy! Get it back, Mommy! Get it back!

MOTHER: Now look what you've done! He's crying! You'd better make it up to him!

YASOHACHI: Sure, sure, I'll get you as many balloons as you like. Hey, balloon man!

KIYOJI: What a waste! We were going to have a drink with that money!

YASOHACHI: Broke my back half a year to grow flax and they rejected the lot! This is all I've got to show for it. Had to sell   the whole damn crop for a tenth of what it's worth! What the hell difference does it make!

KIYOJI: Cut it out now! Smoke a cigarette or something!

YASOHACHI: Listen, Nose, I never started no fire. . . .

KIYOJI: Shut up, will you? Aw, who the hell cares anyway?

YASOHACHI (*buying another balloon*): Look, this time it's the lady landlord! Ah-hah-hah-hah!
The balloon rises into the autumn sky. There is the din of the crowd. The stage grows dark. Music and narration in the darkness.

NARRATOR: Thus, the festival/ Continues into the night.
An interlude of music expresses the din of the festivities and the bustle of the crowd. Gradually, it modulates to the rustic beat of the festival drum.

NARRATOR: Like the arable land of Japan,/ Scarce and divided,/ So are the hearts of the people:/ Even as they move in unison to the   beat of a single drum,/ They are divided against themselves.
The voices of many men and women sing to the rhythm of the drum.

SONG: En'yatto, korayatto!
Dokkoinatto, korayatto!
Ah-ah-ah!
How rare, how precious,
Your voice so sweet,

Whence does it come,
Little nightingale?
Arayatto, dokkoinatto!
The sound of feet dancing to the music.
SONG: Tempered by a waterfall
In your mountain home.
Approach! Let us hear,
Little nightingale!

Act Six: The Festival (Night)

Title slide: ACT SIX: THE FESTIVAL (NIGHT)

SONG: *En'yatto, korayatto!*
   Dokkoinatto, korayatto!
   The song, drum, and dancing continue as the title fades and the lights come up.
   Night has long since fallen. There is no trace of the Vendors whose stalls marked the day. The stone torii is silhouetted beneath the handle of the Big Dipper.   The evening sky is filled with stars like silver sand strewn through the heavens. The scaffold is wrapped in festive curtains with broad red and white stripes.   The drumbeat issues from high atop it and reverberates against the distant volcanic peaks.   Strings of naked light bulbs hang between the trees, and the steamy breath of the dancers can be seen briefly before it dissipates in the cool evening air. Bushclover, red and white spots in the undergrowth, can now be seen.
   Dancers circle the scaffold as they sing.
SONG: Ohhhhhh!
   Swallows stop on telephone poles,
   And trains in stations, too.
   Arayatto!
   Ships stop in harbors,
   My heart stops for you!
   Arayatto!
   Henmi Shino timidly approaches the circle of dancers. She is search-ing for her brother and looks concerned. Adachi Kimi notices her and extricates herself from the circle.
KIMI: Shino! Is it all right for you to be out like this?

SHINO: Have you seen Shōsaku? I'm so worried about him, I can't sit still.

KIMI: What happened?

SHINO: He was like a different person, drinking all that sake.

Hidematsu is standing with Komai Tsuta at the base of the scaffold.

HIDEMATSU (*as the dancers complete one round*): And now, everybody, the moment you've been waiting for: let's break out the sake! I know you're all having a good time, but after you've had a drink and danced one more round, we have to call it a night. We've promised to vacate the grounds by eleven o'clock.

YASOHACHI: How much sake is there?

HIDEMATSU: Five bottles.

YASOHACHI: Apiece?

An explosion of laughter greets this remark. The circle breaks up as the dancers seat themselves on straw mats, stools, and tree trunks and begin to pour each other sake.

TSUTA: I'd just like to say. . . . (*Her words are lost in the tumult.*)

HIDEMATSU (*waving his hands to get attention*): Let's have a little quiet!

TSUTA: I'm not going to waste your time with long-winded remarks. I'd just like to say, enjoy yourselves and watch the time!

The boisterous celebration recommences under the open sky. As Tsuta is about to leave, Tashirogi and several other Youths attired in the uniform of the Young Men's Assocation enter, dragging Seki Tamekichi behind them.

SEKI: Hey, take it easy!

YOUTH 3: Who're you to talk?

TASHIROGI: Come on, you son of a bitch! Oh, Miss Komai, this bastard injured Nenokichi, and. . . .

TSUTA: Injured him?

HIDEMATSU: Where?

TASHIROGI: Between the eyes and on his leg. The first aid team took him to Fukuda Clinic right away. (*To Seki*): Well?

SEKI (*being prodded by his captors*): Sorry . . . I'm . . . I don't know what. . . . It's just that, well, he started in on me all of a sudden, and. . . . I mean, today's supposed to be a holiday, right? He just kept it up and kept it up until. . . . I asked Tashirogi here not to let it get around, but. . . .

TSUTA: Look, no matter what this bastard says, Mr. Hayakawa and I never. . . .

SEKI: But I let Mr. Igarashi know right away. . . .

TSUTA: Then did Igarashi put you up to this?

SEKI: No! I. . . .

ISHI: You'd better apologize, Seki. You could be in real trouble if he's hurt bad.

TSUTA: Never did like this bastard. (*To the revelers*):   Don't pay us no mind. You all just go ahead. . . . As a matter of fact, Seki, I heard you were bad-mouthing me at the meeting the other day.

SEKI: All I said. . . .

TSUTA: Nenokichi told me all about it. So you think this village will never get subsidies as long as I'm around?

SEKI: Tha . . . that has nothing to do with. . . .

TASHIROGI: Just apologize to the lady, you son-of-a. . . .

SEKI: No, you don't understand!

TSUTA: I'm in the business of lending money. What fault is it of mine if Henmi bought his fertilizer in cash?

SEKI (*shaking off his captors*):   Let me go! I want to get a word in edgewise! It's not just us up in east two. Everybody's saying the same thing: there's so much competition in both flax and sugar beets, we'll never get subsidies unless we use the company fertilizer. What's wrong with that?

HIDEMATSU: Seki, shut up, will you?

SEKI: The whole point of quiting the farmers' union and setting up cooperatives was to foster cooperation between the farmers and the mills. With renegades like Henmi. . . .

TSUTA: Talkative as ever, aren't you? Of course, being a woman, I wouldn't understand these things, but tell me, Mr. Seki, is the point of this "cooperation" to go around beating up on people?

Laughter from the revelers.

TSUTA: Look, we're spoiling the party for everybody. Tashirogi, bring him along.

TASHIROGI: All right, you bastard, come on!

He tries to force Seki to follow him, but a voice stops him.

VOICE (*from behind Tashirogi*): You tell 'em, Seki!

The voice apparently belongs to Yoshimitsu Yosaburō, who has shouted and then taken refuge in the crowd.

TSUTA (*turning around*): Who said that?

No one answers. Another voice shouts from the opposite side of the crowd.

ANOTHER VOICE: Over here!

Everyone turns around to see Henmi Shōsaku. He has arrived unnoticed and is glaring drunkenly at Tsuta.

SHINO (*the instant she sees him*): Shōsaku! (*She shoves her way through the crowd and goes to him.*) Come on, let's go home, right now!

SHŌSAKU (*shaking her off and coming forward*): Komai, you bitch!

HIDEMATSU: Watch it, mister!

SHŌSAKU: I'll pay you, all right—with the money from Amamiya!

TSUTA: It's all the same to me.

SHŌSAKU: Stupid bitch! It's different as night and day!

HIDEMATSU: Hey, show a little respect! (*He pushes him.*)

SHŌSAKU: So that's the way you want it, eh? (*He grapples with Hidematsu.*)

Ichihashi, Kimi, Ishi, and others separate the two men.

The sound of stools being knocked over, cups breaking.

YASOHACHI (*rescuing the bottles of sake*): Nose, lend me a hand! It'd be the end if these got broke!

TSUTA: Henmi, I'll see you when you come to your senses. I don't have time for drunks and madmen.

Tsuta and the Young Men who grip Seki by the arms exit, leaving the commotion behind them.

YASOHACHI: All right, drink up, everybody!

ICHIHASHI: Henmi, come here and sit down.

SHŌSAKU (*breathless from the excitement*): Give me a drink.

SHINO: You've had enough already. Come on, let's go home.

ICHIHASHI: Hah-hah-hah! If you always had this much energy, you could do the work of half a dozen men!

SHINO: Please don't drink anymore! Come on, let's go home.

ICHIHASHI: Shino, even if you took him home, you wouldn't be able to control him. (*He whispers something to Kimi.*)

KIMI (*looking around*): Maybe, but I don't see anyone she could trust.

TAKASHI: Hey, Tora, now what's going to happen—to the money for the flax, I mean?

TORA: Good question.

SANGO: With his back to the wall like that, there's no telling what he'll do.

JUNZŌ: Don't worry! I'll take care of everything. Now come on, bottoms up!

KANEYO: I was so scared! Men are so awful when they're drunk!

SUE: I think they're cute.

MATSUE: Did you see my old man? Hah-hah-hah!

SHINJI: This sake sure hits the spot, don't it?

SAICHI: If I had a lot of money. . . .

SHINJI: We won't hold our breath. Hah-hah-hah!

SAICHI: No, I'd take it straight to the bank. "I understand the bank foreclosed on Seki's land. Well, I've come to purchase it, yes indeed." "We already sold it to the Hayakawa farm, so get lost." That'd be about the size of it.   They've always got the jump on us somehow. Hah-hah-hah!

SHINJI: I seem to remember someone about two years ago trying the same fool thing! Hah-hah-hah!

KANEYO (*looking at the bushclover*): You think if I put that white bushclover in purple ink it'd turn purple?

MATSUE: That's lilies-of-the-valley, silly!

SUE: I'll go get some. (*She stands.*)

ISHI: Ah, to be your age again! (*To Hidematsu*): First frost'll be in ten days. The soybeans'll suffer if we don't have some warm sunny days after that.

YOUTH 1 (*to Sue, who is picking bushclover*): Hey, cut that out! Where's your sense of civic pride?

SUE: Oh, mind your own business!

TAKASHI: Henmi and Watari go pull a stunt like that. And then Seki as much as chucks the cooperative.

JUNZŌ: You're right. When did I ever deny it? Listening to that damned experimental station . . . must think we're made out of money! Who in his right mind would. . . . I admit I was wrong. That's why I'm willing to help out with Seki!

SANGO: Yeah, Watari, that's great, after you got everybody else involved first.

TAKASHI: What I don't like, see, is . . . I don't see why Igarashi's tenants have to borrow money from that lady landlord.

TORA: That's just the point!

TAKASHI (*looking around*): Henmi, you still here? Stand up and face us like a man!

SHŌSAKU: Who says! (*He begins to get to his feet.*)

ICHIHASHI: Just ignore them.

KIMI: Stop it, everybody. We have to learn to get along. Hayakawa, Igarashi—they're all the same to us farmers.

TAKASHI: Shut up, you whore. You think we're fighting 'cause we like it?

SANGO: We hardly know where our next meal's coming from. We can't afford the luxury of traipsing around like some miller's daughter!

TORA: Yeah! . . . But just 'cause the crop was bad this year, don't stop selling us groceries on credit, all right?

Laughter.

YOSABURŌ: Hey, Kimi, watch yourself on your way home tonight.
Somebody's liable to jump you and leave you in a ditch!
Laughter.

SHINJI (*indicating Yosaburō*): And we'll sure as hell know who it was,
too!
Laughter.

MATSUE: She may not look it, but Kimi's a real man-eater.

ISHI: Shut up, Matsue.

SAICHI (*singing*): Lovely little firefly. . . .
Two or three others join in.

SONG: Basking in the sun by day. . . .

YOUTH 2: You should've seen what I saw up behind the shrine
before. Right there in broad daylight! The safety patrol sure has its
work cut out!
Laughter.

KIMI (*blushing*): Oh, get off it!

SONG: By night a tender morsel,
Along the narrow way!
Laughter.

ICHIHASHI: Cut it out! Is that the best you big men can do?

YOSABURŌ: You tell 'em, Ichihashi.
Laughter.

YOUTH 1 (*pushing a cup at Kimi*): Come on, Madame Kollontai,[4] down
the hatch! Let me show you what the Young Men's Association's made of.

YASOHACHI: Yeah, and I'm a model of filial devotion! (*Sings*): "Oh,
give me the beans I worked so hard to grow,/ More than the flax and
beets I broke my back to sow!"
Laughter. Shōsaku abruptly gets to his feet.

SHINO (*stopping him*): Shōsaku!

ICHIHASHI: Henmi, where're you going?

SHŌSAKU: Leave me alone. I . . . I. . . .

ICHIHASHI: Wait!

SHŌSAKU: I've got to talk to that lady landlord—Komai, you bitch. . . .
(*He weeps.*)

ICHIHASHI: All right. It's all right. I'll go with you. Take it easy.
(*Soothing Shōsaku, he gently pushes him back in his seat.*) Hey, what
happened to all that energy you had a minute ago? Hah-hah-hah!

---

[4]Aleksandra Mikhailovna Kollontai (1872-1952). Soviet diplomat, feminist, and novelist.

Listen, I know how it feels. When I first came up here and settled on
the Nemuro plain—you can't grow anything   up there, believe
me!—open the circle here, will you, fellows?   Anyway, I cut down
the trees and cleared the land—that's when I learned how to burn
charcoal. The only subsidy I got was sixteen yen per acre, not even
enough to dump a bag of superphosphate on the land.

HIDEMATSU: So you were a squatter. I guess that explains it.

ICHIHASHI: Explains what?

Hidematsu does not answer but chuckles knowingly.

ICHIHASHI (*to Shōsaku*): The corn I planted didn't ripen. . . . All told I
   couldn't've harvested   more than two sacks   of buckwheat that   first
   year.   My wife   and child   got sick   and died, and there wasn't   a
   damned thing I could do about it.   I just sat there, stroking the barren
   land. I just wished they'd give me some decent fertilizer and I'd show
   them, I'd. . . . What's wrong, you cold?

SHŌSAKU: Shino, let's go. (*To Ichihashi*): Thanks. I'll be all right
   now. I won't cause any more trouble.

SHINO: Okay, come on. (*To the crowd*): Sorry for all the trouble.
   (*The two of them disappear over the ridge as Shino comforts her
   brother.*)

KANEYO (*watching them leave*): I can't help feeling sorry for her.

SUE (*to Ishi*):   Couldn't you talk her into apologizing to Miss Komai so
   she'd find her some work someplace?

MATSUE: Not until she's finished with this. (*She inidicates Shino's
   pregnancy.*) When salmon are filled with eggs their value increases.
   Too bad it doesn't work that way with people!

KIMI (*to Ichihashi*): Then what happened?

ICHIHASHI: Every time I see a bushclover, I think of Nemuro. I don't
   know why, but somehow the man in charge of us immigrants took a
   liking to me. I must've behaved better when I was young.

YASOHACHI: A likely story!

Laughter.

ICHIHASHI: It's the truth! The problem was that the men in my area
   were a bunch of real hot-heads.   The agreement was that we'd get forty
   sen for each bag of charcoal we burned from the trees on the land we
   rented, and on the strength of that, they refused to take any less and
   withheld the charcoal. All hell broke loose. I got caught in the middle.
   I had a good mind to pretend that my kiln'd caved in and get the
   hell out of there, but. . . .

KIYOJI (*leaning forward with interest*): The same thing happened to you
   before, then?

ICHIHASHI: Who said that? Oh, Nose! Hah-hah-hah! Don't get so familiar, you bastard. Just kidding! Here, have a drink. Oh, yeah, Watari, you receive your eviction notice from Komai yet?

JUNZŌ: What notice? Cut the kidding. I'm not Komai's tenant.

ICHIHASHI: So what? That's half of Seki's problem right there. Henmi got his notice today.

WATARI: That was for what he borrowed last spring.

ICHIHASHI: Nope, this is different. Listen, Watari, you know how interested Igarashi's been in livestock lately? Well, apparently, he sold all the old tenancy agreements for east two to Komai—and at a discount, too, I'll bet! Haven't you heard?

JUNZŌ: I don't know anything about it.

TORA: Ichihashi, you're putting us on, right?

ICHIHASHI: If you think so, ask Henmi. Look, the point is, this is the kind of thing that's going on behind your back. You're a bunch of damned fools, the way you sit around arguing about whose tenant you are—Igarashi this, Hayakawa that. You're sitting around trying to patch up a divorce while the people are off humping like rabbits!
Laughter.

KIMI: Well, Watari? You've been going around telling everybody that you wouldn't give Ichihashi or me the time of day. Now that your creditor's changed, you've got a chance to renegotiate your tenancy. What do you think you can do all by yourself?

JUNZŌ: I. . . . (*He falls silent.*)

HIDEMATSU (*waving his hands*): All right, all right, enough of that! This is a celebration! Drink up!

YASOHACHI (*to Nose*): I sort of like that part about humping like rabbits. Pretty good, eh? Hah-hah-hah!

KIYOJI: Hey, Ichihashi, you just got finished bad-mouthing Komai and Igarashi, but I see that doesn't stop you from drinking their sake!
Laughter.

ICHIHASHI: Hah-hah-hah! You've got me there! But look, once a year they try to make it up to us, right? If we don't drink their sake, what'll they do? I owe them that much, don't you think? Hah-hah-hah!
Laughter.

ICHIHASHI (*turning around*): What do you say, Mr. Demon?

YASOHACHI: I'm not saying nothing. Starting today, I ain't Mr. Demon no more, starting today.
Laughter.

ICHIHASHI (*to Takashi and his cohorts, who are involved in an intense discussion*): Listen, you guys from east two, maybe there's no need to worry, but how'd you like me to get back that money for the flax Seki pocketed?

TORA: What do you say, Takashi?

ICHIHASHI: I wouldn't be surprised if there's a notice from Komai in each of your mailboxes tomorrow.

SANGO: Thanks but no thanks. I wouldn't want to be in your debt. That'd be jumping from the frying pan into the fire!

Laughter.

TAKASHI: Yeah, but maybe we should see what he can do. He's a real good talker.

JUNZŌ: What the hell are you talking about, after all the trouble I've gone to!

HIDEMATSU: All right, that's enough. We're running out of time. One more dance and that's it.

ICHIHASHI: We'll discuss it later, okay?

YASOHACHI: Hey, there's no more sake! Hey, lady landlord, five more bottles, please!

MATSUE (*to Yasohachi, who is shaking a sake bottle upside down*): Now, Mr. Demon, don't be greedy!

HIDEMATSU: All right, let's go! Jimpo, come on, get over here!

The revelers dance and raise their voices into the night sky as they try to savor the last few moments of this day of celebration.

SONG: *En'yatto, korayatto!*

Dokkoinatto, korayatto!

The rains they falls,

The clothes they's soaked!

The baby bawls,

The food's overcooked!

Arayatto!

The neighbor's cat

She steals the fish!

My old man's back,

Not a thing on his dish!

Come here, little baby,

Don't you pay no mind!

The revelry continues beneath the naked lights.

HIDEMATSU (*at a natural pause*): All right, thank you everyone! All good things've got to come to an end.

YOUTH 2: Come on, we still have a little time!

HIDEMATSU: Hey, you guys are supposed to be on my side! (*Waving his hands*): Okay, that's it! We promised to be out of here by eleven, remember?

YASOHACHI: Don't pay any attention! Keep dancing! Keep dancing! Enyatto, korayatto!

HIDEMATSU: I said that's enough! (*He pulls him back.*)

The circle of dancers breaks up. Talking noisily, the merrymakers prepare to return to their homes.

HIDEMATSU (*to Ichihashi and Kimi, who are talking with Takashi and the others*): Okay, take it somewhere else.

ICHIHASHI (*separating himself from the others*): See you tomorrow, then.

ISHI (*to Matsue, who is about to leave with her friends*): You come home with your father, you hear?

MATSUE: I don't want to.

SHINJI (*indicating Yosaburō with his chin*): Shall I tell him you want an escort?

SAICHI: Hey, cut it out! That's enough!

KANEYO (*as she leaves with Sue*): Embracing Genenger,[5] defeated foe.
    . . . Then how did it go?

SUE: You're a regular Olympic fanatic, you know that!

Gradually people disperse.

KIMI (*to Ichihashi*): I wish you'd come with me—I want to look in on Shino.

ICHIHASHI: All right. (*To Junzō, who lags behind*): Watari, you come, too. I reckon you've got a lot to talk over with Henmi.

JUNZŌ: Huh? No thanks. I'm going home. (*He flees.*)

Ichihashi and Kimi continue their discussion as they disappear into the darkness over the ridge.

HIDEMATSU (*who has been arguing with Yasohachi*): And if that wasn't bad enough, this afternoon you ridiculed Miss Komai with some balloon! You're just intolerable these days!

YASOHACHI: Look who's talking! Hey, Nose, there was a balloon with a stupid looking face like this on it too, wasn't there?

ISHI: Yaso, you'd better settle down before you turn the whole village against you.

YASOHACHI: Aw, mind your own business!

KIYOJI: He's just impossible!

---

[5]See note, page 173.

HIDEMATSU: Mind my own business?   All right, you son-of-a-bitch, I've had just about all I can take. I've tried being generous, today being the festival and all, but damn. . .

KIYOJI: Well, he is drunk, you know. . .

HIDEMATSU: Anyway, come along quietly.

YASOHACHI: Where we going, to buy a couple of whores?

HIDEMATSU: Fool! Miss Komai should still be at Fukuda Clinic. You're coming with me to apologize.

YASOHACHI: For what?

HIDEMATSU: You don't even know yourself, do you? Well, today for starters.   And then there's the other day, when you went and made that trouble over the rice.

YASOHACHI: Of course I went! What's wrong with that? There are seventy thousand bags of rice from the Hokkaido administration waiting to be distributed. The new fiscal year begins in November, so what's he doing sitting on it?

HIDEMATSU: You can talk like that after you've paid back what you owe! Come on now! (*He grabs him.*) I said come on!

YASOHACHI (*clinging to a tree*):   Damn you!   I ain't going nowhere!

The crowd that had begun to disperse stops in its tracks and observes this altercation.

HIDEMATSU: So that's the way you're going to be, eh? All right, then I've got something to say. Everybody knows how careless you are with those cigarettes of yours. What were you talking about with my Matsue over at the flax mill, huh? You should remember that much!

Obviously stung, Yasohachi does not answer.

ISHI: Hidematsu! (*She restrains him with her eyes.*)

MATSUE (*from the crowd*):   I don't know anything about it! (*She tries to hide.*)

The commotion in the crowd increases.

HIDEMATSU: All right, forget about the clinic. We're going to the police!

YASOHACHI: Police! (*He shrinks back.*)

HIDEMATSU: Get the message? You do what I say or pay the price!

YASOHACHI: Damn you to hell!   You can take me any damned place you please! You don't scare me, you son-of-a-bitch!

KIYOJI: That's telling him! You don't have to get pushed around by the likes of him! Go yourself! You ain't got nothing to be afraid of!

YASOHACHI: That's easy for you to say, you bastard, it's not your hide! I . . . I . . . (*He is choking back his tears.*) I ain't apologizing to Komai

and that's that! I got nothing to apologize for! Take me anyplace
else you want, see if I care!

HIDEMATSU: Have it your way! (*He grabs him by the scruff of the neck
and drags him off.*)

KIYOJI (*looking for Matsue*): Hey, you're a witness. You come too.
(*He grabs her by the wrist.*)

MATSUE (*being dragged by the hand*): I'm not going anywhere. I don't
know anything about it. No, I said!

ISHI (*frantically*): Leave her alone! Leave her alone!

KIYOJI: Come on, now! Come on!

Struggling, Hidematsu and Yasohachi, Kiyoji and Matsue exit.

ISHI (*pursuing them*): Wait! Wait for me! (*Exits.*)

*The crowd of onlookers gradually disperses. Some follow
Hidematsu with much commotion; others stand and watch them go.
Eventually, only Youths 1 and 2 and two or three others remain.*

YOUTH 2: Some festival, eh?

YOUTH 1: Come on, let's clean up.

Youth 3 runs out of the darkness.

YOUTH 3: Hey, the dancing over already?

YOUTH 1: We're very strict about the time, you know!

YOUTH 3: Old Seki had to go and make all that trouble, didn't he!

*The Youths clean up the straw mats, stools, cups, sake bottles, and
newspapers strewn around the scaffold. In the distance, the sound of a
train crossing a trestle.*

YOUTH 3: That'll be the eleven o'clock express. Really ended things
right on the button, didn't they!

*Youth 1 climbs up on the scaffold and releases the red and white
curtains.*

YOUTH 3 (*asked something by Youth 2*): They caught him just as he was
sneaking back from town on the last bus. He claimed he didn't know
anything about the money, so they clobbered him right between the
eyes!

YOUTH 1 (*lowering the drum by a rope from the top of the
scaffold*): Catch this, somebody!

One of the other Youths complies.

YOUTH 3 (*to Youth 2*): Don't you know anything? Packing that bucket
land down with a roller once or twice doesn't do anything. It still
leaks like a sieve.

YOUTH 1 (*preparing to toss the rolled curtain down from the
scaffold*): Here's some more!

YOUTH 2: I'll take it! (*He catches the bundle.*)

YOUTH 3: It wouldn't pay to roll just one little plot of two and a half hectares, so Seki asked to go in with Miss Komai, and that's the money he owes her.

YOUTH 2: I guess all those new ideas they come up with at the agricultural station cause more trouble than they're worth.

YOUTH 1: Of course they do, you idiot! Where've you been?

YOUTH 2: And on top of that, they're going to start waving his old debts in front of him. Stubborn old Seki's done for this time.

YOUTH 1 (*standing on top of the scaffold*): From this vantage point, a poverty-stricken habitation. . . . Can't see a damned thing! No, there, the bucket land: black as pitch!

YOUTH 2: Times may be bad, but I'd sure like to dance some more!

YOUTH 3: In the old days, they danced until dawn, didn't they?

YOUTH 1 (*from the scaffold*): Here I come, ready . . . or . . . not! (*He leaps to the ground.*)

YOUTH 2 (*to Youth 3*): Hey, we ought to have a, you know, a grand finale like they do at the balls Igarashi throws.

YOUTH 3: I'm game, come on! (*The two embrace and waltz clumsily.*) "Should old acquaintance be forgot/ And never brought to mind!" Hey, this is no fun, dancing with another guy! (*He shoves his partner away.*)

Youth 2 laughs.

YOUTH 1: Okay, here go the lights! (*He disconnects the electricity.*)

The scene grows dark. The Youths pick up the drum and curtain and exit. The sound of their voices and whistling fades into the distance, and the stage is enveloped in a deep silence. The sound of crickets.

The stars shine more brightly than ever. A thick night fog descends.

A Man enters on a bicycle, pulling a wagon behind him. Nenokichi, his leg bandaged, lies on a mattress spread in the wagon bed. The Man is peddling very slowly to avoid jarring his passenger.

NENOKICHI: Hey, stop . . . stop a minute!

MAN (*turning around*): Does it hurt? You want me to peddle slower?

NENOKICHI: No, I'm all right. Just call my sister, will you?

MAN (*getting off his bicycle and shouting offstage*): Miss Komai! Your brother'd like to have a word with you.

TSUTA (*voice only, drawing nearer*): I can't hear you. I'll be right there.

Tsuta and Tashirogi enter carrying flashlights. Tashirogi is drunk and carries a bottle of sake.

NENOKICHI: Tsuta, we've got trouble. I left my wallet on the table in the clinic when they undid my bandage.

TSUTA: You had Seki's note in there! I can't depend on you for anything, can I!

TASHIROGI (*reeling*): Don't worry . . . I'll just run over. . . .

TSUTA: Not in your condition. The papers would be safer where they are.
Tashirogi grunts his assent.

TSUTA (*to Man*): Listen, run back to the clinic for me, will you?

MAN: Yes, ma'am. I'll just drop the wagon off at your place, and. . . .

NENOKICHI: No, go right now. If those papers get lost, I'll. . . . Just hurry up.

TSUTA: I'll make it worth your while.
Man goes back in the direction from which he came.
Tsuta spreads a handkerchief on the base of the torii and sits down.

TSUTA (*smoking a cigarette*): What a place! Two taxis for the whole village!

TASHIROGI: Listen, you can't complain. Mr. Igarashi took one of them into town. (*Bringing a straw mat from around the denuded scaffold*): Here, sit on this.

TSUTA: I'm all right. It's probably all wet anyway.

TASHIROGI (*sitting on the mat to see*): Ah! You're right!
(*He nevertheless lies down on it.*) I'm beat! I played demon all morning and was on first aid duty all night!

TSUTA: I don't know why, but the fog's really thick this year. Nobody paid any attention, and the flax crop showed it. (*To Nenokichi, who has his hand on his bandaged head*): You getting a fever?

NENOKICHI: Naw. I can see we're in for plenty of trouble collecting this year, too, that's all.

TASHIROGI (*on his back, looking at the sky*): What a night! Miss Komai, I'm counting on you to find me a good wife.

TSUTA: Are you kidding? Not until I see more of the stuff you're made of! (*Looking into the shadows offstage*): Who's there?
The three members of the Izumi family enter timidly.

KAMETARŌ: We was just going up to the shrine to pay our respects before we. . .

TSUTA: Is that you, Izumi? You'd better get moving.

TOKU: Yes, ma'am.
They turn up the dark path to the shrine.

HIDEMA (*as Toku pulls him by the hand*): I don't want to! I'm tired! (*Exits.*)

TSUTA (*watching them go*): What're they doing wandering around here? (*To Nenokichi*): You're not going to be in any condition to inspect the charcoal in the marshes tomorrow. Tashirogi . . . Tashirogi!

Humph, listen to him snore! I guess he won't be needing this. (*She takes the bottle of sake.*) He's better looking asleep! Probably look even better as a corpse! Hah-hah-hah!

NENOKICHI: Wasn't it about this time of year when Pa died?

Tsuta glares at him, but she takes a drink without saying anything.

NENOKICHI: Tsuta, I wish you'd. . . .

TSUTA: Not again! I'm sick and tired of your, "Please, Tsuta, break it off with Igarashi"!

NENOKICHI: I just can't stand it! You and him. . . . I'm worse than useless next to you two. Everywhere I go, I'm humiliated. All I ask is five hectares, that's all!

TSUTA: Hah-hah-hah! Five hectares, eh?

NENOKICHI: He's not at any haiku club tonight. You must suspect that much.

TSUTA: Shut up! If you've got the time to worry about Igarashi's whereabouts, you ought to watch where you're laying your wallet! Tashirogi, wake up!

Tashirogi continues to snore loudly.

NENOKICHI: But you're trying to put that big piece of land where the office is in your name. . . . You get too greedy, and you're going to be sorry. Look, if you can't let me have a measly five hectares of land, then . . . I'd settle for being a tenant. If I could just rent a piece of land—good land—until I die, I'd be. . . .

TSUTA: You fool! What're you going to do on a little piece of land like that? You men just don't understand! We're not going to forget what happened.

NENOKICHI: But Pa. . . . Tsuta, you've got it all wrong. He didn't get himself killed because he got caught between Hayakawa and his tenants. . . .

TSUTA: His corpse tell you that?

NENOKICHI: Remember that five yen note we found stuffed in his corduroys? He got that from Mr. Hayakawa. He'd apologized and was on his way home when he got mixed up in that fight on the train, that's all. Let it go, will you?

TSUTA (*getting steadily drunker*): Let it go! How could they do that to him? Pa didn't know anything. First they dragged him into their troubles, then they claimed that he'd lost—what'd they say, "sold out"?—to the landlord, and not one of the bastards showed up at his funeral!

There is the sound of an automobile pulling to a halt offstage. Sagara Tomokichi enters.

SAGARA: Oh, there you are! I just dropped by your house. I wanted to apologize. I understand Seki from our farm. . . . Ah, Nenokichi, I'm sorry about what happened. (*To Tsuta*): Mr. Igarashi asked me to give you this. (*He hands her a letter.*) Of course, he wanted to come personally, but tonight. . . .

TSUTA: How considerate of him. (*She opens the letter and reads it by the light of the lantern on the wagon.*) Thank Mr. Igarashi for me, will you? Of course neither Mr. Hayakawa nor I would ever dream of suing our own tenants! Hah-hah-hah! By the way, tell Mr. Igarashi if he wants to convert any more IOUs into cash for his livestock business, I'd be happy to accommodate him. We can discuss the discount at his convenience.

SAGARA: Yes, thank you. You know, the men at the mill are arguing about that issue, too. They're all excited. Why, just today I was trying to have a quiet drink in the shrine office when a man from the mill showed up and called me back because things were getting out of hand. Well, if you'll excuse me. (*Exits.*)

The sound of a car driving off.

NENOKICHI: What's taking him so long? It'd better still be there. . . . Tsuta, I don't know why you have to go around bowing and scraping like that. After all, you're doing Igarashi a favor, taking those IOU's off his hands.

TSUTA: You'll never understand. Look, old baldy Hayakawa shows up here twice a year from his whorehouse in Gifu, right? He checks every cent I've spent, down to the amount of sake I contributed to the festival. You don't expect me to rely on his generosity for my old age, do you?

Nenokichi does not answer.

TSUTA (*her face pale, her drunken eyes staring*): Just wait and see. It won't be long. I'll get enough money, and I'll fuck somebody who'll really get old baldy's goat—I don't give a damn who it is. Then I'm getting out of here for good!

NENOKICHI: But then what'll happen to me?

TSUTA: Hah-hah-hah! Neno, that's what I like about you, you're so easy going! Hah-hah-hah!

MAN (*running back*): Sorry to take so long. The place was all locked up. I had to pound and pound. . . .

NENOKICHI: Here, let me see that! (*He takes the wallet.*) It's here, it's still here! What a relief!

TSUTA: Thanks. Shall we go, then? (*She takes the remaining sake in her mouth and sprays it over Tashirogi's face.*) Hah-hah-hah!

TASHIROGI (*waking with a start*):   What the! . . . Miss Komai, I can see you're in a good mood, what with Mr. Igarashi off at his "haiku club" surrounded by beautiful women. . . .

TSUTA: Don't be a fool!

Tsuta and Tashirogi exit beside the wagon that carries Nenokichi. The Izumi family emerges from   the shadows along the path leading to the shrine.

HIDEMA: I'm sleepy. Let's go!

KAMETARŌ: You're the one who wanted to play around all day.

TOKU: Leave him alone. Don't take it out on him. I'm beat, too. I couldn't take another step if I wanted to. (*She sits down on the mat spread at the base of the gate.*) Come over here, Hidema. (*She embraces him on her lap.*) Pa and I are going to talk things over, and then we'll take you someplace nice to go to sleep.

HIDEMA: But I thought we were taking the train tonight?

TOKU: I'm afraid we're not going to make it, being on foot and all.

HIDEMA: Then let's take a taxi. When I was pulling the float, that's what you said. You said we would at ten. Come on!

KAMETARŌ: We don't have any money.

HIDEMA: Don't try to fool me! I know better than that! Come on, let's go! . . . What're you crying for, Ma?

TOKU (*to Kametarō*): Don't you have any idea how the boy must feel? Remember Miss Komai's little girl, dancing so pretty like? You saw how happy Hidema was, pulling the float. . . .

KAMETARŌ: I don't want to talk about it. Leave me alone.

TOKU: You don't want to talk about it? Then how about the show you put on for that scatterbrain, ? He thought you didn't have any money and tried to make a fool of you. So you had to squeeze blood from a stone and give him first fifty sen, then a whole yen just to save your pride! It's no wonder you don't have any "five hundred yen cash on the barrelhead"!

KAMETARŌ: How many times you going to say the same thing over and over?

TOKU: It's all we can do to get to Otaru. We don't even have enough money to take the bus to the station or buy a box lunch on the train!

Pause. Hidema yawns.

TOKU: You're probably going to yell at me again, but you don't even have the guts . . . the guts to accept your own grandchild! It's about time you stopped being so pig-headed!

Kametarō is silent.

TOKU: I didn't suspect a thing, but if Jirō and Shino loved each other that much, then the baby must be. . . .

KAMETARŌ: Don't be stupid!   How are we supposed to know whose baby it is?   If I hadn't gone to discuss settling the suit with Miss Komai that time. . . . You never seen anything like it: There she was, sitting by this big fireplace in the living room with Amamiya's kid, brazen as all get out. I'll be damned if she wasn't ready to marry him right then and there! I mentioned Jirō and she just started bawling and ran out.

TOKU: Well, . . . that's what you say, but . . . we'll have to wait and see what Jirō says.

Pause.

KAMETARŌ: Toku, about Otaru, you're not thinking of? . . .

TOKU: No, it's too late for that.   I was just worrying that even if we get to the Satake's, they'll turn us away, that's all.

KAMETARŌ: I thought I told you not to worry about that. I wrote to them, remember?   You gave me hell for it, but. . . . Hah-hah-hah!

TOKU (*to, Hidema without responding to her husband*): Come on, now, don't fall asleep! I can't hold you. You've gotten so big!

KAMETARŌ: Satake's wife's really something, you know. Remember what I told you? She laid out that sea otter coat for me and said how she and her husband had a son who'd gotten into trouble and how her husband had to quit his job with the Chamber of Commerce and was spending all his time just waiting for the boy to come home. "You've got children waiting for you," she told me. "Go home and look after them. We'll be here any time you need us. Don't worry." She even gave me money for the train.

TOKU: If you were so worried about your kids, how come you treated Jirō so he stopped talking to us and walked out?   Now our place is all boarded up—even if he writes, . . . You were in such a hurry, we didn't even ask Ichihashi to look after things.

The Man has dropped Nenokichi off and enters on his bicycle, the empty wagon behind him.

MAN: You still here?

KAMETARŌ: Yeah. We just visited the shrine, and. . . .

MAN: If you were planning to take the express, it pulled out a long time ago. You're going to miss the last train too if you don't get going.

KAMETARŌ: Don't worry about us. A taxi'll get us to the station in less than thirty minutes.

MAN: Taxi! Forget it! They're booked solid. Hey, I've got an idea. You can ride in this. It'll hold three people easy. I'll give you a special rate.

KAMETARŌ: What? Oh, no. No, thanks.

MAN: But. . . . (*Understanding*): I see! I thought it all sounded too good to be true! (*He exits.*)

TOKU: How long you going to keep this up? They even threw you out of the shrine before!

KAMETARŌ: I wish I'd never come back to this place. I'd have been better off if they'd just carted me off to prison.

TOKU: Don't talk like an idiot!

KAMETARŌ (*looking into the offstage shadows*): Shhh, there's someone coming. Let's go.

TOKU: Go? Where?

Teramachi Tamaki enters, lost in thought.

HIDEMA: Mr. Teramachi! (*He runs to him.*)

TERAMACHI: Izumi! What are you doing out this time of night?

HIDEMA: Pa lied. He told everybody he had a lot of money, but he doesn't even have enough to get to town.

TERAMACHI: What? (*After looking at Kametarō and Toku*): I see. . . . Actually, I was afraid of that. Look, I know I'm a little out of line here, but if you'd like, how about spending the night at my place?

HIDEMA: No! If we don't leave tonight, they won't take me at the school in Otaru!

TERAMACHI: Oh. . . .

HIDEMA: If I go to that school, I won't have to go around collecting pencils anymore.

KAMETARŌ: Hidema! Mr. Teramachi, I'm so ashamed to have you see us like this.

TERAMACHI: Never mind about that. How about it, really?

TOKU: I'm sure we'd be imposing. . . .

TERAMACHI: Nonsense. My father passed away and my wife just sits around since she lost her job. . . . I was just thinking I'd never get to sleep tonight anyway, so. . . .

TOKU: Yes, but. . . .

TERAMACHI: I won't breathe a word to anyone. You can take the first bus in the morning. Leave that much to me. I'm afraid it's about all I can offer, but. . . . Hah-hah-hah! (*To Hidema*): I'll write a note to your teacher in Otaru, how would that be?

HIDEMA (*doubtfully*): You know him?

TERAMACHI: Mm. All right? (To Kametarō and Toku): Please. (He goes ahead.) Hidema, let me tell you something. The Ainu used to live around here, but each village had its own chief, so they were divided against themselves, and they wasted their time making war and spilling each other's blood. . . .

Teacher and pupil exit, talking. The old couple follow them in silence.

Ichihashi and Adachi Kimi enter over the ridge.

ICHIHASHI: Ten kilometers in the middle of the night! It'll be dawn before I get home!

KIMI: But I'm glad you came with me. I thought you really gave Shino some good advice.

ICHIHASHI: And tomorrow's an inspection at the kilns! That reminds me: afterwards I've got to come back here to discuss the money for the flax crop. I don't want to sound like Jirō, but I'm afraid it'll be like talking to a stone wall.

KIMI: I learned something myself. (*Stopping*): Aren't they beautiful, these big bushclover?

ICHIHASHI: Big? If you think these are big, you should see the bushclover in Nemuro! I don't know whether it's the soil or what, but bushclover's the only thing that grows up there—even the bamboo looks like moss on the ground. The bushclover's so tall, you ride a horse down those stony paths, and you're lucky if you don't get your eyes scratched out! (*They reach the fork in the road.*) Well, I guess this is it.

KIMI: Yes. (*She remains standing where she is.*)

ICHIHASHI: Your place is near here, isn't it? Go ahead, I'll watch till you get inside.

KIMI: Good night. (*She starts to leave but immediately returns.*) Listen, about what we were saying before—when I was working at the tractor farm, you don't think I. . . . No, of course you don't. I'm sorry. . . .

ICHIHASHI: No. Even if I did believe it, it wouldn't matter. After all, I had a wife and child myself once. But Kimi—now don't take this wrong—are you sure you want to get involved? Aren't you, you know, taking the easy way out?

KIMI: The easy way out?

ICHIHASHI: Maybe you're finding it hard to be independent and just want to get away. I mean, they give you a hard time at home and nobody'll hire you. . . .

KIMI: Is that what you think?

ICHIHASHI: I don't want to.

KIMI: To be honest, I used to wonder if I had it in me to spend day after day firing a kiln and getting black with soot. But not anymore. Believe me.

ICHIHASHI: Then I'll be honest, too. I've had this feeling you might be getting too dependent on me. I just want you to know I'm no one to depend on. I just . . . when I came up to Nemuro, like I was saying before, I just stood there watching those newly cleared fields, not being able to give them the fertilizer they needed, and all the while my wife and kid were growing paler and paler, and I thought, if this is what it means to be a farmer, then there's not a more god-forsaken. . . . Anyway, I just wanted you to know.

KIMI: But it made you so strong.

ICHIHASHI: See what I mean? There you go again! Hah-hah-hah!

KIMI: You thirsty?

ICHIHASHI: Not particularly.

KIMI: Why don't you stop by the house? There should be a melon cooling in the well.

ICHIHASHI: No, thanks. But listen, if that fellow Aoki—that's his name, isn't it?—if he wants you to go back to work at the station, I think you should.

KIMI: All right. . . .

ICHIHASHI: Look, I know you really want to settle down and learn farming. There's nothing wrong with that. Far from it! But, you said something before. . . .

KIMI: You mean about feeling like being in a vacuum tube?

ICHIHASHI: That's it. If you ask me . . . now don't get mad, okay? . . . you really do act like the miller's spoiled little girl the way you pick and choose when there's work to be done. You see what I mean?

KIMI (*after a pause*): I'll think it over. Take care. .   . . (*She starts to leave.*)

ICHIHASHI: Kimi, don't get me wrong. . . . Look at me, talking like this, bald as an eagle and all, but . . . hah-hah-hah! It's not that I don't feel anything for you. . . . Well, I guess that doesn't matter right now. We can talk about it some other time.

KIMI: Yes. . . . Well, good night. (*Exits.*)

ICHIHASHI (*into the shadows offstage*): Hey, don't walk backwards! Watch where you're going!

KIMI (*voice only*): Good night!

The raucous sound of a dog barking.

ICHIHASHI: Hah-hah-hah! See, you stepped on the poor mutt! Don't you know enough to let a sleeping dog lie? Hah-hah-hah!

Curtain.

Act Seven: Before the Dawn

Music in the darkness expresses the turbulence of a storm. Gradually its intensity diminishes, and a title appears on the screen.

Title slide: ACT SEVEN: BEFORE THE DAWN

The gentle strains of the music are replaced by the real sound of autumn rain, and through it, the clear tones of a woman's voice can be heard on the radio.

RADIO: The typhoon left devastation in its wake, but at this hour the danger has passed, and the weather is improving. The rainfall set a new record for our usually dry region, however: 49.93 millimeters since last night. Landslides remain a real danger in the mountain passes between Tokachi and Ishikari, and the National Railroads has added extra crews along endangered sections of track.

The title fades and the lights come up as the weather report continues.

The scene is the same as Act Two. All that remains of the intense downpour of the previous night is a light drizzle that descends in silver streaks through the September darkness outside the window.

Amamiya Teruko stands before the radio in a corner of the room and listens intently.   Stray strands of hair along the white nape of her neck are visible over the collar of her serge kimono.

RADIO: Thanks to their efforts, all trains are presently on schedule. However, traffic on highways through the mountains has been stopped since the storm commenced. This concludes our report, prepared in the newsroom of *The Northern Japan Daily News.*

Teruko switches off the radio. For a few moments she stands lost in thought.

While the setting is the same as Act Two, the atmosphere has changed completely. Gone are the gay new year's decorations and party preparations; a round coffee table stands forlornly in their place. Gone also is the sputtering sound of the stove. Indeed, the room resembles nothing so much as an empty cavern, and even the familiar pieces of furniture exude an aura of mutual alienation that is reinforced by the rain on the slate roof. Only the bellflower in a vase near the wall provides a touch of color in the pale light of the chandelier.

Teruko hesitantly goes to the writing table, opens the briefcase standing there, and begins searching through it. Nothing. She opens the suitcase on the floor. Again nothing. Turning to the bookcase, she pulls books at random from the shelves and examines them. Inadvertently she knocks five or six volumes to the floor and hastily retrieves them. Finally, she comes to a drawer in the writing table and removes a sealed envelope. At first she hesitates but then rips it open. She extracts a sheaf of ruled paper covered with writing and begins to read. From the look on her face, it is apparent that her worst fears have been confirmed.

The headlights of an automobile shine through the window. Startled and momentarily confused, Teruko finally puts the papers back in the drawer. The doorbell rings. She straightens her garments, becalms herself, and goes to the door.

Aoki Yoshie appears through Door A.

AOKI: Sorry to be late.

TERUKO: I'm sorry to put you to all this trouble.

AOKI: I brought him back with me.

TERUKO: Was he still there?

AOKI: No, he'd left Lake Akan early this morning as you said.

Teruko nods her acknowledgment.

AOKI: I didn't realize he'd been using an assumed name, so it took me some time to track him down.

TERUKO: Yes, I'm sorry, I forgot to tell you. I only realized it after you'd left. (*Looking out through Door A*): Tōru, what's wrong? Come inside.

AOKI (*softly, from behind her*): I'm afraid he's had a little too much to drink.

TERUKO: He has? Where?

AOKI: Well, ma'am. . . .

Tōru appears on the doorstep in a wet raincoat. His face is pale and inebriated.

TERUKO: You're dripping! Take off your coat! Where were you?

Aoki helps Tōru off with his raincoat. Beneath it he wears a brand new suit.

TŌRU: Well, actually. . . .

Aoki removes the sketchbook rolled up in the pocket of the raincoat, places it on the coffee table, and proceeds toward the door.

TERUKO: Well, never mind. I'll find out from Mr. Aoki. Right now, why don't you start getting ready to leave?

TŌRU: Sure. (*He collapses on the sofa and stretches out.*)

TERUKO: Tōru, please! I don't want to get letters saying, send me this and send me that. You're going a lot farther than Sapporo this time, remember.

TŌRU (*prostrate on the couch*): Mother, I'm not leaving tonight.

TERUKO: Of course you are. Don't be silly! (*She picks up the sketchbook on the table and pages through it.*) You spent three whole months up at Lake Akan, and you didn't make a single sketch?

Tōru does not answer. He just lies there, staring at the ceiling. Aoki returns with his luggage.

TERUKO (*opening the sketchbook from the other side*): Oh! I didn't know you stayed in an Ainu village!

TŌRU (*laughing*): I'm surprised Aoki didn't mistake me for one of the natives! Pretty good for someone who was plastered at the time, wouldn't you say?

TERUKO (*to Aoki*): It really is quite amazing how you found him in a place like this.

AOKI: Yes, when I got back to the station, I discovered that he'd checked his luggage, so I asked around and. . . . Well, I still have a lot of work to do. If you'll excuse me?

TERUKO: Of course. I'm really very sorry to have put you to all this trouble. Was there anybody with him?

AOKI: Well, as a matter of fact. . . . (*To Tōru*): What was his name?

Tōru does not respond.

AOKI (*to Teruko*): He graduated from middle school here—an artist. . . .

TERUKO (*taken by surprise*): Oh! (*To Tōru*): Is your friend Sugai back?

TŌRU: Mother, look a few pages ahead.

TERUKO (*flipping the pages*): My word!

AOKI: I'll be going then. . . .

TERUKO: Mr. Aoki, I don't know how to thank you. Won't you stay and have some tea or something?

AOKI: No, thank you. I'm afraid I'm a bit pressed for time.

TERUKO: I see. But you must be tired after your long trip through this rain.

AOKI: Yes, ma'am . . . I mean, no, ma'am. Tōru, I'll take you to the station later. (*To Teruko*): You know, the driver was saying it was lucky Tōru was up at Lake Akan, where they've just built that scenic drive. If he'd been in the mountains between here and Sapporo, we'd never have been able to fetch him. It would've been too dangerous.

Teruko sees Aoki out through Door A. Tōru remains lying on the couch. Teruko returns and picks up the sketchbook again.

TŌRU: Surprised, eh? I was surprised myself. Listen, when we got back, I stood for the longest time in front of this poster. I'll bet you can't guess which one. (*He sits up.*)

Teruko continues looking at the sketches.

TŌRU: A recruiting poster for salmon fishermen to go up to Kamchatka. (*Laughs*): All of a sudden I hear my name called and someone puts his hand on my shoulder. Well, . . .

TERUKO: And did you tell him that your father has given you permission to go to art school?

TŌRU: Mother, you know the exams you take in art school?

TERUKO: Yes?

TŌRU: There'll be a plaster bust of, say, Moliere—you know, one with hair down to here? (*He indicates shoulder-length.*) You sit around on three sides and draw it, right?

TERUKO: Yes, that's what you told me.

TŌRU: Well, if you get a seat with a window at your back, the bust looks all white, and it's almost impossible to draw. You can't grasp it.

TERUKO: I know! I was so worried, I made some inquiries, and you know what they said? Even if you spent the next six months commuting to the art center in Kasuga, you'd still have a difficult time. Didn't Sugai warn you?

TŌRU: You don't have to make that face, Mother. Sugai's not going to be a bad influence. Not any more.

Teruko does not understand.

TŌRU: Otherwise why would he come back here? He says he's been given a seat in this society with a window at his back. But, if you're really talented, then even if your subject appears all white—or completely enveloped in shadows for that matter—you should still be able to produce a reasonable likeness. I remember, this is Sugai talking—I don't want to start making excuses before I've even tried my hand. . . . (*He pauses, as if trying to control his emotions.*) Anyway, that's all he had to say at the bar tonight. Of course, his feelings are a lot more complicated—I'm not really doing him justice. But . . . but it was enough for me.

TERUKO: Was that really all he said?

TŌRU: Then . . . then. . . . (*Wanting desperately to change the subject*): You know, they say hard cider's just like champagne, only without the bubbles. *(Laughs.)* I wonder if Sugai's ever had champagne? But what a motley crew, eh? Sugai and me and that Russian. (*Mimicking*): "No, no. Me Japanese. Name Nobugorō." *(Laughs.)* He cracks me up. He claims his name's Nobugorō because he was born in Nizhni Novgorod!

TERUKO: Tōru, before you leave, I. . . .

TŌRU: Come on, listen. He said there was a palace with a dome shaped like an onion, and the Tartars used to set up a market called a yarmarka. I don't know whether there's any truth to it, but Kovankov claims that when Shalyapin was young, he was his star pupil. The man can hardly carry a tune, but he sings this special version of "The Song of the Flea" that he says Shalyapin taught him.[1] We have it, Mother, let's listen to it. (*He stands up.*)

TERUKO: Never mind about that now.

TŌRU: Come on, it'll be fun! (*He goes to the phonograph.*)

TERUKO: Tōru, you're really impossible! Start packing, this instant! Come on, I'll help you.

TŌRU (*looking through the record collection*): It's not here. Hey, Debussy's not here either. Did you lend them to somebody?

TERUKO (*noncommittally*): Ye . . . yes.

TŌRU: Why didn't you say so? (*Coming back to the sofa*): And then there's Gorki—he died while I was in exile. That reminds me: according to the paper, it seems you really made a mess of things at that meeting of your Women and Society group.

TERUKO: Don't be ridiculous.

TŌRU: What's wrong with holding a memorial for the man? It's only natural. I don't care much for his work—although even Aoki seems to have read *The Mother*—but the idea that a Johnny-come-lately like that should be considered one of the world's great authors absolutely scandalizes Kovankov. "I knew him when he was nothing but a bellboy on a Volga river steamer," he says. *(Laughs.)* So Sugai says, "Yes, but there's no such place as Nizhni Novgorod anymore—today it's called Gorkigrad!"

TERUKO: You see, you just contradicted yourself.

TŌRU: I did?

TERUKO: About Sugai's leanings.

---

[1] Fyodor Ivanovich Shalyapin (1873-1938). Russian vocalist. The song referred to here is "Mephistopheles' Song of the Flea" by Musorgsky.

TŌRU: Well, hear me out. Anyway, in the end Kovankov starts crying!
(He laughs.) "When in Rome, do as Romans do," he says. That
Russian bastard even knows stuff like that. I may be drinking cider
now, he says, but. . . . *(Again, he imitates the Russian.)* "Please,
please, you believe! Me nobility. Russian nobility!" That was fine,
but then he left, and Sugai said something that really floored me. "All
you have to do is substitute you-know-what[2] for 'Russian nobility,'"
he said, "And that's exactly how I feel!" Mother, that was Sugai, who. .
. . *(He stops, profoundly disturbed.)*
Teruko is silent.

TŌRU: Then Aoki said we had to leave, and that was that. . . . Where's
Father?

TERUKO: He's not back yet. He's probably still in his laboratory. I
wonder if he's finished his report.

TŌRU: Mother, I'm not going. I don't want to be banished to Tokyo.
Would you explain to Grandfather that I won't be staying with the
Takimotos in Tokyo after all?

TERUKO: Then you really don't plan to leave tonight?

TŌRU *(with growing conviction)*: That's right.

TERUKO: No, Tōru, you leave tonight as planned.

TŌRU: Just me? What about Father?

TERUKO: You read my letter, didn't you? The plan was for you to go to
Sapporo with your father and then as soon as the conference of
station directors is over to. . . . No matter how much your father
disliked it, I wanted him to see your grandfather and ask him
personally to have the family in Tokyo look after you. I'd hoped that
if they got together, they'd patch up their differences. But, the way
things are going. . . . Well, never mind about that. In any case, I
understand the situation precisely, and we simply can't have someone
with your disposition here or at school in Sapporo. With that scandal
hanging over you. . . . If you could have handled it responsibly,
what need would there have been to send you up to Lake Akan?
Tōru does not respond.

TERUKO: There's no sense in dwelling on it now, but even if I'd tried to
stop your father . . . I just hope you won't hold it against him. That
would be a terrible mistake. Your father. . . .

TŌRU *(suddenly, with vehemence)*: Don't be stupid! Who the hell are
you to talk!

---

[2] I.e., Communist.

TERUKO: Tōru!

TŌRU: When we came back from Komai's place, what did you say, right here in this room? That it was my fault for taking these farm girls seriously. You're disgusting, you know that! You even attacked father! To hell with your "Kingdom of God"! Father told me over and over on the way home that I'd accepted responsibility for what I'd done and that was what counted. He said it would be wrong to let one incident poison my attitude toward the farmers. He said it to me real soft, so Shino wouldn't hear. You're really low, you know that, Mother?

TERUKO: Low? Look who's talking! But let's stop. I don't like arguing with you like this. But do you think that you can just decide not to take the entrance examination for art school and everything will be all right between you and your grandfather? He's professor emeritus at the university, and look how you've sullied his good name! You've just completed your punishment. If you throw it all away now and say you just want to paint. . . .

TŌRU: You see, that's it. You're always like this. You're always dragging Grandfather into everything.

TERUKO: Of course! There's never been anyone in the world as important to me as your grandfather.

TŌRU: Mother!

TERUKO: But Grandfather, fine a man as he is, also has his evil side. And that's where you get it. Do you understand? How do you think my mother, your grandmother in Tokyo, died?

TŌRU: I've heard about it before.

TERUKO: No, you haven't, not about the cause of her death. It's hard to admit, but . . . tonight before you leave, I want you to know, just you. Even your father isn't aware. I was only a child, but it seems like yesterday. It was new year's. Mother sat up the whole night beneath the decorations, her face like wax, staring into space. . . . (*She weeps.*) For a while, I couldn't stand the sight of new year's decorations. They still remind me of her.

Tōru stares at his mother.

TERUKO: Even after we moved to Sapporo, it kept on . . . or, I should say, it happened again. Can you imagine? The same thing that forced Grandfather to leave Tokyo is forcing you to leave here! Late one night, I went to meet the brother of the woman. I took some money. Someone found out about it and suggested that I. . . . My whole future was. . . . I suffered terribly, until we moved here. But that's beside the point. In the end, I was able to protect Grandfather and preserve his reputation as an   outstanding agronomist.   But you're a different matter, Tōru. . . .

TŌRU: Then. . . .

TERUKO: That's why . . . that's why I was against your getting involved with people like artists and their loose morals from the start. I didn't want you to come under their influence.

TŌRU: I don't believe it! How could you be so stupid! Not all artists have loose morals! Look at Sugai! Sugai. . . . (*He starts to speak but is overcome with a sense of futility and hangs his head.*)
Pause.

TERUKO: So, you see?   The relationship between your father and grandfather is one thing, but even the women in my Women and Society group have turned against me because of this Shino affair. Even that business about Gorki—all I did was suggest that we commemorate his death with a small, private reading instead of a public observance, and just look how it got blown out of proportion! I could just. . . . But the point is, you're about to get what you've always wanted. Now you can buckle down and really study painting. What kind of an artist do you expect to be if you spend three whole months at Lake Akan and don't make a single sketch? Please, Tōru, when you get to Tokyo. . . . No, I can't imagine your getting involved like Sugai. I've always known there'd be no danger of that. So work hard and try to get your work into the Second Division Show—the Modern Japanese Show would do nicely too.[3] The sooner the better. It would make me so happy to see something you painted on a postcard at the Kikumaru Department Store! (*She weeps.*)
Tōru does not respond.

TERUKO (*taking an envelope from the sash of her kimono*):   It's not much, but take this with you—just in case.

TŌRU: I don't want your money!

TERUKO: It's all I can do for you now. Hard as it may be for you to accept. . .

TŌRU: I said I don't want it! So that's why you were against my going? Stupid! You stupid old woman! I've always wondered why I didn't go

---

[3]The Second Division Society (*Nikakai*) was established in 1914 by Western-style artists like Umehara Ryūzaburō and Yasui Sōtarō, who had been influenced by the Impressionists and early Post-Impressionists, as an alternative to the government-sponsored Bunten exhibit. The Modern Japanese Exhibit (*Kokuten*), was sponsored by the Society for the Promotion of Modern Japanese-Style Painting (*Kokuga sōsaku kyōkai*), which had been established in 1918 by Murakami Kagaku and others in a similar break with Bunten.

to Tokyo right away when Sugai sent for me. Now I understand. I always thought I was no good because I didn't go. I understood why Sugai sent me that book of Brueghel's paintings, and I had nothing but contempt for myself because all I wanted to do was sit around here and paint snowscapes. But when I saw Sugai tonight, I realized. . . . Mother, I'm not going to Tokyo . . . *(with self-derision)*: and I'm obviously not going to Kamchatka . . . but I'm not going back to my lodgings in Sapporo either. I'm finished. I'm not doing anything anymore!

TERUKO: No, Tōru. Your father will be back soon. He may not go with you, but in either case, you leave for Tokyo tonight.

The doorbell rings.

TERUKO *(softly)*: You'd better not let your father see you in this mood. Go inside and start packing. *(She wipes her eyes and goes to Door A.)*

Tōru does not move. Teruko returns with an unexpected visitor: Komai Tsuta.

TERUKO *(to Tōru)*: I said, go inside and start packing!

TSUTA: Sorry to be calling so late, but. . . . *(Toward the door)*: Come in, will you?

Tōru abruptly gets up to leave.

TERUKO: Where are you going?

TŌRU: Never mind. I won't be back tonight.

TERUKO: Tōru!

Tōru tries to exit but he is impeded by Henmi Shōsaku who is coming through the door.

TSUTA: Tōru, you're in fine spirits! Now don't go out and get involved with another Shino! *(She laughs.)*

Tōru exits without replying.

SHŌSAKU *(timidly)*: Sorry to bother you like this. . . .

TSUTA: You see, ma'am. . . .

TERUKO: Wait a minute, will you, please?

She goes through Door A. There is the sound of arguing in the foyer.

SHŌSAKU: Miss Komai, I. . . .

TSUTA: Just leave everything to me. One peep out of you, and I wash my hands of the whole affair. You should never have listened to that Ichihashi.

Teruko returns, trying to conceal her emotions.

TSUTA: You seem preoccupied. . . .

TERUKO: Not at all. I apologize. Please, have a seat. *(She sits, facing them.)*

TSUTA: You see, ma'am, this is a busy time for the farmers. The weather's good, and Henmi here says he has to work in the fields until dark. We knew we'd be imposing, but tonight was the only time—

TERUKO: I see. Well, if you'd like to see my husband, I'm afraid he's leaving for Sapporo tonight. Perhaps you read in the paper about the conference of agricultural station directors?

TSUTA: I'm afraid not. . . . *(She looks up at the clock.)* Will he be taking the eleven o'clock express? Then he'll be coming home before he leaves, I suppose?

TERUKO: Yes, perhaps. I'm just waiting for him to ring me. I may have to take his bags and meet him at the station.

TSUTA: Is that so? Well, since it's so difficult for us to get together, perhaps you'll hear us out. I'm afraid it's not the most pleasant business, but. . . . *(Laughs.)*

TERUKO: Well, I don't know. . . .

TSUTA: Actually, we were wondering if something couldn't be done about the note Mr. Amamiya countersigned for Henmi here? You see, it's overdue, and. . . .

SHŌSAKU: I . . . I don't know what to say . . . how to apologize. When I asked your husband to help me last spring, I never expected. . . .

TERUKO: I think perhaps you should discuss this with my husband.

TSUTA: We'd be more than happy to, ma'am, but as you know, there have been certain changes at the Igarashi farms. Young Mr. Igarashi has gone off the deep end with this livestock project of his, and he's trying to get his money out of the farms, so. . . .

TERUKO: I see.

TSUTA: Now I wish I'd never got involved, but I thought I'd do a good turn, you see, and took over some of the old debts of Igarashi's tenants. Well, you know what Igarashi said? "I've known those people so long, I didn't have it in me to rake them over the coals, so I sold the notes to Komai at a loss." How do you think that makes me look? *(She laughs.)*

SHŌSAKU: I don't mean to change the subject, but. . . .

TSUTA: You just keep out of this! I know you and Mr. Amamiya are generous people, too, so even if I hadn't taken over those debts. . . . There isn't a farmer around nowadays who isn't in arrears, but Henmi here's in a class by himself. He hasn't had the crops to pay his land tax, and his loan's been refinanced several times to the tune of six hundred yen, so in all fairness I have to start collecting with him.

SHŌSAKU: I don't know how many times I asked them to let me repay the loan Mr. Amamiya countersigned for me first, but when I spoke to

Mr. Igarashi, he said he was going to confiscate my soy and adzuki bean crops, and. . . .

TERUKO (*raising her eyebrows*): My word, you'd have nothing left!

TSUTA: And then there's the little matter of Shino. Of course, it wouldn't be fair to bring that up, now would it? (*She laughs.*) But perhaps you could consider it a gift to Shōsaku here. (*She removes the loan document from her sash.*) It's really a pittance to you. You could just pretend you misplaced one of your diamond rings.

SHŌSAKU: Miss Komai, let's come back some other time. We're really imposing, and. . . .

TSUTA: You see what I have to put up with? The night of the festival he drank too much and started yelling, "If you want your money, go collect it from Amamiya!"

SHŌSAKU: I never said that! Please don't believe her. I could never face Mr. Amamiya if. . . .

TSUTA (*laughing*): Put yourself in his place. Think how he must feel. Your son knocks up his sister, and here he is apologizing! (*She laughs.*)

TERUKO (*fiercely*): Wait just a minute. I don't think I have to sit here and listen to that, Miss Komai.

TSUTA: Oh, I am terribly sorry. It just slipped out. The last thing in the world I want to do is offend you! (*Laughter.*)

TERUKO: You know, Miss Komai, I've heard quite a lot about you. Won't you reconsider? As I understand it, you were originally a tenant farmer yourself, just like Mr. Henmi.

TSUTA: Yes, indeed, and despite appearances, I'm doing all I can to be of service. But you know what they say: the child knows not the parent's heart. I go around being solicitous, accepting their kimonos and chests of drawers as security, and how do the tenants repay me? They say I do it out of guilt for having moved up in the world! (*She laughs.*)

TERUKO: That's not what I had in mind. It's the matter of your father. I really didn't want to mention it, but. . . . He died such a wretched death, and the funeral was hardly over when you. . . . (*Fiercely*): You're in no position to discuss other people's morals!

TSUTA: Oh, I am sorry! I misunderstood. You see, my father was a real weakling, and when Mr. Hayakawa took over as landlord, he got himself caught between him and the tenants and was killed. (*Brazenly*): Forgive me for thinking I was better off becoming Hayakawa's mistress than selling myself to a whorehouse in Nemuro!

TERUKO (*contemptuously*): Well, I never!

TSUTA (*unfazed*): You've never experienced a day of hunger in your life! What would you know?

SHŌSAKU: Miss Komai, please. We really should excuse ourselves.

TSUTA (*suddenly shouting*): I told you to shut your trap! We're in the right here! (*She takes out a cigarette and begins smoking.*) Mrs. Amamiya, if you have something to do, please go ahead. We'll just wait until we get satisfaction!

TERUKO (*rising*): I'll thank you to leave! I have to get ready to go to the station.

The doorbell rings. Teruko goes to Door A.

SHŌSAKU: Miss Komai, please. . . .

TSUTA (*interrupting him*): Shh, that's Amamiya's voice.

Amamiya enters from Door A, followed by Teruko. He is dressed in his usual black suit.

AMAMIYA: Well, hello! Sorry to have kept you waiting. (*He signals with his eyes for Teruko to leave them.*)

Teruko shoots Tsuta an angry glance, then exits through Door B.

AMAMIYA (*sitting down opposite his guests*): I wrote and had Aoki call on you several times. I really would have preferred that you kept my wife out of this.

TSUTA: Well, she was being so unreasonable, I'm afraid I may have lost my temper. *(Laughing)*: Please excuse me.

AMAMIYA: Actually, you see, I just finished working on my report, and I really have to leave tonight or I won't make it to Sapporo in time for the conference.   I'll only be gone three days. We'll clear up this business as soon as I get back.

TSUTA: I see. But. . . .

AMAMIYA: I've seen Henmi and heard about his situation. You can rest assured that something will be done. (*To Shōsaku*): Come back after I've returned, will you? Tonight I'm rather in a hurry.

SHŌSAKU (*timidly*): Mr. Amamiya, sir, I. . . .

AMAMIYA: Yes?

SHŌSAKU: I'm afraid I'll just make matters worse by saying this, but I don't want to be accused of trading my sister for money, that's all. I appreciate you're wanting to make things right, but . . . I just can't ask you to pay. . . .

AMAMIYA: I see. (*He considers.*)

SHŌSAKU: People are already talking, and. . . .

TSUTA: After all I've tried to do for you! . . .

AMAMIYA: Now, just hold on a minute. (*To Shōsaku*): I understand. That's very honorable of you. The last thing in the world I want
is to have you soil your good name. How about this? Let's separate
this matter from Tōru's . . . indiscretion. As for Miss Komai, we'll
take the necessary steps to avoid any further inconvenience.

TSUTA: May I have your word on that?

AMAMIYA: Of course. And as for you, please consider the money an
indefinite loan. How would that be?

SHŌSAKU: That's very generous, but. . . .

Teruko appears in Door B.

TERUKO: Excuse me, but. . . .

AMAMIYA (*turning around*): What is it?

TERUKO (*still in the doorway*): Could I have a word with you here for a
moment?

AMAMIYA: Later.

TSUTA: Well, thank you very much for your consideration. Now, before
I offend Mrs. Amamiya any further. . . . *(She laughs.)*

Teruko closes the door.

SHŌSAKU: Mr. Amamiya, I'm afraid this whole thing's my fault. You
know, I listened to your radio talk, and I wanted to discuss it with
somebody, but I never should have mentioned it to Watari. The rat
won't even speak to me these days. He sees me coming and walks the
other way.

TSUTA: That's enough apologies already.

AMAMIYA: No, if anyone's to blame, it's me. Karasawa claimed that
all the company wanted was to see the yield increase on the plots that
received incentive subsidies. But the fact of the matter is that unless
you bought company fertilizer on credit, they wouldn't do a thing for
you.

SHŌSAKU: Yessir. And that's all the more. . . .

AMAMIYA: Even something as simple as getting help transporting the
harvested flax to the mill—the cooperative's the unit for that assist-
ance, so if someone like you tries to be independent, they just get left
out in the cold. I should have realized that. All I knew was that the
target of the incentive policy had changed from individuals to
groups. I didn't realize what it really meant.

TSUTA: You see, for all your learning. . . . I know I don't have any
business butting in here, but . . . supposing a man has three hectares
and plants half in beets and half in flax. What's the big deal about
buying fertilizer on credit until the fall harvest? And if someone says
the company fertilizer's too expensive, I always tell him, look, you

wouldn't think anything of borrowing money for six months, so don't think of it as borrowing fertilizer and seed but as borrowing money and it won't bother you so much.

AMAMIYA (*unamused*): No, that's just the point. (*To Shōsaku*): The problem is the influx of company capital and increasing company control over the land. But, well, tonight. . .

TSUTA: Of course. Sorry to have imposed like this. (*She stands.*) Oh, by the way, about the bucket land we've been consulting you about since the bank put it up for sale. . . . (*Laughing*): Look at me, coming in here and making all kinds of demands! I completely forgot to thank you! I wanted to let you know that after I spoke to you, we ran a roller over it, and it's made a big difference. Now I've gained control of all the independent plots, and I'm considering paving the irrigation ditches with concrete, but the tenants are up in arms about the assessments, and. . . . (*She goes to Door A as she speaks.*)

SHŌSAKU (*in the doorway*): Mr. Amamiya, I don't know how to thank you. I'm going to talk things over with Ichihashi and make a fresh start.

AMAMIYA (*nodding*): Fine, fine. All the best to Shino. It won't be much longer now, will it? (*He sees them out.*)

Teruko enters through Door B. Amamiya returns.

AMAMIYA: I understand Tōru was here.

TERUKO: Akira, what are doing, taking Henmi on like that?

AMAMIYA (*sardonically*): Doing? What else is there to do? That reminds me, we have to return this book of paintings to Tōru. (*He climbs up on the ladder and removes a book from one of the higher shelves. Noticing something different about the arrangement of the books*): Have you been meddling with these books?

He turns to Teruko. A thought comes to him. He descends the ladder and goes to the writing table.

Teruko reaches the desk an instant before him and grabs the envelope in the drawer.

AMAMIYA: You fool! What are you doing?

Fending off her husband, Teruko rips the envelope in two. They face each other in icy silence.

AMAMIYA (*at last*): Have you no shame, going through my things when I'm away?

TERUKO: Shame? Aren't you ashamed to have hidden this from me?

Pause.

AMAMIYA (*trying to control himself*): All right. Sit down over there. (*He sits down, too.*)

TERUKO: Please, as a favor to me, delay your departure just one day, just until tomorrow morning. Let's talk this over one more time, please?

AMAMIYA: If I wait until tomorrow, there won't be any point in going. All the data relevant to my work is going to be reported on the first day of the conference. Can't we discuss it after I return?

TERUKO: I know that you've been involved in this debate since the spring, and I appreciate your not wanting to give in now, but. . . .

AMAMIYA: Think of you and the children, not just my work, is that it? I'd like to think that in my own way I. . . .

TERUKO: No, that's not it. It's something you told me some time ago. You mentioned that recently they've been using electricity in crop rotation experiments.

AMAMIYA (*dubiously*): Yes?

TERUKO: And, well, is it true that the Ministry of Agriculture and Forestry is anticipating the work of the main experimental station and using refrigeration units to . . . simulate, is that the word? . . . to simulate the effects of cold and frost on crops?

AMAMIYA: That's true, but who in the world told you about that?

TERUKO: I'm ashamed to have to admit it, but all these years I haven't taken the slightest interest in your work. I've been too preoccupied with other things. The point is, if your experiments are going to be that complex in the future, then perhaps you would be better off giving in this time around.

AMAMIYA: I see. Well, if it were simply a question of my work. . . .

TERUKO: No, it would be for the good of the farmers, too.

AMAMIYA: Listen, you began this technical discussion, so let me continue. (*He smiles.*) You know, this is the first time we've talked like this? Of course, I'm sure you paid attention to what I had to say on the radio and so forth, but...

TERUKO: That's why I. . . .

AMAMIYA: Never mind. What's done is done. Now listen, in this region there are presently 200,000 hectares under cultivation. Now, if all told there are 280,000 hectares of arable land—that is, land suitable for cultivation—then since the land under cultivation increases at the rate of about 10,000 hectares per year. . . . Are you following me?

TERUKO: Yes.

AMAMIYA: If you take 200,000 from 280,000, that means in seven or eight years, all the arable land in this region will be under cultivation. We'll reach the saturation point. My point is that we have to get away from primitive methods of land management like depletion farming—you know, the thing your father and I had that big fight about over by the sugar beet fields—we have to stop simply exploting nature—of course, it's not only nature that's being exploited—and work toward creating new, intensive farming methods. If we wait until every centimeter of land is being tilled and then have crop failures or damage from the cold, there'll be hell to pay. It's a question of life and death for the farmers whether we can make a smooth transition from one method of land management to another. Can't you see that?

TERUKO: Yes . . . but if it's that simple, why should Mr. Saegusa have written what he did in his article?

AMAMIYA: It was just malicious, that's all. For example, I was arguing that instead of common vetch . . . well, never mind the details. Everything I had to say was based on the results of actual experiments. It was just absurd for him to fault my conclusions without considering my data! I doubt that anyone at this conference. . . . Oh, I see! Then you think my position is going to prevail! That's why you want me to give in!

TERUKO: That's just the point! Take the matter of that money for the Neubauer apparatus. With your relationship in such a state, what alternative was there but to pay Father back out of the children's savings? Even if we're eventually reimbursed out of the station's operating expenses, how many years do you think that will take? Then you decided to change the motor, and, well, there's just nothing left. Please, whatever you do, don't resign! What sort of research do you think you'd be able to do if you quit as director of this station?

AMAMIYA (*nodding his assent*): You're right on that score. But this idea of making a strategic retreat in order to avoid a head-on collision—that's just what Saegusa and the others want. They want this whole matter left up in the air so they can ignore the needs of the farmers and remain in control for years to come. Of course you're right, without the facilities or the money to conduct research, I'd be like a fish out of water. But, look, if I stand up for what's right, somebody's bound to . . . I can't believe that I'm the only agronomist with any principles. Well, I'm running out of time. Is Tōru packed? Here, take this book—I'm sure I'll forget it.

Teruko does not take it. Demoralized, she does not move. Finally, she rises from her seat without a word.

AMAMIYA: Teruko, what's the matter?

Teruko goes toward Door B without replying.

AMAMIYA (*into the interior of the house*): Tōru! Tōru!

TERUKO (*turning back in the doorway, icily*): He's gone.

AMAMIYA: Where?

TERUKO: How should I know? (*She reenters the room. Supporting herself precariously on the writing table*): Please! Tōru isn't the kind of child who can study painting under difficult conditions. I don't care what happens to me, and in four or five years Reiko will. . . .

AMAMIYA: You see! That's all you can think of! Somebody put those ideas into your head, and you just mouthed them like a parrot. And I have a pretty good idea who it was, too!

TERUKO (*falling to her knees*): Please! Don't go to this meeting!

AMAMIYA: Look, you have to trust. . . . You just can't ask this of me. Even if his studies are difficult, Tōru will do at least as well as I've done.

TERUKO: I see. I should never have thought that I could be worthy of your trust.

AMAMIYA: Oh, stop it! Don't be ridiculous!

Teruko manages to get to her feet and move unsteadily to Door B. Amamiya quietly collects the scraps of paper his wife has torn and disposes of them in the waste basket. Then he seats himself with dignity before the writing table and begins to prepare ink with an ink stick. He spreads a sheet of lined paper on the desk and picks up a brush.

Reiko bursts in through Door A.

REIKO (*seeing her father*): Father! I was afraid I'd miss you! Shimura's so slow at her homework!

AMAMIYA (*putting down the brush*): Welcome home.

REIKO (*looking at the flower in the vase and going toward it*): I didn't know we had such a pretty flower in the house! I could have painted this! Let's see, how many petals are there? . . . Oh, that reminds me. Father, want to know what I found out? That Mrs. Shimura really hates to be outdone! She went out and bought just the same records as we have! (*She shrugs.*) Of course, they're second-hand, but there's the "Song of the Flea" and the "Pre— (*Realizing*): Oh, you're busy, aren't you!

Amamiya nods.

REIKO (*noticing the book of paintings*): Are you going to give this back to Tōru?

AMAMIYA: Yes.

REIKO: Then I'll take it to him right away. (*She picks up the book.*) Father, you want to know a secret? Tōru's been taking this down and looking at it every now and then. (*She exits through Door B, leaving peals of laughter in her wake.*)

Amamiya writes, forming each character with great care. He folds the paper carefully and inserts it in an envelope.

REIKO (*entering through Door C*): He's not here. I looked everywhere. (*She exits through Door B.*)

There is the sound of an argument offstage, then the sound of a glass breaking.

REIKO (*voice only, from behind Door B*): Father, come quick!

AMAMIYA (*sealing the envelope*): What is it?

REIKO (*sticking her head through the doorway*): Hurry! Mother took some white medicine!

AMAMIYA: It's probably just a sedative. Reiko, come here. You'd better leave her alone for a while.

REIKO (*running to him*): It's not a sedative!

Teruko appears in Door B. She stares unblinking at her husband and daughter.

AMAMIYA (*startled by her expression*): Teruko! What have you done? What did you take?

Teruko does not respond.

AMAMIYA: Teruko! (*He goes toward her.*)

TERUKO: I'm fine. You needn't concern yourself with the likes of me. (*She moves unsteadily toward Door A.*)

AMAMIYA: Teruko, where are you going?

TERUKO: My face is so hot, I want to cool it in the rain. (*She shakes him off and tries to leave.*)

AMAMIYA (*pulling her back*): That's enough! What if someone sees you looking like this?

TERUKO: I don't care. I'm going to get on the train and go straight back to Sapporo just like this.

AMAMIYA: You fool! Fool! (He strikes her.) Do you want to ruin my work and everything! You fool!

Teruko breaks her fall on the sofa. Suddenly, she begins weeping uncontrollably.

REIKO (*holding him back*): Father! Stop it! Father!

The doorbell.

REIKO: Who could that be? (*Flustered, she goes to Door A.*)

AMAMIYA (*whispering in his wife's ear*): Get out of here. Teruko! Get out! (*He tries to pull her roughly to her feet.*)

Aoki Yoshie appears through Door A.

AOKI: Mr. Amamiya . . . I'll get Dr. Nakaide right away. (*He places the package he is carrying on the coffee table.*) Here are your reports.

AMAMIYA: Thanks. (*Lifting Teruko in his arms*): Come and lie down inside.

REIKO (*sticking her head through Door A as she puts on her coat*): Never mind, I'll go. It's not far. (*Exits.*)

AMAMIYA (*carrying Teruko through Door B, to Aoki, who is following*): You stay here. If anybody comes, send them away, will you?

AOKI: Yes, sir.

Aoki remains behind in the living room.   A few moments pass, then Teruko's unconsolable weeping begins again. Aoki paces uncomfortably around the room. After a time, he picks up a copy of The Journal of the Agronomy Association from the table, but he is unable to concentrate. He stands and looks out the window. A few moments pass, then he notices someone approaching the house. Quickly he goes to Door A. The front door opens, and there is the sound of an argument, but it is impossible to make out what is being said.   Finally, Karasawa Katsumi enters through Door A, pushing Aoki aside as he does so.

KARASAWA: There's no reason you can't at least let me use the phone!

AOKI: You can't just come barging in like this!

KARASAWA: How many times do I have to tell you? All I want to do is call the train station and have a word with Mrs. Amamiya. *Mrs.* Amamiya, do you understand?

AOKI: But. . . .

KARASAWA (*spying the luggage*): You see, Amamiya's suitcase is still here. (*Clucking his tongue*): You've got me all wrong. If I hadn't received a letter, why would I be wasting precious time. . . . You must know about the fire we had at the mill.

AOKI: They're not here, neither of them. . . . (*He points to the luggage.*) I'm supposed to deliver. . . .

KARASAWA (*taking a letter from his pocket*):   Here it is.   The professor's terribly worried. He says. . . . Listen, tell this to Amamiya: Professor Takimoto goes so far as to recognize a certain validity in his position. But despite its validity, if Amamiya tries to force his point at the conference, it will simply be rejected.   Not only that, Tsuji has already been selected as the next director . . . . that is to say, Professor Takimoto has already been consulted about possible replacements for Amamiya, and naturally Tsuji's name has come up. Anyway, as soon as I read this, I hurried over here. I knew that even if I told Amamiya

directly he'd never listen to me, so I hoped his wife would see me, and.
. . . It takes a big man to write a letter like this, Aoki. Can you
understand that?

AOKI (*searching for a reply*): Of course . . . I'm sure that both Mr. and
Mrs. Amamiya will appreciate the trouble you've taken, but at the
moment. . . .

KARASAWA: Hell, there's no point in talking to you! I'm going in.
(*He strides forward toward the interior of the house.*)

AOKI: You're not supposed to. . . . (*He stands in his way.*)

Amamiya appears in Door B. He beckons to Aoki with his eyes. Aoki
listens to Amamiya, then proceeds through Door B.

AMAMIYA (*forcing a tense smile*): It's been a while.

KARASAWA: I'm not here to see you.

AMAMIYA: Well, I'm afraid Teruko's not here just now, so I'll have to
ask you to leave.

KARASAWA: You won't let me see her, even if I have a message from
her father?

AMAMIYA: In that case, I'll see that she gets the message.

KARASAWA: I see. Well, for old time's sake, then. (*He pushes the*
letter at him.) Try not to blush when you read it.

Amamiya takes the letter and reads it. Karasawa sits down near the
coffee table and watches Amamiya's expression as he reads.
Pause.

KARASAWA: Well? Professor Takimoto's in a class by himself,
wouldn't you say?

AMAMIYA (*finishing the letter*): I see.

KARASAWA: I wept when I got to the end. If I were you, I'd
reconsider. . . .

Reiko bursts in through Door A.

REIKO (*seeing Karasawa*): Oh! (*She hesitates but realizes nothing can be*
done. Into the foyer): Please come in.

Dr. Nakaide enters and is led by Reiko toward Door B. Nakaide bows
to Amamiya and exits.

KARASAWA: Is she sick? Why didn't you say so in the first place?

Amamiya returns the letter in silence.

KARASAWA (*taking the letter*): Is it serious?

AMAMIYA: It's nothing. . . .

KARASAWA: Of course, in that case it would be out of the question to
show her this. But, what do you say, Amamiya? Here's one of the
foremost authorities on Japanese agriculture humbling himself before
you, asking you to let things be as they were when you were in

graduate school, and suggesting that you submit a joint report that combines the best points of both your arguments. I can't tell you the admiration and esteem he inspires in me!

Amamiya is silent.

KARASAWA: If it were a joint effort, you wouldn't have to settle for *The Journal of the Agronomy Assocation*; you could publish your ideas in a much more prestigious forum. And you'd be a cinch to get your doctorate, too. Moreover, your findings would be applied almost automatically. Why, everything would turn out just the way you hoped!

AMAMIYA: I'm not so sure.

KARASAWA: Can't you even see that much? Look, take my advice, forget this conference and buckle under just this once. You won't regret it. *(He laughs.)*

Reiko enters through Door B. She approaches her father and whispers something to him.

AMAMIYA: I see. I'll be right there.

Reiko exits.

AMAMIYA *(rising)*: Well, if you'll excuse me.

KARASAWA: I'll just look in on her. . . .

AMAMIYA *(interrupting)*: I'm afraid I'll have to ask you to leave.

KARASAWA: Why? There's something strange going on here.

AMAMIYA: Get out!

KARASAWA: I see. Well, just one more thing, then. You owe me that much common courtesy.

Amamiya nods.

KARASAWA: Amamiya, you know what they say, genius is a product of its times. Of course, I'm in no position to know whether your theory's a work of genius or not. As far as I'm concerned, Professor Takimoto and Saegusa at the main station—and our own staff at the mill for that matter—have known all along what you propose. The reason that even an authority like Professor Takimoto hasn't spoken out, though, is that so long as Hokkaido remains in its underdeveloped state, there's no alternative to primitive methods of land management.

AMAMIYA: I see. And?

KARASAWA: As a scholar, don't you think it's a little childish of you to be prancing around, acting as if you'd just invented the wheel?

AMAMIYA: Childish? Maybe so. But if I'm just being childish, what need is there to shut me up?

KARASAWA: Shut you up? Who's trying to shut you up? Professor Takimoto?

AMAMIYA: Isn't he?

KARASAWA: What's the matter with you? (*He slaps Amamiya's chest with the letter.*) Didn't you read this? Professor Takimoto's aware that your theory's damaging to his position, but he accepts it anyway—to a point. He even goes out of his way to give examples from other countries. He admits that it was hasty of Saegusa to draw conclusions based on data taken from soil where the three basic nutrients hadn't been sufficiently supplied—and I have to admit my own embarrassment on that score—but the whole thing's based on the expectation of reciprocity. And all you can do is throw it back in his face!

AMAMIYA: There's no point in going on. These days I've gotten into the habit of looking for ulterior motives in everything people say.

KARASAWA: Ulterior motives? I see. Then there's nothing left to discuss. What you're trying to say is that you can't even trust your own father-in-law, the mentor to whom you owe so much?

AMAMIYA: I suppose it comes down to that.

KARASAWA: All right, then that's what I'll tell him. No wonder your wife got sick. Or perhaps she's more than just ill?

AMAMIYA: That's enough. Get out!

KARASAWA: I wouldn't stay if you begged me. Amamiya, we're through! (*Barking these words, he exits through Door A.*)

Amamiya tries to calm himself and starts toward Door B, but just then Dr. Nakaide emerges.

AMAMIYA: Oh, Doctor, I was just going in to see you. Please, have a seat. (*He offers him a chair. To Door B*): Reiko! Make some coffee, will you? I'm sorry for all the trouble, Doctor.

NAKAIDE: Not at all.

AMAMIYA: How is she?

NAKAIDE: I don't think there's anything to worry about. The amount was a little. . . . But, it was a regular sleeping preparation, and, well, in a lot of cases like this, the shame . . . that is, the sense of having failed continues to plague the mind, and . . . well, let's just say that there have been cases where the individual tries again. In that respect, I would advise caution.

Short pause.

AMAMIYA: As a matter of fact. . . .

NAKAIDE (*simultaneously*): Usually. . . .

AMAMIYA (*yielding*): Please.

NAKAIDE: Was there something else?

AMAMIYA: No, please.

NAKAIDE: This may be beside the point, but I remember something that happened to me about ten years ago. It was just about this time of year. I was on my way back from a physicians meeting in Asahikawa when a man was struck by the train one stop from here.

AMAMIYA: I see. (*He looks at the Doctor.*)

NAKAIDE: Perhaps because I'm a doctor, the idea of death didn't particularly disturb me tonight. I suppose I'm resigned to the idea that I'm going to have to witness a certain number of deaths before I'm through. (*He laughs.*) On that particular occasion, though—as a doctor, I'm ashamed to have to admit it—the thought of dealing with death terrified me, so I hid until a conductor of my acquaintance recognized me and dragged me out to the site of the accident.

AMAMIYA (*his mind occupied with other things*): I see.

NAKAIDE: The victim was a country fellow, well on in years. Well, as you know from the assassination of Prime Minister Inukai,[4] dying men repeat reflexively the words and actions
they were speaking before they were injured. . . .
Reiko enters with coffee through Door C.

REIKO: I'm afraid I'm not very good at this.

AMAMIYA (*taking the tray from her*): I'll take care of it.
Reiko exits.

NAKAIDE: Anyway, this old man was writhing and trying to take something out of the pocket of his ragged old corduroys. He kept saying, "Give it back for me!"—"Give it back fer me," I guess it was, since he was from the country. (*Laughing, he sips the coffee.*) He kept repeating it over and over. Now, a layman might think that the wheels of a train would cut you right in two, but the fact is they just crush you; and the blood clots in the vessels, so there's not much bleeding. But that "Give it back fer me," over and over, really got to me. As soon as the police doctor arrived, I let him take over. I wonder what he had in his pocket? I'm telling you, this is some business I'm in! (*He laughs.*) Well, I guess I'd better. . . . (*He rises from his chair.*)

AMAMIYA (*stopping him*): I'm not sure it's proper to ask, but. . .

NAKAIDE: Yes?

AMAMIYA: Will you have to report this?

NAKAIDE: I see. Well, if the substance in question were more dangerous, the first question would be the source, but in a case like

---

[4]Inukai Tsuyoshi (1855-1932) was assassinated by ultranationalists on May 15, 1932.

this, where the family is socially prominent, I'm sure it would be counterproductive to involve the authorities.

AMAMIYA (*nodding*): Thank you.

NAKAIDE: Let's just keep an eye on her, and. . . . Oh, yes, I read about your plans in the paper. . . .

AMAMIYA: Yes, as a matter of fact, that's what. . . .

NAKAIDE: The head of the household really should remain at home for the next day or so. Observing things as I have, I know how important this conference is to you, but as a doctor. . . .

AMAMIYA: Of course, I understand.

NAKAIDE: Well, then, take good care of her. (*He rises from his seat.*)

AMAMIYA: Thank you for everything you've done, Doctor. (*He sees him out through Door A.*)

The telephone rings on the vacant stage. Aoki appears through Door B, and an instant later Amamiya returns through Door A.

AOKI (*picking up the receiver*): Hello? Oh, Tsuji. Yes? Yes, he's still here. Yes, I see. (*He covers the mouthpiece.*) He says they're waiting at the station and if you don't hurry you'll miss the train.

Amamiya whispers something to him.

AOKI (*into the receiver*): Hello? Mr. Amamiya's sorry for all the trouble, but he says he won't be leaving tonight. What? A reporter? Just a minute. (*Again, he listens to Amamiya's instructions.*) Hello? He'd like you to explain the situation for him. What? No, tell him he's just not prepared.

AMAMIYA (*taking the phone*): Amamiya here. Sorry for all the inconvenience. What? No, of course I haven't lost confidence in my ideas! Don't be ridiculous. All right. All right. No, something's come up. Something personal. What? No, there's nothing for you to do here now. I'll see you in the morning. What? Yes, all right. Good-bye. (*He hangs up.*)

The two men look at each other. Pause.

AOKI: If Tsuji's going to suggest you're caving in, then let me tell you something, too. I met Adachi Kimi the other day on my way to Komai's.

AMAMIYA: Yes?

AOKI: She said that Tsuji was probably behind that card. She also said that he'd gone behind your back and told her to cover the flax seeds in the plots without potassium as usual but in the experimental plots where we'd supplied the three nutrients to cover the seeds with four centimeters of soil to inhibit germination.

AMAMIYA: She said that?

AOKI: Perhaps he fired her because he was afraid she'd give him away.
In his most recent report, he spends most of his time writing about the
ratio of nitrogen, phosphorus, and potassium in the fruit and never gets
around to analyzing the stem. It seems like a clear case of sabotage to
me. You'd be sure to find more potassium in the stem if you did
the analysis properly.

AMAMIYA: That's enough for the time being. Let's leave it.

Reiko enters from Door B.

REIKO: Father, please come. Please stay with Mother.

Amamiya does not answer.

REIKO: She's delerious. Please, Father!

AMAMIYA: All right. . . .

AOKI: Reiko, your father. . . .

REIKO: She   just   keeps   babbling   about motors and new year's
decorations.   (*She begins to sob.*) Why did she do it? Please, Father,
come on!

AMAMIYA (*shaking his head almost imperceptibly*): No. (*He slowly
covers his face with his hands.*)

REIKO (*looking questioningly at her father with tear-filled eyes*): Father,
you're cruel!

AOKI (*rising*): Reiko, please don't be too hard on him just now. Come
on, I'll go with you. (*Comforting her, he leads the wailing Reiko
through Door B.*)

Pause. Amamiya remains with his head hanging, immobilized.

*The clock strikes eleven. A steam whistle pierces the quiet, rainy
night. Then there is the sound of a train. After a cruel eternity, the
sound fades into the distance.*

*Amamiya looks up. Quietly he rises and goes to the table where his
reports are stacked.*

AMAMIYA (*picking them up one by one*): "Report Number 125:
The Proportional Distribution of the Three Basic Nutrients in
Volcanic Ash Soil." "Report Number 126: Application of the
Neubauer Seedling Method to. . . . " (*His voice becomes choked, and it
is impossible to make out what he is saying.*)

*Aoki appears at Door B. He does not say anything but remains
standing in the doorway, watching the anguished scholar he so highly
esteems.*

AMAMIYA (*to Aoki, who has quietly reentered the room*): Aoki, if you
don't mind, would you stay here with me tonight?

AOKI: I was just going to ask if I could. There's not much point in going
home now, and. . . .

AMAMIYA: You're used to burning the midnight oil, eh?

The two men laugh cheerlessly together.

AOKI (*after a moment*): The other day you told me you'd stake your professional life on your work this time. Well, I've been staying up late, just staring out the window. . . . I've been working on those yield statistics for sugar beets planted after clover that I showed you this morning. Anyway, I remember a book I read as a child. I can't recall the title, but the story took place somewhere in the tropics. It was about how an army of ants crosses a stream. Those in the vanguard drown and their black bodies form a bridge.

AMAMIYA (*thinking of something else*): I see.

AOKI: Finally, those who follow are able to cross to the other side on the backs of their fallen comrades. The moral of the story is that human progress is made the same way—I still remember. The work you're doing is so important. Compared to that. . . . I'm ashamed I ever considered leaving. I just couldn't get what happened to Michiko out of my mind.

AMAMIYA: Of course.

AOKI: You were kind enough to encourage me, but I decided if I had to choose, I'd rather split up with Michiko than sacrifice my work.

AMAMIYA (*suddenly alert*): What? Divorce your wife?

AOKI: Yes.

AMAMIYA: What seems to be the problem? Is she opposed to what you're doing?

AOKI: Oh, no, sir! It's not that. We only disagree about, well, your attitude toward Tōru. Michiko will say something disparaging, and, well, since I remember what happened with her. . . .

AMAMIYA: But that's no reason for divorce! I'm on the verge of breaking up my own home, so I'm in no position to give advice, but if Michiko's willing to follow you and try to understand what you're doing, then . . . (*emphatically*): take good care of her! If I'd taken a different approach with Teruko, then perhaps. . . .

Both men fall silent. Pause. Amamiya casually picks up a copy of The Journal of the Agronomy Association *from the table. As he reads, he is drawn into the article.*

AMAMIYA (*eventually looking up*): Aoki, do you think they're wrong—my conclusions, I mean?

AOKI: No, sir! Absolutely not. All the figures indicate. . . .

AMAMIYA: No, that's not what I mean. Of course, we're responsible for guiding agricultural production—as Saegusa says, for increasing the yield per hectare—but do you think, as it says here, that we're wrong to see any larger social implications in our work?

AOKI: Well. . . .

AMAMIYA: After all, my conclusion—the conclusion that true intensive agriculture is predicated on a large-scale farming system— derives from my attempts to increase yield per hectare, doesn't it?

AOKI: It's just cowardly, the way Saegusa tried to rebut your arguments by calling you . . . of course, I made a bad joke myself once and called you. . . .

AMAMIYA: A socialist? Look, Aoki, you know as well as I do that I've never given a thought to anything but the capitlist system for agriculture. But if you start calling people names like Saegusa, why . . . . . take the Hachisuka farm . . . back when Director General Saito̅, Professor Takimoto's teacher, formulated his theory of large-scale agriculture, he argued that the area of land under cultivation should be reapportioned at least on the scale of Belgium, the smallest country in Europe. Eighteen eighty-nine or ninety, I think it was.

AOKI: Yes, I think that's right.

AMAMIYA: After the American-style large-scale system of that farm collapsed and it was broken up into tenant farms, . . . Look, we've got the same problem today—take the failure of the sugar company's mechanized farm. If you went along with Saegusa, you'd have to call Shimura and Director General Saito̅ the same dirty name as me! Of course, Shimura's reprehensible, but for other reasons.

AOKI: Yes, but. . . .

AMAMIYA: But just because I suggested large-scale land management, I hardly think I. . . . Look, is there a single socialist book on these shelves? If we're going to be ridiculed by Saegusa and those of his ilk, then maybe that tells us something about what we're doing. I mean, maybe somewhere in all of this there's a hint of something more important than the difference between soil conditions in Japan and other countries!

AOKI: Sir, won't you consider leaving tonight? I'll look after things here. If you take a car and leave now. . . .

AMAMIYA: After this storm, I'd never make it.

AOKI: No, I suppose not.

AMAMIYA: I'm such a fool, Aoki. I've finally begun to have some inkling of what the farmers are up against, and. . . .

The doorbell rings. Aoki rises to answer it.

AOKI (*peering out through Door A*): It's Tsuji.

Amamiya grimaces.   He whispers something to Aoki, who has returned to his side.   In the meantime, Tsuji Shōhei enters the room, followed by Miyake Tetsuya.

TSUJI: I understand Mrs. Amamiya's not feeling well. What seems to be the trouble?

AMAMIYA: Who told you that?

TSUJI: You know that old cafe at the end of the row of acacias? We just ran into Karasawa coming out of there. He's always full of gossip.

AMAMIYA: I see. By the way, sorry to have made you go all the way to the station. . . .

TSUJI (*helping himself to a seat*): Sir, I know it's not my place to say this, and I don't know how ill Mrs. Amamiya is, but isn't there some way you could make it to the conference?

Amamiya does not answer.

TSUJI: The reason I say that is, well, I've witnessed your lonely struggle since last spring, and, of course, it's audacious of me to say so, but I just want to let you know I consider it a great honor to be working under your command, sir. That's all the more reason why I feel you should go tonight. . . . I mean, even if all of your recommendations should be rejected by the conferees—which seems unlikely—still. . . .

AMAMIYA: You think I'm afraid of that?

TSUJI: No, sir, You misunderstand me. I. . . .

MIYAKE: Sorry to interrupt. Maybe this is a stupid question, but, you will be continuing your debate in the *Journal*, won't you? Whether you go or not, I mean.

AMAMIYA: Well, yes, if there's space.

TSUJI: How about this, sir? Even if you don't arrive on the first day of the conference, you could still leave first thing in the   morning, and. . . . Otherwise, I'm afraid I'd feel completely bereft.

MIYAKE (*ironically*): Why, Tsuji, what have you got to worry about?

TSUJI: What do you mean?

MIYAKE: Even if Mr.   Amamiya loses his position here, assuming you're promoted from assistant director, who better to carry on his work and defend his theories! *(He laughs.)* Right, Aoki?

Aoki smiles.

TSUJI: Miyake, I hardly think that's funny! Mr. Amamiya, I hope I haven't offended you—I'm sure you're very tired—but I just wanted you to know that I hope you won't compromise, that's all. I'm sure you understand me, even if others don't.

AMAMIYA: Thank you for your concern.

TSUJI: Well, in that case, I'll call again in the morning?

AMAMIYA: Yes, do that.

TSUJI (*getting up, to Miyake*): Are you coming?

Miyake does not answer. Aoki sees Tsuji out through Door A.

MIYAKE: You know, Mr. Amamiya, I feel terrible. Call it a journalist's sixth sense if you like, but somehow I feel I understand your situation.

Aoki returns.

MIYAKE (*after a moment's reflection*): Well, I guess I'd better be going, too. Don't worry about my article. I'll stress the point that you haven't abandoned your position.

AMAMIYA: I'd appreciate that.

MIYAKE: This may be the last time I see you in my unpleasant role as a reporter.

AMAMIYA: Why is that?

MIYAKE: They're forcing me to resign at the end of the month.

AMAMIYA: Why?

MIYAKE: Well, I interviewed the father of that athlete, Morita? Busy as you are, you probably didn't see the article. Anyway, the son of one of the workers at the Igarashi Lumber Mill went to the Olympics in Berlin. It seems he was really living high on the hog over there. Apparently if you walked around with a pair of glasses on your nose and a Leica slung around your neck, people could tell a mile away that you were Japanese. Well, here's this fellow who ordinarily has to struggle to pay his tuition painting Berlin red, and I thought something must be up. So when I heard that he'd written a long letter to his father, I went to ask about it and quoted the whole thing in the paper. *(He laughs.)* That was the last straw for my bureau chief, and the rest is history.

AOKI: I read that article.

AMAMIYA: But that hardly seems reason to. . . .

MIYAKE: Well, we've been working up to this ever since I wrote that piece about Kovankov and the snowplow tractor. *(He laughs.)*

The telephone rings.

AOKI (*picking up the receiver*): Hello? Yes. Miyake? Yes, he's here. All right. (*To Miyake*): It's for you, from your office. They've been looking all over for you.

MIYAKE (*looking quizzically*): Now what do they want? (*Into the telephone*): Yes? Yes, I'm writing it now. What? Now? (*Becoming upset*): I'm sure it'll keep till morning. Why is it my fault if our paper's the only one late with the story? What? Yes. Well, in any case, count me out. Find somebody else. What? No, absolutely not. Good-bye. (*He puts down the phone.*) Damn, they're going to order me around till the day they give me the axe!

AOKI: Did something happen?

MIYAKE: Not really, just a landslide in the Karikachi Pass. They want me to visit the scene. I missed the express, so now they want me to go by company car. (*Suddenly*): Mr. Amamiya!

AMAMIYA (*simultaneously*): Miyake!

AOKI: That's it!

MIYAKE: Let's go after the train! They stop this side of the pass to bring the engine around in back. It takes. . . .

AMAMIYA: Twenty-five minutes at that stop!

MIYAKE: We'll make it, I'm sure of it. And with a press flag on the car, we can get through the roadblocks, too. Of course, we might slip off a cliff on one of those sharp curves, but if I have to die, it might as well be in illustrious company! (*Laughs.*)

AMAMIYA (*modestly*): Miyake, thank you.

MIYAKE: Even if they find out later—let me borrow the phone—so what, I'm finished anyway. (*He draws his finger across his neck. Then, laughing, he picks up the phone.*) Hello? Sorry to bother you so late, but ring two-six-zero for me, will you? *The Northern Japan Daily News*, that's right. (*With the receiver to his ear, he turns to Amamiya.*) You know, it's been ten years. . . . (*Into the mouthpiece*): Hello? This is Miyake. Let me speak to the chief. (*Turning to Amamiya again*): It's been ten years since I became a reporter, and I'm sorry to say. . . . (*Into the mouthpiece*): Hello, Chief? I've decided to go after all. Yes. Yes, I'm sorry. I'll be more careful in future—for the next two weeks. (*Cheerfully*): I'd be happy to apologize. Yes, please send the car around to the Amamiya's right away. I'll leave straight from here. What? My article? Yes. Listen, send someone with the car to pick it up, will you? What? I don't think you understand. Reporters from the other papers took the eleven o'clock express, didn't they? I want to be the first on the scene. Photographer? Anybody but Kawabe. I've had it with that fool. Right away, then, okay? Thanks. (*He hangs up.*) Damn! I haven't felt this good in I don't know how long! Mr. Amamiya, it's been ten years since I became a reporter, and I'm sorry to say this is the first worthwhile assignment I've had! (*He laughs.*)

The three men laugh. Amamiya, with the aid of Aoki, is absorbed in packing his papers and personal effects in his valise.

MIYAKE (*writing feverishly*):   "Overcoming all obstacles, Amamiya Akira, director of the local agricultural station, left last night for. . . . " Rats! What a waste!

AOKI: Waste?

MIYAKE: I've got a scoop here! If I had the time, I could sell it to some other paper for a lot of money!

Again the three men laugh together.

MIYAKE (*finished writing*): That does it. All right, I'm going to watch for the car. As soon as we've dropped the fellow who's coming to pick this up. . . .

AOKI: I know! You can save time by cutting across the compound. I'll open the gate.

The two of them exit into the rain through Door A.

Amamiya is alone.   Quietly, music begins. Reiko enters through Door B.

REIKO (*seeing her father dressed for travel*): Oh! Are you going after all?

AMAMIYA: Reiko. . . . (*He beckons to her with his eyes.*)

REIKO: I'll be right back. (*She picks up the bellflower in the vase near the wall.*) I'll just leave this next to Mother's bed. (*She exits momentarily through Door B, then returns.*) Yes, Father?

AMAMIYA: Reiko, you called me cruel before. I just want you to know that . . . well, I'm not a strong man. I was afraid that if I sat down next to your mother, I'd never get up again.

Reiko weeps.

AMAMIYA: Reiko, suppose, just   suppose that your mother and I decided not to live together anymore. Which of us would you like to stay with? Hm?

REIKO (*crying*): How should I know? I've never thought about it, not ever!

AMAMIYA: I see.

REIKO: Father? I love you more than anybody, more than I can say. But—but why did you have to treat Mother . . . You shouldn't have. . . .

Pause. Music.

REIKO: Father, will you do something for me?

AMAMIYA: What is it? That's right, I never did buy you that bicycle!

REIKO: No, that's not it. Listen, when you go before the conference —you know how nervous you get when you have to speak formally. You get flustered and mix up your words.

AMAMIYA: Yes?

REIKO: Well, when you get up in front of all those people, imagine me standing there. Just relax, and don't let anything disturb you.

AMAMIYA: All right.

REIKO: Don't say am . . . ammonium sulfate instead of potassium sulfate, all right? (*She sobs.*)

AMAMIYA (*laughing through his tears*): You've learned something, haven't you?

Pause. Music. Father and daughter wipe their eyes.

AMAMIYA: How's the rain?

REIKO (*getting up and going to the window*): It's almost stopped. You remember what I said that time? The rain's so fine it reminds you of volcanic ash.

AMAMIYA: Volcanic ash, eh? You know, if there are five million hectares of arable land in Japan, then this plain from here to Nemuro comprises about ten percent of the total. Reiko, volcanic ash is going to fall on this plain again before long, mark my words.

REIKO: What? What are you talking about?

AMAMIYA: Mt. Tokachi and Mt. Ishikari are going to erupt again. The only question is what it will be like for us under the debris.

Reiko stares at her father. The headlights of a car flash across the window.

AOKI (*voice only*): Sir!

AMAMIYA (*through the window*): I'll be right there.

He puts his letter of resignation in his breast pocket and is about to pick up his valise but stops. He goes to Door B but thinks better of it and turns back.

AMAMIYA: Reiko, I'm going to leave without seeing your mother. Everything's just going to have to wait until I get back. Take good care of her. (*He picks up his valise and briefcase and strides through Door A.*)

Reiko follows her father through Door A. There is the sound of the doorbell as it shuts, then Reiko races back into the room and throws open the window. There is the sound of a car driving into the distance.

REIKO (*to the father who is already beyond her reach*): Father!

Pause. As if pursuing the men in the speeding car, the music rises to a crescendo, then gently stops.

In the stillness, the only sound is the falling rain.

There is a voice at the entrance.

VOICE: Is anybody home?

REIKO (*half hanging out of the window*): Who is it?

VOICE: Would Henmi Shōsaku be here by any chance?

REIKO: He left a long time ago.

VOICE: I see. I must've passed him on the way.

REIKO: Is something wrong?

VOICE: No, I just dropped by his place and found that the baby's been born.

REIKO: You mean Shino's baby?

VOICE: That's right! She used to work here, didn't she?

The face that appears in the window is that of Ichihashi Tatsuji. He stands bare-headed in the rain.

ICHIHASHI: Then tell everyone, will you? It's a cute, little baby boy—the spitting image of Izumi Jirō!

Curtain.

Appendix

Scientific Names of Major Plants
Mentioned in the Text

Translation	Term in Text	Scientific Name
Adzuki	*azuki*	*Vigna angularis* (Willd.) Ohwi and Ohashi.
Alfalfa	*umagoyashi*	*M. sativa* Hortus Third, 1976, p. 721.
Apple	*ringo*	*Malus pumila* Mill.
Ash	*yachidamo*	*Fraxinus mandshurica* Rupr.
Bamboo	*kumazasa*	*Sasa Veitchii* (Carrière) Rehd. Hortus Third, 1976, p. 1007.
Bamboo grass	*sasa*	*Sasa* spp.
Beans	*tebō* [*ingenmame*]	*Lablab purpureus* (L.) Sweet
Bellflower	*kikyō*	*Platycodon grandiflorus* (Jacq.) A. DC. Hortus Third, 1976, p. 884.
Bushclover	*hagi*	*Lespedeza bicolor* Turcz. Hortus Third, 1976, p. 651.
Buckwheat	*soba*	*Fagopyrum esculentum* Moench
Burdock	*gobō*	*Arctium Lappa* L. Hortus Third, 1976, p. 99.
Chinese milk vetch	*genge*	*Astragalus sinicus* L.
Citrons		*Citrus aurantium* L. var. *daidai* Makino (=*C. daidai* Sieb.)
Common vetch	*komon betchi*	*Vicia sativa* L.
Corn	*tōmorokoshi*	*Zea mays* L.
Elm	*nire*	*Ulmus* spp.
Firs	*todomatsu*	*Abies sachalinensis* (Friedr. Schmidt) M. T. Mast. Hortus Third, 1976, p. 2.
Flax	*ama*	*Linum usitatissiumum* L. Hortus Third, 1976, p. 669
Grapes	*budō*	*Vitis vinifera* L.
Ground cherries	*hōzuki*	*Physalis* Alkekengi L.

Hare's ear	*hotaru-sō*	*Bupleurum falcatum* L. Hortus Third, 1976, p. 190
Knotweed	*akamanma*	*Polygonum* species
Lillies-of-the-valley	*suzuran*	*Convallaria majalis* L.
Mandarin Orange	*mikan*	*Citrus reticulata* Blanco
Maples	*itaya*	*Acer mono* Maxim.
Melon	*makura-uri*	*Cucumis melo* L. var. *makua* Makino
Millet	*inakibi [kokibi]*	*Panicum miliaceum* L.
Mugwort	*yomogi*	*Artemisia vulgaris* L.
Oak	*nara*	*Quercus* spp.
Oats	*enbaku*	*Avena sativa* L.
Peas	*endō*	*Pisum sativum* L.
Pigweed	*akaza*	*Chenopdium album* L.
Pines	*matsu*	*Pinus* spp.
Poplar	*doroyanagi [doronoki]*	*Populus Maximowiczii* A. Henry Hortus Third, 1976, p. 901.
Potatoes	*imo*	*Solanum tuberosum* L.
Red clover	*reddo klōbaa*	*Trifolium pratense* L.
Reeds	*ashi*	*Phragmites communis* Trinius
Rice	*kome*	*Oryza sativa* L.
Rye	*rai-mugi*	*Secale cereale* L.
Sakaki	*sakaki*	*Cleyera japonica* Thunb. Hortus Third, 1976, p. 286.
Smartweed	*mizosoba*	*Polygonum Thunbergii* Sieb. et Zucc. (=*Persicaria Thunbergii* Gross)
Soybeans	*mame [daizu]*	*Glycine max* (L.) Merr.
Spring elms	*akadamo [harunire]*	*Ulmus davidiana* Planch. var *japonica* (Rehd.) Nakai, Hortus Third, 1976, p. 1138.
Sugar beets	*biito [tensai]*	*Beta vulgaris* L.
Wheat	*mugi*	*Triticum aestivum* L.
Yews	*onkō*	*Taxus cuspidata* Sieb. and Zucc. Hortus Third, 1976, p. 1099.

CORNELL EAST ASIA SERIES

For ordering information, please contact the Cornell East Asia Series, East Asia Program, Cornell University, 140 Uris Hall, Ithaca, NY 14853-7601, USA, (607) 255-6222.

9-93/.5M/BB